IFIP Advances in Information and Communication Technology 360

IFIP – The International Federation for Information Processing

IFIP was founded in 1960 under the auspices of UNESCO, following the First World Computer Congress held in Paris the previous year. An umbrella organization for societies working in information processing, IFIP's aim is two-fold: to support information processing within ist member countries and to encourage technology transfer to developing nations. As ist mission statement clearly states,

> *IFIP's mission is to be the leading, truly international, apolitical organization which encourages and assists in the development, exploitation and application of information technology for the bene t of all people.*

IFIP is a non-profitmaking organization, run almost solely by 2500 volunteers. It operates through a number of technical committees, which organize events and publications. IFIP's events range from an international congress to local seminars, but the most important are:

- The IFIP World Computer Congress, held every second year;
- Open conferences;
- Working conferences.

The flagship event is the IFIP World Computer Congress, at which both invited and contributed papers are presented. Contributed papers are rigorously refereed and the rejection rate is high.

As with the Congress, participation in the open conferences is open to all and papers may be invited or submitted. Again, submitted papers are stringently refereed.

The working conferences are structured differently. They are usually run by a working group and attendance is small and by invitation only. Their purpose is to create an atmosphere conducive to innovation and development. Refereeing is less rigorous and papers are subjected to extensive group discussion.

Publications arising from IFIP events vary. The papers presented at the IFIP World Computer Congress and at open conferences are published as conference proceedings, while the results of the working conferences are often published as collections of selected and edited papers.

Any national society whose primary activity is in information may apply to become a full member of IFIP, although full membership is restricted to one society per country. Full members are entitled to vote at the annual General Assembly, National societies preferring a less committed involvement may apply for associate or corresponding membership. Associate members enjoy the same benefits as full members, but without voting rights. Corresponding members are not represented in IFIP bodies. Affiliated membership is open to non-national societies, and individual and honorary membership schemes are also offered.

Jürgen Becker   Marcelo Johann
Ricardo Reis (Eds.)

VLSI-SoC: Technologies for Systems Integration

17th IFIP WG 10.5/IEEE International Conference
on Very Large Scale Integration, VLSI-SoC 2009
Florianópolis, Brazil, October 12-14, 2009
Revised Selected Papers

 Springer

Volume Editors

Jürgen Becker
Karlsruhe Institute of Technology, Institute for Information Processing
Vincenz-Prießnitz-Str. 1, 76131 Karlsruhe, Germany
E-mail: becker@kit.edu

Marcelo Johann
Ricardo Reis
Universidade Federal do Rio Grande do Sul, Instituto de Informatica
Campus do Vale, Av. Bento Goncalves, 9500, 91501-970 Porto Alegre, RS, Brazil
E-mail: {johann, reis}@inf.ufrgs.br

ISSN 1868-4238   e-ISSN 1868-422X
ISBN 978-3-642-27072-7   ISBN 978-3-642-23120-9 (eBook)
DOI 10.1007/978-3-642-23120-9
Springer Heidelberg Dordrecht London New York

CR Subject Classification (1998): B.7-8, C.0, F.2, J.2-3, C.2.1

Typesetting: Camera-ready by author, data conversion by Scientific Publishing Services, Chennai, India

Printed on acid-free paper

Springer is part of Springer Science+Business Media (www.springer.com)

Preface

This book contains extended and revised versions of the best papers that were presented during the 17th edition of the IFIP/IEEE WG10.5 International Conference on Very Large Scale Integration, a global System-on-a-Chip Design and CAD conference. The 17th conference was held at the Jurerê Beach Village Hotel, Florianópolis, Brazil (October 12–14, 2009). Previous conferences have taken place in Edinburgh, Trondheim, Vancouver, Munich, Grenoble, Tokyo, Gramado, Lisbon, Montpellier, Darmstadt, Perth, Nice, Atlanta and Rhodes.

The purpose of this conference sponsored by IFIP TC 10 Working Group 10.5, the IEEE Council on Electronic Design Automation (CEDA) and by IEEE Circuits and Systems Society, with the In-Cooperation of ACM SIGDA, is to provide a forum to exchange ideas and show industrial and academic research results in the field of microelectronics design. The current trend toward increasing chip integration and technology process advancements brings about stimulating new challenges both at the physical and system-design levels, as well in the test of these systems. VLSI-SoC conferences aim to address these exciting new issues.

The 2009 edition of VLSI-SoC maintained the traditional structure, which has been successful at the previous VLSI-SoC conferences. The quality of submissions (81 papers) made the selection process difficult, but finally 27 papers and 18 posters were accepted for presentation at VLSI-SoC 2009. Out of the 27 full papers presented at the conference, 8 regular papers were chosen by a Selection Committee to have an extended and revised version included in this book. The book also includes two chapters related to the keynote talks of the conference. The chapters of this book have authors from Brazil, France, Germany, Portugal, Spain, Switzerland and the USA.

VLSI-SoC 2009 was the culmination of many dedicated volunteers: paper authors, reviewers, Session Chairs, invited speakers and various Committee Chairs, especially the local arrangements organizers. We thank them all for their contribution.

This book is intended for the VLSI community mainly to those that did not have the chance to take part in the VLSI-SoC 2009 conference. The papers were selected to cover a wide variety of excellence in VLSI technology and the advanced research they describe. We hope you will enjoy reading this book and find it useful in your professional life and toward the development of the VLSI community as a whole.

June 2011

Juergen Becker
Marcelo Johann
Ricardo Reis

Organization

The IFIP/IEEE International Conference on Very Large Scale Integration-System-on-a-Chip (VLSI-SoC) 2009 took place during October 12–15, 2009 in the Jurerê Beach Village Hotel, Florianópolis, Brazil. VLSI-SoC 2009 was the 17th in a series of international conferences, sponsored by IFIP TC 10 Working Group 10.5 (VLSI), IEEE CEDA.

General Chair

Ricardo Reis — Universidade Federal do Rio Grande do Sul, Brazil

Program Chair

Juergen Becker — KIT, Germany

Local Chair

José Luís Güntzel — Universidade Federal de Santa Catarina, Brazil

Publicity Chair

David Atienza — Complutense University of Madrid, Spain

Publication Chair

Marcelo Johann — Universidade Federal do Rio Grande do Sul, Brazil

Finance Chair

Gustavo Wilke — Universidade Federal do Rio Grande do Sul, Brazil

PhD Forum Chair

Lisane Brisolara de Brisolara — Universidade Federal de Pelotas, Brazil

Web Chair

Cristina Meinhardt   Universidade Federal do Rio Grande do Sul,
                                   Brazil

Steering Committee

Manfred Glesner   TU Darmstadt, Germany
Salvador Mir   TIMA, France
Ricardo Reis   UFRGS, Brazil
Michel Robert   LIRMM, France
Luis Miguel Silveira   INESC ID, Portugal

Technical Program Committee

Ioannis Andreadis   Nathalie Julien
Federico Angiolini   Hsien-Hsin S. Lee
David Atienza   Jean-Didier Legat
Nadine Azermad   Tiziana Margaria
Sergio Bampi   Salvador Mir
Magdy Bayoumi   Vincent Mooney
Juergen Becker   Alex Orailoglu
Mladen Berekovic   Vassilis Paliouras
Holger Blume   Marios Papaefthymiou
Dominique Borrione   Zebo Peng
Joao Cardoso   Dionisios N. Pnevmatikatos
Luc Claesen   Massimo Poncino
Gero Dittmann   Franz Rammig
Joan Figueras   Flavio Rech Wagner
Georgi N. Gaydadjiev   Ricardo Reis
Dimitris Gizopoulos   Renato Ribas
Manfred Glesner   Marcos Sanchez-Elez
Matthew Guthaus   Donatella Sciuto
Josef Haid   Dimitrios Serpanos
Domenik Helms   Cristina Silvano
Ahmed Hemani   Luis Miguel Silveira
Renato Hentschke   Stylianos Siskos
Klaus Hofmann   Thanos Skodras
Tang Hua   Dimitrios Soudris
Michael Huebner   P.A. Subrahmanyam
Marcelo Johann   Eugenio Villar

Table of Contents

Emerging Technologies and Nanoscale Computing Fabrics

Ian O'Connor[1,4], Junchen Liu[1], Jabeur Kotb[1], Nataliya Yakymets[1],
Renaud Daviot[2], David Navarro[1], Pierre-Emmanuel Gaillardon[3],
Fabien Clermidy[3], Maïmouna Amadou[4], and Gabriela Nicolescu[4]

[1] University of Lyon, Lyon Institute of Nanotechnology UMR 5270
Ecole Centrale de Lyon, 36 avenue Guy de Collongue, F-69134 Ecully cedex, France
[2] University of Lyon, Lyon Institute of Nanotechnology UMR 5270
CPE Lyon, 43, boulevard du 11 novembre 1918, F-69100 Villeurbanne, France
[3] CEA – LETI – MINATEC
17, rue des Martyrs, F-38054 Grenoble, France
[4] École Polytechnique de Montréal, Computer Science Department
Montréal, QC, H3C 3J7, Canada
ian.oconnor@ec-lyon.fr

Abstract. This chapter describes a reconfigurable computing architecture based on clusters of regular matrices of fine-grain dynamically reconfigurable cells using double-gate carbon nanotube field effect transistors (DG-CNTFET), which exhibit ambivalence (p-type or n-type behaviour depending on the back-gate voltage). Hierarchical function mapping methods suitable for the cluster of matrices structure have been devised, and various benchmark circuits mapped to the architecture. This work shows how circuit and architecture designers can work with emerging technology concepts to examine its suitability for use in computing platforms.

1 Introduction

Computing power recently broke the petaflop/s barrier within a single machine and is expected to continue to scale to exacomputing over the next decade [1] (fig. 1). The main hardware vectors behind this spectacular evolution have been a) increase in intrinsic chip functionality through scaling and b) massive parallelism and increasingly efficient interconnect topologies. While scaling has now for a few years been mainly limited to improving the number of functions per chip rather than clock speed, other factors (such as cost, reliability, static power) render necessary the exploration of other technologies and computing paradigms to pursue the quest for performance.

Indeed, it is widely recognized that transistor scaling, as a vector for the pursuit of performance levels predicted by Moore's Law and required by future applications, will not last through the next decade. Alternatives must be found, be they at the architectural level (e.g. exploring multiple core architectures) or at the device level (heterogeneous or nanoelectronic devices). In this context, the emergence of new research devices offers the opportunity to provide novel logic building blocks and to elaborate non-conventional techniques for digital design. Ultimately it will be

J. Becker, M. Johann, and R. Reis (Eds.): VLSI-SoC 2009, IFIP AICT 360, pp. 1–20, 2011.

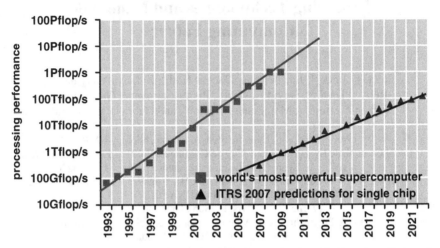

Fig. 1. Best observed processing performance for a single machine [1] (a) and predictions for processing performance in a single chip [2] (b)

possible to reconsider the paradigms of computing architectures to achieve orders of magnitude improvements in the conventional figure of merit (MIPS / volume*power). In this way, future computing platforms are likely to cover broad ranges of applications, from traditional number-crunching (counting and calculating) to emerging neuromorphic (recognizing and reasoning). These very different classes of algorithm will require suitable hardware platforms, with the additional constraints of occupying small volume and low-power.

It is also expected that the necessary structuring of the projected tens of billions of elementary, unreliable, nanometric devices to achieve the computing capacities necessary for future software applications will lead to the emergence of reconfigurable platforms as the principal computing fabric before the end of the next decade. The reconfigurable approach allows volume manufacturing and reduces the impact of the evolution of mask costs, projected to move above the $10M mark in 2010. It can also efficiently cover a broad range of applications while exceeding performance levels of programmable systems, and couples naturally to fault-tolerant design techniques for robust architectures. Reliability is clearly an increasingly important issue given the lack of reliability at individual device level: leading to the rise of self-x (self-configuration, self-repair ...) at architectural and/or software levels.

However, the organization of such reconfigurable cells in a system is uncertain – integration density and switchbox overhead concerns are a growing issue. These point to the rising probability of fixed interconnect topologies between individual cells organized into clusters, and the use of switchboxes or network approaches only between clusters of cells. In parallel, the unreliability of individual devices will lead to a loss of accessible functions in certain cells. This can be circumvented by reformulating cluster configurations based on the incomplete set of identified operators. In this context, the development of methods capable of mapping complex functions onto clusters of reconfigurable cells with incomplete sets of operators is a key milestone to exploiting the full potential of future reconfigurable systems.

In addition, recent technological breakthroughs have led to the proposal of area- and power-efficient reconfigurable cells based on emerging devices such as double-gate carbon nanotube transistors (CNTFET) with incomplete operator sets [3]. CNTFETs have attracted much attention in recent years, and benchmark figures against state-of-the-art planar and non-planar silicon logic transistors are favourable. They have shown in particular that the high mobility, achievable current density, theoretical transition frequency and Ion/Ioff ratio place CNTFETs among the most promising nanodevices in line to succeed the MOS transistor from the standpoint of their integration into future nanoelectronic systems on chip [4]. Some work has been carried out to explore the use of the unique properties of multiple diameter and ambipiolar CNTFETS with respect to CMOS for new computing paradigms ([5], [6]). The emergence of double gate devices, with four accessible terminals, also opens the way to solutions specifically exploiting the additional terminal for reconfigurability purposes. In the case of the double gate CNTFET [7], completely new prospects for reconfigurability are possible due to its ambivalent (n- and p-type) behaviour. Using this property, logic cells can be built that offer fine-grain reconfigurability not available with MOSFET technology, at comparable or better speed and power figures, and improving over current reconfigurable systems in terms of the number of devices used to realize a single function.

These considerations have recently led to the emergence of the concept of nanofabrics [8], or nanoscale computing fabrics. A nanoFabric can be defined as an array of connected nanoscale logic blocks (nanoBlocks), where a nanoBlock is a circuit block containing programmable devices to compute boolean logic functions and means to route data. From a technological point of view, such systems are usually based on a hybrid approach (on a silicon die, or with CMOS compatibility). They are a combination of a bottom-up structure, using chemical self-assembly for dense and regular arrangement of elements, and a top-down structure, using conventional process options for interconnect or for computation. In this work, we do not consider memory issues but it is clear that memory integration is also paramount.

This chapter begins by describing the structure and properties of a DG-CNTFET based dynamically reconfigurable logic cell to be used in a computing nanofabric. We then explore ways in which this cell can be used to form a regular and dense matrix structure, as well as a method to map function graphs to such matrices, and clusters of matrices, of reconfigurable cells for on-the fly and partial reprogrammability. The method is applied for various benchmarks in order to evaluate the capability of the architecture to execute complex functions. We finally conclude with a discussion on the insights of this work, and future challenges.

2 Carbon-Based Nanofabrics

For high-performance FETs, short gate lengths and high channel mobility are required. Since nanotubes typically exhibit very small diameters (allowing excellent gate control) without suffering from mobility degradation, they are promising candidates to overcome the limitations of nanometric silicon devices. Fig. 2 shows the structure of a novel DG-CNTFET [7], fabricated with an aluminium front gate placed under the nanotube between the contacts of the source and the drain and controlling the electrostatics and switching of the nanotube bulk channel in region B. The Schottky

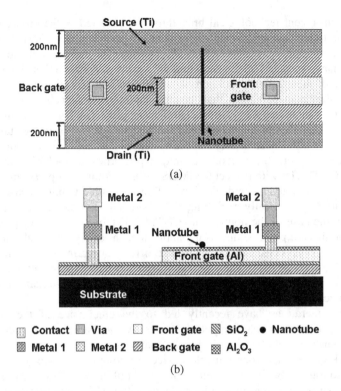

Fig. 2. Double-Gate CNTFET structure [7] (a) top view (b) cross-sectional view

barriers (SB) at the nanotube/metal contacts are controlled by the silicon back gate (substrate), which also prevents the electrostatics in region A from being influenced by the front gate. The SBs at the contacts are not affected by the front gate voltages.

The behaviour of this DG-CNTFET device is strongly dependent on the potential of the silicon back gate, which we call V_{gs-bg}:

- when V_{gs-bg} is sufficiently negative (some hundreds of mV), the device functions like a p-type FET with a negative threshold voltage.
- when V_{gs-bg} is sufficiently positive (some hundreds of mV), the device functions like an n-type FET with a positive threshold voltage;
- when V_{gs-bg} is floating, the sub-bands with the contacts are not affected by the bias of the front gate, and the device is in the off state with a very weak current ($I_{off} < 100fA$).

The impact of the back gate voltage polarity on the transistor channel transport characteristics opens up new opportunities for using CNTFETs in logic circuits. We have built a reconfigurable logic block which can be configured to any one of fourteen basic binary operation modes. This functionality is impossible to achieve in CMOS technology without resorting to far more complex circuitry (and therefore silicon real estate and system power) than the cell structure described here. The polarity (n-type or p-type) of each transistor is controlled by the back-gate bias voltage values. The dynamically reconfigurable logic cell (DRLC_7T) is shown in fig. 3; while tab. 1 describes the 3-input configuration, corresponding basic binary logic functions and power figures for operation at 4GHz and 250MHz extracted from transient simulations using a Verilog-A model adapted from [3] and parasitic capacitances extracted from layout estimations.

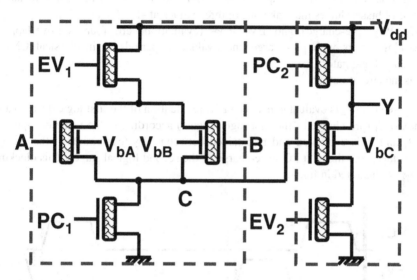

Fig. 3. Dynamically reconfigurable logic cell (DRLC_7T) transistor-level schematic

Table 1. 3-input configurations for reconfigurable cell with 3 logic levels (+V, 0, -V) and corresponding 14 basic binary logic functions

V_{bA}	V_{bB}	V_{bC}	Y	P_{tot}@4GHz (nW)	P_{tot}@250MHz (nW)
+V	+V	+V	A↓B	1.87	1.076
+V	+V	-V	A∨B	1.85	0.99
+V	0	+V	¬A	1.83	0.84
+V	0	-V	A	1.81	0.82
-V	-V	+V	A∧B	1.84	0.9
-V	-V	-V	A↑B	1.82	0.814
+V	-V	+V	B↛A	1.86	1.05
+V	-V	-V	B→A	1.84	0.96
0	+V	+V	¬B	1.82	0.8
0	+V	-V	B	1.79	0.79
0	0	0	1	1.12	0.04
0	0	-V	0	1.82	0.2
-V	+V	+V	A↛B	1.84	1.03
-V	+V	-V	A→B	1.82	0.95

DRLC_7T is made up of 7 CNTFETs arranged in two logic stages: the first stage performs an elementary logical operation and the second stage works either in follower or inverter mode.

- A and B are boolean data inputs (voltages at A and B vary between 0V and 1V);
- V_{bA}, V_{bB}, V_{bC} are control inputs which configure the circuit according to tab. 1 (control bias voltages may take one of three values at -1V, 0V and 1V);
- PC_1, PC_2 (pre-charge) and EV_1, EV_2 (evaluation) are four non-overlapping clocking inputs with pre-charge and evaluation periods as in classical CMOS dynamic logic gates;
- Y is the circuit output.

We can see that V_c is evaluated between EV_1 (evaluation of the first logical stage) and the next PC_1 (pre-charge of the first logical stage) according to the value of inputs A and B; and Y is evaluated and maintained between EV_2 (evaluation of the second logical stage) and the next PC_2 (pre-charge of the second logical stage). This clocking scheme is illustrated in fig. 4.

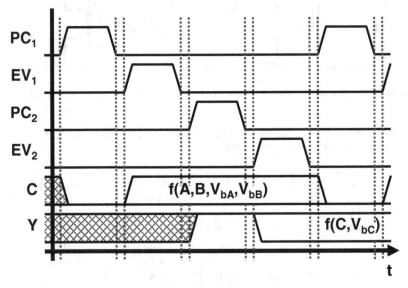

Fig. 4. Two-stage dynamic logic clock signal scheme

An example illustrates how this logic gate works. When $V_{bA}=V_{bB}=V_{bC}=1V$, CNTFETs T_{c1}, T_{c2} and T_{c3} (shown in fig. 3) are all configured as n-type FETs, as indicated in the previous section. When PC_1 is enabled, the first stage is pre-charged, and the voltage of the internal node C (V_c) is discharged to 0V. If for example either of the data inputs A or B=logic "1", then when EV_1 is enabled, the first layer evaluates its output such that the internal node C is set to logic "1". Then PC_2 is enabled (pre-charge of the second stage), and the output Y is charged to logic "1"; and when EV_2 is enabled, the output is evaluated and Y is evaluated to logic "0". In fact in this configuration, the only situation where C is not set to logic "1" and Y therefore evaluates to logic "1" (since Tc_3 is off) is when both A and B=logic "0". This shows that for $V_{bA}=V_{bB}=V_{bC}=1V$, DRLC_7T is configured as a NOR operator, as specified in tab. 1. Simulation results of DRLC_7T in this configuration are shown in the left half of fig. 5 (up to 8ns) at 500MHz operation. After this point, V_{bA}, V_{bB} and V_{bC} change to -1V, such that CNTFETs T_{c1}, T_{c2} and T_{c3} are all configured as p-type FETs. When PC_1 is enabled, the first stage is pre-charged, and the voltage of the internal node C (V_c) is discharged to 0V. If for example either of the data inputs A or B=logic "0", then when EV_1 is enabled, the first layer evaluates its output such that the internal node C is set to logic "1". Then PC_2 is enabled (pre-charge of the second stage), and the output Y is charged to logic "1"; and when EV_2 is enabled, the output is evaluated and Y is evaluated at logic "1". The only situation here where C is not set to logic "1" and Y therefore evaluates to logic "0" (since Tc_3 is on) is when both A and B=logic "1". This shows that for $V_{bA}=V_{bB}=V_{bC}=-1V$, DRLC_7T is configured as a NAND operator.

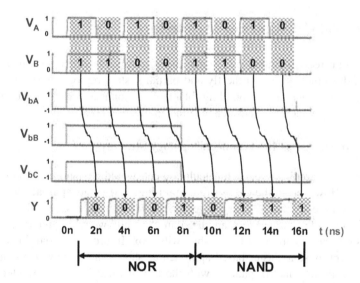

Fig. 5. Simulation results of dynamic reconfiguration of reconfigurable cell DRLC_7T from NOR operator to NAND operator

It is thus clear that this gate can realize several functions and can be dynamically reconfigured during the calculation.

Tab. 1 also gives the power consumption when DRLC_7T (working with 2-logic-stage control bias voltage) operates at 250MHz and 4GHz.

It should be noted that as this is prospective work, no technology as yet exists to build this circuit, although a single DG-CNTFET has been fabricated and characterized [7]. Further, significant technological advances have been made recently to achieve 95-98% horizontally aligned semiconducting CNTs [9] and, separately, hybrid integration with CMOS [10]. This enables us to envisage systems using "substrates" of many aligned semiconducting CNTs with conventional metallization and lithography techniques creating interconnections. In terms of device design, much work has focused on improving drive current (and therefore maximum frequency and insensitivity to noise) and reliability by using an array of parallel single-walled carbon nanotubes as multiple channels in a single transistor with good directional and spatial control [11]. This device can pass currents of up to 1.5mA and has achieved a record current gain cutoff frequency of 8GHz. These performances are still dominated by parasitics but recent advances project that this device should reach a current gain cutoff frequency of 31GHz. Double-gate transistors using the same principle for the channel should not pose any technological obstacle.

Here we have given only one example of the family of dynamically reconfigurable logic cells. By changing the number of the transistors we have developed 3 other logic cells which can realize different logic function sets [3].

3   Clusters of Cell-Matrices Architecture

Such fine-grain reconfigurable gates open the way towards structures which can be configured dynamically, for on-the-fly and partial system reprogrammability. In this section, the way elementary building blocks are connected and programmed is explored to achieve increased efficiency at the application level.

3.1   Fixed Intra-matrix Interconnect Topology Strategy

In a conventional architecture, each calculation cell would be connected to the switch box directly. However, in the case of fine-grain logic cells, this approach would lead to a loss of efficiency due to a large overhead in terms of device complexity. In the case of DRLC_7T, 7 transistors are used in the cell, while a similar number of transistors (at least 6) are used for a 1-bit switchbox. In order to avoid this overhead problem, we propose a cluster-based approach as shown in fig. 6, which consists of assembling cells in a matrix pattern, with the use of fixed intra-matrix interconnect between layers of cells. Here, the identifier f^{xy} corresponds to the configured function of the cell and the {x,y} coordinates of the cell within the matrix. Inputs A and B are shown, as is the output Y (duplicated); precharge and evaluation connections are not shown to avoid making the figure overly cumbersome. Considering the whole of this cluster set as a new coarse grain element, switchboxes could be used for inter-matrix interconnect. It is interesting to note that matrix architectures are also particularly well-suited to CNTFET-based logic cells, since it is possible for single nanotubes to span several cells in the same column.

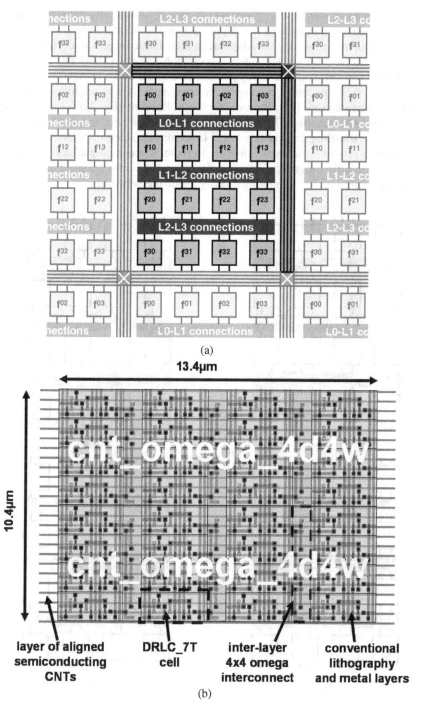

(a)

(b)

Fig. 6. Tile-based approach for the integration of regularly structured matrices of reconfigurable cells (a) conceptual schematic (b) layout for two tiles of 4d4w Modified-Omega topologies

For intra-matrix interconnect, and taking wiring complexity into account, we eliminate any total interconnectivity topologies at the outset. Instead, and through analogy to computer networks, we adapt incomplete interconnection sets to the matrix architecture. In fact, Multistage Interconnection Networks (MIN) are designed to interconnect layers in an efficient way and can be applied in this context.

Of course, there are many topologies or combinations, but we focus principally on 4 typical permutations [12]: Banyan (fig. 7(a)), Baseline (fig. 7(b)), Flip (fig. 7(c)) and Modified-Omega (fig. 7(d)), where the modifications to standard Omega maximize the shuffling in this topology. In computer science, MINs are used to interconnect layers of switchboxes in order to route information packets only. In this application, the main difference is that switchboxes have been removed and replaced by logic cells, introducing computing directly inside the network.

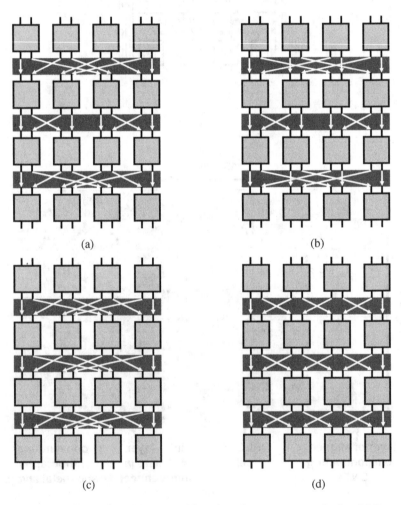

(a)   (b)

(c)   (d)

Fig. 7. Matrix of 16 reconfigurable gates with various interconnect topologies: (a) Banyan (b) Baseline (c) Flip (d) Modified-Omega

3.2 Matrix Programming

It is useful to combine such novel types of nanodevice-based reconfigurable cell with the exploration of new function mapping methods in anticipation of the deployment of incomplete-operator cluster-based systems. A primary objective is to analyze the limits of such architectures when mapping a complex software application onto it. Many parameters must be considered to program the nanodevice-based architectures:

- the number of cells in matrix
- the topology of cells interconnections
- potentially, the faults present in the matrix

Moreover, several metrics have to be optimized (computation speed, area, etc). Therefore, new CAD tools meeting these requirements are mandatory in order to explore the potential of nanodevicebased architectures during the prototyping phase. One of the key issues is the automatic mapping of complex functions onto nanodevice-based architectures. Several mapping methods defined for conventional architectures have been proposed. However, these methods fail to reach the ultra-fine granularity specific to nanodevice-based architectures. Furthermore, they do not consider connectivity restrictions and dynamic reconfiguration opportunities.

While the application is quite close to logic synthesis and network routing, the fact that we have introduced computing inside the matrix means that we cannot use routing algorithms or synthesis algorithms directly. We present in this section a mapping method designed to map a logic function graph onto the architecture described above. First, we will describe the method, and then we will give an example to show how this method works.

3.3 Functional Description

The described method inputs the function graph to map and the physical connectivity matrix and outputs the map of logic elements onto physical cells. The algorithms work

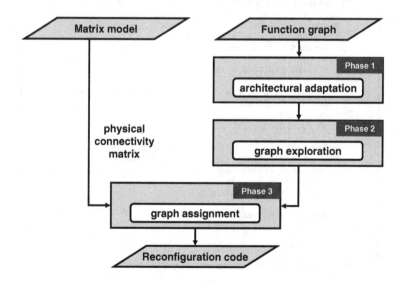

Fig. 8. Mapping method functional stream

using adjacency matrices. In such matrices, (i,j) refers to the intersection of the row i and column j. A 1 at the position (i,j) means that the point i is connected to the point j. These matrices are essential to subsequent processing steps, described in fig. 8.

Phase 1: Pre-processing of function graph

In a first operation, we have to adapt the logic function to our architecture. Due to the layered structure, the system is pipelined. Function graphs have to be processed by adding necessary synchronization elements (to extend input and output paths of data), as well as removing jumps over logic layers (to conform to the physical topology). To identify logic layers in function graphs, we divide the associated adjacency matrix into small matrices C_{nm}. C_{nm} is the adjacency matrix between the points in the logic layer n and those in the logic layer m. We therefore pay particular attention to matrices where $m \neq n+1$ because the presence of any non-zero element in these three matrices identifies a connection which "jumps" at least one logic layer. Such a direct connection cannot be realized in the topology since the interconnect topology is physically fixed. The solution is to add synchronization elements (i.e. create a path instead of a jump), then repeat the process until no more connections jump logic layers.

Phase 2: Recursive exploration

The processed function graph is then analyzed in depth, meaning that for each node in the structure, child branches are identified and recursively explored.

Phase 3: Node assignment

Logic nodes are then assigned to cells. This is done according to the physical interconnections. Each layer's connections are compared to the relevant inter-layer

```
Current node = First node
LOOP
   IF (children/parents of current node already placed) THEN
      IF (empty cell connected to childs or parents) THEN
         Map the node at the first empty position
         Store other solutions
         IF (Remaining node to map) THEN
            Current node = Next node
         ELSE
            MAPPING FINISHED - END LOOP
      ELSE
         IF (Previous node has a non explored solution) THEN
            Try next solution
         ELSE
            NO SOLUTIONS - END LOOP
   ELSE
      IF (free cell at the corresponding stage) THEN
         Map the node at the first empty position
         Store other solutions
         IF (Remaining node to map) THEN
            Current node = Next node
         ELSE
            MAPPING FINISHED - END LOOP
      ELSE

         NO SOLUTIONS - END LOOP
```

Fig. 9. Mapping algorithm (pseudo-code)

connectivity matrix – allowing (or not) the assignment of functions to cells. Branching (i.e. the exploration of the immediately preceding alternative) is used when the arbitrary choice leads to a dead-end, and the process is repeated until all functions are assigned to cells. The algorithm of this step is shown in fig. 9.

The algorithm has been implemented in Matlab, and executes in under 0.1s for a complete 16-node mapping operation using a standard 2GHz PC. While this approach enables the mapping of simple functions to the fixed-interconnect matrix based on the reconfigurable cells, function partitioning and merging methods will be required to map more complex functions over several matrices.

3.4 Mapping Example

As an example, we consider a matrix which is 4 cells deep and 4 cells wide (4d4w) using a Banyan interconnect topology (fig. 7(a)). Individual cross-connectivity matrices X_{nm} (X_{01}, X_{12} and X_{23}) between logic cell stages of depth n to m are shown in eq. 1.

$$
X_{01} = \begin{bmatrix} 1 & 0 & 1 & 0 \\ 0 & 1 & 0 & 1 \\ 1 & 0 & 1 & 0 \\ 0 & 1 & 0 & 1 \end{bmatrix}, X_{12} = \begin{bmatrix} 1 & 1 & 0 & 0 \\ 1 & 1 & 0 & 0 \\ 0 & 0 & 1 & 1 \\ 0 & 0 & 1 & 1 \end{bmatrix}, X_{23} = \begin{bmatrix} 1 & 0 & 1 & 0 \\ 0 & 1 & 0 & 1 \\ 1 & 0 & 1 & 0 \\ 0 & 1 & 0 & 1 \end{bmatrix} \quad (1)
$$

The function to map is represented by a graph, generated by a random graph generator for test purposes. During the graph adaptation step, we pay particular attention to the matrices C_{02}, C_{03} and C_{13} containing 1's. As mentioned previously, such matrices represent connections which "jump" at least one logic layer, and are impossible to realize. In this example, the connections between points (2, 6), (5, 8) and (4, 9) are the three connections to be adjusted.

The graph exploration is then launched and we obtain the following sequence (p* represents synchronization nodes):

p_1-p_4-p^*-p_9-p_5-p_7-p_3-p^*-p^*-p^*-p_8-p_2-p^*-p_6-p^*

Finally, the graph assignment is performed. In the example, the first point p_1 is assigned to the cell f^{00}. According to the path defined in the previous step, p_4 is the next point to assign to a cell in the matrix. Since f^{00} is physically connected to f^{10} and f^{12}, the cell with lower y-index (here f^{10}) is arbitrarily chosen for p_4 assignment, and the other possibility is memorized. In our example, the final programmed matrix is shown in fig. 10. In this figure, we can see the nodes of the logic function graph and the nodes added for synchronization purposes (circles with no names) correctly placed on the cell matrix.

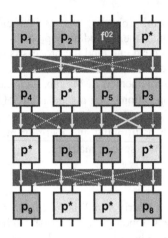

Fig. 10. Matrix after function mapping

3.5 Evaluation Methodology

The aim of this part of our work was to evaluate and compare performance metrics for the 4 interconnect topologies. Our study was made on a 4d4w matrix using the previously mentioned intra-matrix interconnection topologies. 4d4w matrices have been chosen because of a good balance between complexity and simulation time. We evaluated various metrics: the success rate of mapping function graphs, the fault tolerance and the average interconnection length. We have carried out detailed analyses to compare the efficiency of the different intra-matrix interconnect topologies. We use a random graph generator to generate static sets of function graphs containing 6-16 points, in order to have fixed comparison criteria between topologies. No graphs contain isolated nodes, as here we focus on fixed interconnect layers, which are severely penalized by isolated nodes. We consider therefore these cases to be an overload issue to be solved by specific architectural customization. Each set, corresponding to a given number of points in the function graph, contains 1000 samples. Using the previously described mapping method, each function is programmed onto the 4d4w matrix using the various intramatrix interconnect topologies, ideal or faulty, and metrics are calculated. Fig. 11 summarizes the evaluation methodology and the associated parameters.

Applying static sets to ideal interconnect topologies, we can test the ability of the matrix-topology ensemble to have complex functions mapped onto it. Considering the percentage of function graphs successfully mapped onto matrix with respect to the number of samples in the set, we obtained the success rate. Fig. 12 shows the comparison of success rates for 4d4w Banyan, Omega, Flip and Baseline topologies. For Banyan, Flip and Baseline interconnect topologies, the success rate is about 80% when the function graphs have 6 points. At 12 points, the success rate is about 25%. The difference between these two topologies is thus relatively small. However for the Omega interconnect topology, the success rate is about 90% for 6-point function graphs and about 40% for 12-point graphs. This clearly shows that the Omega interconnect topology is more suitable for this type of matrix.

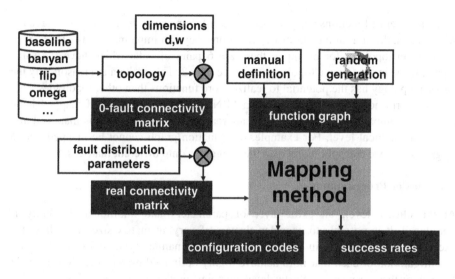

Fig. 11. Evaluation method

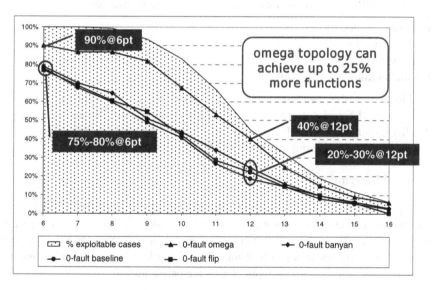

Fig. 12. Programmability success rates for Banyan, Omega, Flip and Baseline interconnect topologies within 4d4w matrices

This is because this topology is has less symmetric redundancy than the other topologies and spreads calculations over cells occupying less width, which seems to correspond better to typical function graphs. In fact in the matrix, there are pairs of cells which have the same inputs. For two cells which have the same inputs, the sum of the number of functions they can achieve is 14. For two cells which do not have the same inputs, the sum of the number of functions they can implement is 14+14 = 28. In the Banyan topology for example, there are 6 pairs of cells which have the same inputs, while in the Omega topology, there are only 2. This is the main reason why the Omega topology has the potential to realize more functions than other topologies.

It is worth noticing that the use of a MIN reduces the number of mapped logic functions, compared to traditional LUT approaches. Such a problem is managed at a higher hierarchical level. For example, if a function graph cannot be mapped onto a single matrix, we can split it and map the subgraphs onto different matrices.

3.6 Cluster Programming

At the cluster level, an extra layer of parameters and additional flexibility is introduced. It is possible to consider clusters of varying matrix size, as well as the execution of functions in parallel, and the dynamic (potentially cycle-level) reconfiguration of each matrix to achieve highly optimized graph execution. In order to explore these aspects, a cluster-level mapping model is proposed. This mapping model places applications onto the complete architecture composed of several matrices, such that multiple metrics are optimized. These metrics are:

- communication cost
- configuration cost
- execution time
- number of unused logical cells.

The objective of the mapping model is to optimize the placement of a complex function onto the architecture. It considers the structure of the architecture, the scalability requirement as well as the dynamic reconfiguration implying a high-level of pipelining and parallelism. It combines GA and partitioning approaches.

3.7 Model Description

The proposed model is shown in fig. 13. It takes as inputs a function graph and the architecture model and generates the reconfigurable code of the mapping as output. In general, complex functions cannot be mapped onto a single matrix. For this purpose, functions are partitioned into sub-functions. Thus, in order to map a complex function onto a cluster of matrices, two mapping levels are performed:

- Firstly, each sub-function is mapped onto a matrix using the method described in the previous section;
- Then, the dependency graph of sub-functions is also mapped onto the cluster of matrices.

The function to map is represented as a Direct Acyclic Graph (DAG) $G_f = (E_f, V_f)$ where V_f is a set of nodes representing logic operations, and E_f a set of direct edges dependency relations between nodes.

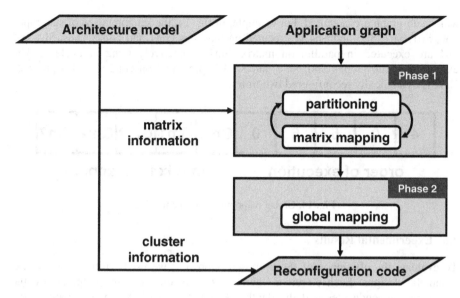

Fig. 13. Mapping model

Phase 1: Partitioning and matrix mapping

The aim of the first step is to partition a function graph into smaller sub-graphs so that each sub-graph fits in a single matrix. For this purpose, partitioning and matrix mapping methods are processed. To be valid, a partitioning result must respect the following constraints:

• The total number of operation in the sub-graphs is the same as the one in the initial graph
• There is no cyclic dependency.

Each sub-graph obtained during partitioning is mapped onto the matrix using the matrix mapping method defined previously. An exhaustive research is performed to ensure that the best mapping is found. If the matrix mapping fails, the partitioning is modified and new matrix mappings are performed. This exploration loop, represented in fig. 13 through a feedback arrow, is performed until the sub-graphs fit in a single matrix. The result of the first step is a new graph composed of subgraphs and a set of mapping solutions associated to each subgraph.

Phase 2: Global mapping

The second phase maps the set of sub-graphs obtained during the phase 1 onto the cluster of matrices. The objective is to find a mapping and an execution order minimizing the communication cost, the configuration cost, the number of cells non-used and the execution time. A Fast Elitist Non-Dominated Sorting Genetic Algorithm (NSGA II) [13] is used to minimize these metrics.

A mapping solution is encoded as a two part chromosome (fig. 14): the first part represents the execution order of the subgraphs; the second part gives the matrix on which sub-graph are executed. For example, in fig. 14, the set composed of subgraphs Sb0, Sb1, Sb2, Sb3 and Sb4 is executed on matrices Gm1 and Gm2. Thus, Sb1 and Sb4 are executed in parallel on matrix Gm1 respectively Gm2 at cycle 0. The execution of sub-graphs Sb0, Sb 2 and Sb 3 is pipelined on Gm2. For this purpose, Gm2 is dynamically reconfigured two times.

order of execution   **matrix for mapping**

Fig. 14. Global mapping solution encoding

3.8 Experimental Results

To evaluate the efficiency of the proposed approach, we used Xilinx-Virtex-4 [14] schematic designs. Each circuit is characterized by the number of operations, the number of dependencies and the depth (i.e. the length of the longest path in the circuit). The designs are modified to reach the granularity required for the logic cell (two 1-bit inputs and two 1-bit outputs). The target architecture is based on Modified-Omega clusters of 4d4w matrices. The experimental results are given in tab. 2, in terms of the number of sub-functions obtained after the partitioning phase, the number of dependencies between sub-functions, the ratio between the number of logic operations and the number of sub-functions (fill factor) and finally the number of failures for matrix mapping during partitioning.

These results depend on the following factors:

- the size of the circuit: In the partitioning, no cyclic dependency is allowed between sub-functions. Moreover, the restriction of connectivity must be respected in order to route data coherently in matrices. So, partitioning results depend on number of dependences and the size of the circuit.
- failures on matrix mapping: During partitioning when a sub-graph cannot be mapped onto a matrix, the sub-graph has to be partitioned until it can be mapped. This case occurred twice for CMP8, i.e. the corresponding graph was reduced three times.

Table 2. Experimental cluster mapping results for Xilinx-Virtex-4 benchmark functions

Benchmk circuit	No. operations	No. dependencies	Logical depth	No. sub-functions	No. dependencies	Fill factor (%)	No. hw placement failures
ALU2	45	64	14	6	9	46.9	1
CMP8	59	75	11	9	14	40.6	2
ADD8	101	132	22	11	18	57.4	0
ADSU8	133	180	25	18	30	45.8	0
CMP16	142	189	22	19	41	46.7	2
ADD16	197	260	38	21	36	58.6	0
ADSU16	261	356	41	27	49	60.5	1

4 Insights and Future Challenges

In this work, we have firstly explored some of the opportunities opened up by the electrical behaviour of the double-gate CNTFET. We focused primarily on a specific property, namely the enabling of p-type or n-type device behaviour to be achieved in the same CNTFET according to the voltage applied to the back-gate. We have developed a family of dynamically reconfigurable logic cell, based on these devices and configured by the set of back gate bias voltages. These fine-grain reconfigurable cells have been considered as a universal reconfigurable cell enabling the synthesis of any Boolean function.

We then introduced a cluster-based matrix architecture useful for fine-grain reconfigurable logic cells based on emerging devices. This cluster-based architecture uses fixed interconnection topologies in order to reduce the overhead induced by conventional approaches. We have proposed a method to map specific functions to the matrices of reconfigurable cells. This method has been used to analyze intra-matrix topologies with respect to various metrics and shown that the mapping success rate is about 90% for 6-point function graphs and about 40% for 12-point graphs when using the Modified-Omega interconnect topology in a 4x4 matrix. This new function mapping method is a key step towards using fine-grain reconfigurable cells for the on-the fly and partial reprogrammability.

Finally, we proposed a methodology for mapping applications onto the cluster-based architectures. This model enables the exploration of the potential of this type of architectures for future applications and was used successfully to map complex benchmark functions onto the architecture. The model consists of two main steps accomplished through three complementary methods: partitioning, matrix mapping and cluster mapping.

The experience gained through this work lead us to believe that carbon-based computing fabrics can be a suitable support for pervasively deployment in many industries such as communications, energy, transport and healthcare. Tomorrow's computing platforms must achieve high computing throughput at very low power, while maintaining a level of robustness and capacity to be redeployed to new applications via software programming on very flexible hardware. In this way, engineers and scientists can benefit from almost unlimited computing power and can concentrate on developing imaginative and high added-value applications, while seamlessly supported by highly flexible and automatically configurable hardware and software programming models.

Such design of nanofabrics is at the interface between two scientific communities: that of nanoscience and nanotechnology on one hand, and that of data processing and embedded systems on the other. Critical challenges from the design point of view are to be able to understand how such devices can best be used in architectures and indeed if they can be expected to deliver significant benefits at this level, and to extend existing design and simulation approaches to take into account the nanoelectronic approach. Close collaboration between designers and technologists is key to the strengthening of mutual design approaches necessary for the development of nanoelectronic systems and the generation of truly original designs exploiting the specific properties of nanodevices. The outcome of such collaboration is a clearer understanding of choices among the broad spectrum of potential devices and possible technologies capable of challenging conventional approaches in future nanoscale applications.

In our view, technology is evolving at such a rate that it is necessary to break the traditional technology – device – compact model – circuit – architecture development cycle by focusing on the fast-track integration of new devices into many-core computing platforms, through the implementation of a vertical and integrated research approach. In this way, circuit and architectural design activities are based on reasonable hypotheses issuing from device and technology work, and the development of the aforementioned devices and technology is focused towards the needs of high-level architectures.

References

1. TOP 500 Supercomputing Sites (2009), http://www.top500.org
2. International Technology Roadmap for Semiconductors (2007), http://public.itrs.net
3. O'Connor, I., et al.: CNTFET Modeling and Reconfigurable Logic-Circuit design. IEEE Trans. Circuits and Systems 54(11), 2365–2379 (2007)
4. Chau, R., et al.: Benchmarking Nanotechnology for High-Performance and Low-Power Logic Transistor Applications. IEEE Trans. Nanotechnology 4(2), 153 (2005)
5. Raychowdhury, A., Roy, K.: Carbon-Nanotube-Based Voltage-Mode Multiple-Valued Logic Design. IEEE Trans. Nanotechnology 4(2), 168–179 (2005)
6. Sordan, R., Balasubramanian, K., Burghard, M., Kern, K.: Exclusive-OR gate with a single carbon nanotube. Appl. Phys. Lett. 88, 053119 (2006)
7. Lin, Y., Appenzeller, J., Knoch, J., Avouris, P.: High-Performance Carbon Nanotube Field-Effect Transistor With Tunable Polarities. IEEE Trans. Nanotechnology 4(5) (September 2005)
8. Moritz, C.A., et al.: Fault-Tolerant Nanoscale Processors on Semiconductor Nanowire Grids. IEEE Trans. CASI 54(11), 2422 (2007)
9. Ding, L., Tselev, A., Wang, J., et al.: Selective Growth of Well-Aligned Semiconducting Single-Walled Carbon Nanotubes. Nano. Lett. 9(2), 800 (2009)
10. Akinwande, D., Yasuda, S., Paul, B., Fujita, S., Close, G., Wong, H.S.P.: Monolithic integration of CMOS VLSI and carbon nanotubes for hybrid nanotechnology applications. IEEE Trans. Nanotechnology 7(5), 636 (2008)
11. Beyhoux, J.-M., Happy, H., Dambrine, G., Derycke, V., Goffman, M., Bourgoin, J.-P.: An 8-GHz ft Carbon Nanotube Field-effect transistor for Gigahertz Range Applications. IEEE Electron Device Letters 27(8), 681–683 (2006)
12. Adams, G.B., Agrawal, D.P., Siegel, H.J.: A Survey and Comparison of Fault-Tolerant Multistage Interconnection Networks. Computer 20(6), 14–27 (1987)
13. Kalyanmoy, D.: A Fast Elitist Non-Dominated Sorting Genetic Algorithm for Multi-Objective Optimization: NSGA-II. IEEE Trans. Evol. Comput. 6(3), 149 (2002)
14. Xilin, X.: Virtex-4 Libraries Guide for Schematic Designs (2009)

Challenges and Emerging Technologies for System Integration beyond the End of the Roadmap of Nano-CMOS

Sergio Bampi and Ricardo Reis

PGMicro/PPGC, Instituto de Informática,
Universidade Federal do Rio Grande do Sul
Porto Alegre, Brazil
{bampi,reis}@inf.ufrgs.br

Abstract. By 2020 it is very likely that nano-CMOS will reach the end of the scaling roadmap. Such end will not mean the demise of silicon technology at all. While there are uncertainties as to what will be the show-stoppers, there is a large number of transitional and compatible to CMOS technologies that will be more important than just 2-D scaling. This paper discusses possible limitations bringing the end of scaling and also proposes a likely scenario for hardware technology evolution and related challenges for integrating systems in the next 20 years. The scenario beyond the end of the roadmap is drawn, in which key technologies will be developed to be compatible with nano-scaled CMOS in silicon, and not to replace it entirely. Transitional technologies will rather co-exist and be built upon a basic CMOS-like technology platform of silicon-on-insulator. Radically new devices at the 1-10 nm scale will most likely be built on a silicon substrate with the same technical requirements (such as cleanness, lithographic resolution, long-range ordering, etc) of near end-of-roadmap CMOS industry. The end of scaling will not necessarily lead to the onset of a post-silicon era. Advanced materials research has not pointed so far to a non-silicon scenario well beyond 2020. The computing systems challenges will be dealt with new forms of integration, hierarchically ordered from the micron-level, to sub-micron level (500nm to 100nm) non-digital, down to nano-scaled transistors on silicon further down to 10 nm. In this hierarchy, at the bottom, it is highly possible that disruptive molecular-level devices (self-assembled in the scale of 2 to 10 nanometers) will eventually be production-worthy for 100 Giga- to Tera-scale devices integration. Structures like graphene-based carbon tubes or planes are the most viable candidates for molecular devices. In this presentation the computer-systems relevant issues of systems power dissipation, noise, hardware design complexity, and resilience to systems failures in the presence of device variances and faults, are addressed as the challenging computing research topics that will guide future research in computing architectures at the tera-scale integration beyond 2020.

Keywords: Nanoelectronics, Beyond CMOs, Roadmap, CMOS.

J. Becker, M. Johann, and R. Reis (Eds.): VLSI-SoC 2009, IFIP AICT 360, pp. 21–33, 2011.
© IFIP International Federation for Information Processing 2011

1 Introduction

CMOS (complementary metal-oxide-semiconductor) circuits on silicon substrates of various types (bulk, silicon-on-insulator SOI, strained silicon with silicon-germanium alloys, etc) have been the dominant devices on which ICT (digital information and communication technologies) hardware and software have been developed for about 30 years. The integrated circuit and discrete silicon devices industries are even older, namely 50 years old in 2009 since Jack Kilby's patent in 1959 [1]. Reliable estimation is that the worldwide semiconductor industry reached US$261.9 billion revenue in 2008 [4], a 4.4 % decline from 2007, due to the 2008-2009 economic downturn worldwide. In 2007 the revenue in this industry topped at US$273 billion per year, a dollar-mark that is forecasted to be surpassed only in 2011, after the economic recovery expected in 2010. Electronics manufacturing worldwide produces an output of roughly US$1.6 Trillion per year, and it has grown about 3 percentage points over the average growth of the rest of the world-manufacturing sector, consistently in the period 1996-2008. IT services enabled by equipment produced by this industry will continue to grow at even higher rates, powered by software as-services and by the increasingly pervasive communication services that will grow above the average world GDP growth rate for the next decades. IT and wireless communications devices are forecasted to move into most objects the humans relate to. Chips with simple processors and communicators will be embedded into buildings and most life-related engines, as ubiquitous as paints or information ducts. The ever-decreasing cost of chips in this micro- and nano-worlds provides the efficiency gains that will make this IT explosion viable. The integration paradigm in semiconductor circuits – reliable and low-cost due to mass-production - will ultimately make it viable to connect 10^{11} to 10^{12} objects simultaneously to the internet, roughly hundreds of IP-powered systems or nodes per individual, in average.

The grand challenges in computer science will be shaped by this tera-scale number of complex embedded hardware, autonomous systems and communicating devices, all interacting much like general-purpose computers do today over the Internet protocols. What will be the key enablers to this internet-of-things? In our view, towards 2030 the main-stay of the electronics integration technology will continue to be nano-scaled CMOS devices manufactured on silicon wafers. To which disruptive, yet-in-research devices will be added, to be made compatible with silicon ultra-clean in-fab processing. For instance, solid-stage storage devices with 5-10 nm-sized devices for each 1-bit of RAM, integrated in the range of 256Gbits/chip is within reach of mass-production in the next 10 years. Still manufactured in CMOS. Also other types of sensors, which will be compatible with – if not on the same - silicon substrate as the dense CMOS devices, will bring the "sensing-and-computing" hardware integration into a great variety of products and applications. With great benefits resulting thereof for health-care, cheap communications, and intelligent machines. These will sense tens of environmental variables, do analog and digital processing in CMOS, and then act more and more autonomously.

Mature electronic packaging technologies at the 10-100 micron scale will continue to evolve to provide increasing hardware power efficiency. The 3-D integration will make new systems into compact volumes – with silicon dies in them, interconnected by fine wires (10 μm to 40 μm wide). While this is an evolutionary scenario drawn in this paper, its enormous technical and scientific impacts in terms of building ever-more complex systems have to be modeled, designed and fabricated as computer systems in the giga-scale era. Most importantly, because such systems are of heterogeneous nature, in which sensing physical events is as important as communicating information over RF devices; all with many digital processors and dedicated software embedded at their core. Moreover, one can assert that the impact on Computer Science brought by disruptive device technologies, even at the molecular level, is most often a change of focus at the system to model, instead of the introduction of a radically new scientific methodology in Computer Science. Hence, Computer Systems research will continue to thrive on this method: system modeling, verify/refine the computing model, actual design, and finally, realize and fabricate those complex systems. Designing them today is an extremely complex task, in which hardware integration capabilities in silicon already surpass the capacity to design complex systems-on-chip timely. Impacts on the ICT (information and telecommunication technologies) due to this heterogeneous integration will be enormous. The companies that may lead the pack in modeling, specification, designing and also manufacturing of those nano-circuits are poised to rip the most economic benefits in the world ICT market. Clever and IP-powered electronic devices will also unveil new large IT applications and markets

This paper is organized as follows: in section 2 we address the ITC grand challenges and the ITRS roadmap for the world electronics industry. Section 3 briefly addresses roadblocks to continuing down-scaling (size reduction) of circuits on planar structures and the emerging alternatives for silicon. Section 4 presents the systems-on-chips challenges, which are more relevant to overcome when dealing with computer systems design. In Section 5 the impacts for the future of the hardware industry will be addressed, while section 6 concludes this paper.

2   Related Work

The advances in ICT technologies present grand challenges for advanced research in computing systems [2]. The most likely scenario in the global nano-electronics industry hints for transitional and non-replacing integrated technologies to be introduced with silicon devices – far from full replacement of the latter. For reasons that are dealt with in sections 3 and 4 of this paper, it is very likely that a transition to non-silicon IC technologies will not take place in the next 20 years.

The most comprehensive industry expert's panel publishes the ITRS (International Technology Roadmap for Semiconductors) roadmap [3]. The roadblocks to future progression in terms of integration into a silicon surface are well mapped, and several problems with yet unknown technical solutions are pointed out and updated yearly in that roadmap. The significance of those roadblocks is by no means saying that silicon will be replaced as the implementation technology – instead it is pointing to likely events that could be "*showstoppers*" for more integration onto silicon. Once overcoming them, the industry envisions the goal of fabricating flash memories with densities up to 256 to 512 Gbits/chip by 2021, compared to 16G - 32G bits/chip today. The industry forecasts these densities using nano-CMOS, still on silicon chips. Table 1 shows the predictions by experts of the ITRS panel up to the year 2024, for several circuit-meaningful dimensions in CMOS technologies: half-pitch in flash memories uncontactedpolycides (polysilicon with silicides on top), photoresist printed gate length, and physical gate lengths in state-of-the art microprocessor in mass production (MPUs, in Table 1). The technology roadblocks that exist for the continuing scaling down to 7 to 8 nm technology by 2024, with physical gate lengths of such quantum-confined electron wavelength, are too many to discuss in short. Compared to 23nm of nano-CMOS 32nm technologies currently (2010) in production in selected state-of-the-art nano-electronics production facilities, areal densities can be improved by a factor of about10-15 times. Producing such physical channel lengths of the order of the silicon wavelength will mean effectively quantum devices, where energy bands will considerable differ from the bulk semiconductor.

Table 1. Evolution of CMOS Scaling [ITRS, 2009]

Year of Fabrication	2009	2012	2015	2018	2021	2024
Uncontactedpoli-Si ½ pitch [nm]	38	25	18	12.6	8.9	6.3
MPU/ASIC Metal_1 ½ pith [nm]	54	32	21	15	10.6	7.5
MPU Printed Gate Length [nm]	47	31	22	15.7	11.1	7.9
MPU Physical Gate length [nm]	29	22	17	12.8	9.7	7.4
Bits/chip DRAM production [Gb]	2G	4G	8G	16G	32G	64G
Bits/chip FLASH production [Gb]2 bits/cell	22G	32G	64G	256G	512G	2048G

The minimum physical length evolution in the past and future is shown in Figure 2, in a log y-scale, to show the enormous scaling achieved in microelectronics since 1970. This dimension downscaling alone does not provide the full picture. A factor of 4 to 5 in the transistor length reduction, from today to 2020, can lead to a 10-15X (maximum 20X) integration gain, at best, if measured in logic gates per square millimeter of silicon area, considering the logic part of a system-on-chip design. The point is that logic gates are very different than digital cells for storing bits. For this reason, we foresee a large divergence in the semiconductor industry paths for two kinds of products: a) memory chips, b) processing (analog or digital) chips, named MPU/ASIC in Table 1. For both types, the 3-D integration will provide another leap in terms of systems integration. With gains on the order of 10X - 100X in integration density, at a lower cost than planar-only downscaling and integration.

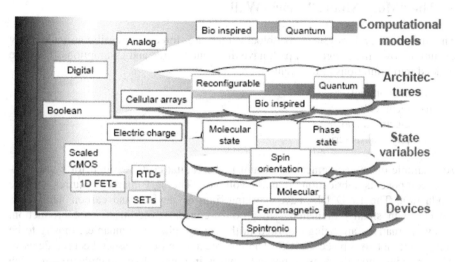

Fig. 1. Conceptual hierarchy of alternative computing devices (ITRS, 2007)

The ITRS industry panel assesses continuously the emerging devices, which are candidates to replace silicon. Figure 1 from ITRS conceptually separates the emerging devices in terms of the state variables used to enable in the physical world the digital state abstraction (charge, as in CMOS devices, phase state of a molecule or atom, and spin or magnetic number state of a given electron level or molecule, respectively). The devices in the red polygon (resonant tunneling device - RTD, single-electron SET switch) are non-conventional devices also fabricated on silicon planar technology. Currently the carbon nanostructures (single plane, carbon nano-tubes - CNTs, multi-walled tubes, etc) are the most likely candidates for the non-silicon transistor. These devices are being pursued at the research laboratories precisely because they can be manufactured by keeping compatibility with conventional planar CMOS silicon fabrication. Low dimensionality structures (2-D monoatomic layers) require an extremely clean surface on which to be built, like those of silicon wafers today. In fact, 2-D mono-layers of atoms on semiconductors were demonstrated in labs since the late 1970s. The aforementioned compatibility is the main reason as to why CNTs are considered the alternative transistor, replacing nanowires of silicon – or most likely sharing the silicon wafer surface with silicon nanowires over insulators. The alternatives in spintronics or molecular devices will not be described here, even though they deserve careful discussion as revolutionary alternative candidates in the future technology roadmaps. These emerging devices are being pursued in pre-competitive research phase exactly because they do not rule out the compatibility with current silicon technologies. These alternatives are in the infancy of materials and devices research, well behind the systems integration capability of current nano-CMOS technologies.

3 The "More Moore" Brick-Walls

The technical and physical roadblocks that are forecast for silicon technology evolution down the integration path have different natures and assumptions. They are divided into limitations of different natures, namely:

i)   economical
ii)   technical,
iii) electrical and
iv)   physical/materials.

An example of an economical constraint is the capital costs required for system-on-chip components fabrication in mass volumes. The ICT market requires volume production. The R&D labs have working 5nm Si devices and carbon nano-tubes devices with smaller diameter – in proof-of-concept experiments, not production. Many alternatives are being explored in the semiconductor companies, mostly to be compatible not to replace CMOS. The complexity and cost issues become decisive when moving those to densely packed devices in high-volume manufacturing. High fabrication costs today already require larger and larger chip volumes to recover the capital costs incurred on fabricationinfrastructure. Memory chips are one class of components that find very large market demand to justify such investments. The processors+memory (general purpose multi-processors in fact) paradigm is another typeof such component. Integrated optical cameras are another class of product in high volumes today. Other products for high volumemanufacturing are rare to emerge.

The limits or "brick-walls" imposed to silicon scaling that are of a physical nature are shown in Figure 2. The oxide thicknesses in MOSFET transistors today have reached 1 (one) nanometer to 1.5 nm, which is the lower limit for direct metal-to-semiconductor electron tunneling through the insulator. This limit cannot be surpassed, and the solution was to replace silicon-dioxide by another insulator with a higher dielectric constant. This material solution is already in production at leading fabrication of 45nm nano-CMOS today. Device structures at 10nm sizes have quantum-mechanical behavior since the conduction band electron wave-length for a thermal-voltage average energy is typically around 10nm. This limit will be attained by the physical gate lengths (Lg) of production transistorsin the year 2020, as predicted by ITRS in Table 1.

In Figure 2 any dimension below 0.3 nm is certainly hypothetical, since this is just the separation between individual nuclei of the atoms in the silicon solid, which is a physical scale at which the electron orbital's are probabilistically distributed as quantum particles binding the atoms. This limit is marked in Figure 2, and it is clearly physically unattainable in the gate oxide thickness. Instead, higher-K dielectrics will be used to surmount this barrier. Those are limits to the evolution of current CMOS silicon chips, which combined to the economics of this industry will eventually call for a " show-stopper" in terms of CMOS down-scaling in the Lg (physical gate length) curve in Figure 2.

The first ITRS roadmaps (ITRS, 2007) were introduced to predict the evolution of the CMOS technology in the time period marked in Figure 2 by the top arrow. Some industry experts forecast that at 16nm CMOS node (for which 7 to 9 nm Lg will be the physical transistor length, the same magnitude of the in-band electron wavelength in Fig. 2), the circuits will be at the limit of its technical and economical viability, at least for processors. And this could occur before 2020. Memory devices could experience even further downscaling, hence an increasing divergence between memory and processor CMOS technologies is forecasted by the authors. It is important that the challenges for CMOS downscaling be understood as a combination of factors of the natures above-mentioned: i) economical ii) technical, iii) electrical, and iv) physical or materials.

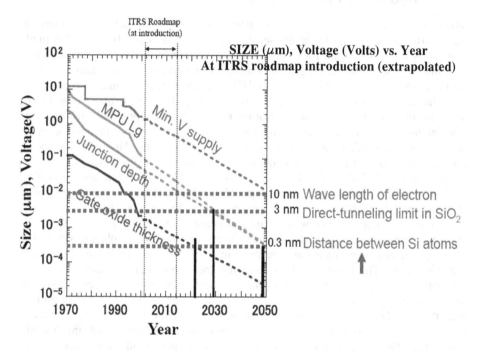

Fig. 2. Evolution of CMOS technology: the minimum supply voltage, oxide thickness and junction depth. Comparison to basic physical limits – electron wavelength in conduction-band and distance between silicon atoms [5].

While those roadblocks combined may hinder the mainstream use of 16nm CMOS in 2020, they will not drive silicon technology out of the mainstay, or make current silicon technologies less viable. The "more-Moore" brick-walls will not be dealt with in detail here, since they are most out of the scope of architectural challenges. The relevant point is that no other economically and technically viable integration technology other than CMOS is within sight. The economic gains of the hardware systems integration will be moved into the "more than Moore" devices, which are addressed in the next section.

4 Grand Challenges for Systems-on-Chips Integration

The most important computing devices in the future will be at the leaf-end of the Web, as always-on, ambient-aware micro-devices. For their impact to be far-reaching, they will have to be compact, resilient to failures and attacks, communicating through RF. They are ubiquitous, in most senses of their operation. This will be the economic driver to sustain the growing of the computing infrastructure into most objects. The main challenges for the design of this new hardware are listed below, according to the characteristics of the hardware architectures that will need considerable research and breakthroughs.

4.1 Heterogeneous Hardware Integration

Silicon integration technology will not reach the end of affordable fabrication on planar structures on-wafer in the foreseeable future. Going below 10nm CMOS in all film levels is still uncertain for technical reasons aforementioned. The new trend of 3-D, multi-stack, multi-die integration will be an enabling technology that will push the integration level not only a factor of 100 over conventional planar silicon: it will allow heterogeneous integration of systems-in-package that will contain: transducers to electro-optical devices, sensors, actuators, besides the usual processor and memory subsystems. The so-called more-than-Moore path to integration will provide more complex and new functions of high value for the IT devices. The 3-level stack of mass-produced digital cameras is today just an example of a system technology that has just begun. By 2020 3-D integration will make viable powerful massively parallel computers on few cubic centimeters, with 1K to 10K CPUs, for which the power efficiency and dissipation is the single most important design constraint.

An important impact on computing and communication will happen with the opto-electronics integration. Currently the transducers like lasers and photodetectors for serial optical communication links are done in III-V (like InP, InGaAsP) compound semiconductors. This is a niche market that may merge into 3-D packages with silicon substrates. Recent developments on photonic devices with nano-structured silicon show promising perspectives for optic emitters on silicon – an important breakthrough. This will provide more integration, not an optical computer, since these new devices are well suited for serial communication links, not information processing. The photo-electronics systems in the future could move onto silicon substrates, narrowing the market for III-V semiconductor devices like LEDs and discrete semiconductor lasers.

4.2 Nano-power Computing for Autonomic Systems

The research on autonomic systems will strive on a technology that has yet to be discovered: computing systems that can reliably compute in bursts, at very low MIPS rates, and still be able to communicate to the next hierarchy at the network, using average nano-watts over long periods of time (years) and few micro-watts over short communication times. Heterogeneous integration will be key again to provide intelligent energy scavenging from the environment for such devices. This is a well-known research field in CS, which still requires breakthrough-engineering solutions at the circuit level.

4.3 Design and Architectural Complexity

The sequential computing paradigm and the ever-increasing complexity of systems-on-chip are considerable challenges to be overcome at the system design tools. Massively parallel systems are viable to integrate for general computing onto single chips. The applications and the parallel programming models are key to demonstrate an efficient use of such parallelism. The restrictions are well known since the mid-80s research on parallel – and room-scaled systems: While few parts could be computing, other parts sit idle wasting power. For this reason, the software stack necessary to exploit effectively the massively parallel systems also needs challenging innovation.

The application-specific complex systems can decompose the applications and map it beforehand to specific silicon cores. Some could be programmable cores, some certainly dedicated cores. These systems are, for instance, multiprocessors SoCs that are specifically designed for certain applications. This is viable for network processing, media processors (audio & video streams), and pattern matching processing. General computing is a different challenge though. Designing in parallel and making effective usage of hundreds of processors simultaneously is a methodology yet to be dealt with effectively in the computer science research community.

4.4 Simple IP Objects – Sense-Compute-Communicate

The future Net or Internet will have 10^{11} to 10^{12} objects interconnected – from PDAs to vehicles to mundane appliances. Communication hardware has to be cheap (integrated in silicon, with processors and memory), hence mass-produced. And this ubiquitous computing era will be enabled in silicon chips – not in molecular level devices, for certain. Molecular devices will find applications in dense memories at Tera-scale bits/cm^2, but for radiation fields for communication over 1m to 100m the technology requires tens of µW or even mW power, and this RF systems requires much larger silicon area than Mbits of storage. The first appliances to reach 100% connectivity arethe communication and entertainment gadgets (like phones, audio and video systems) that empower individuals to communicate.

The market driver for electronics now and into decades ahead will be at the leaf-cells of this net-of-things, in local wireless personal networks (PANs). And these PANs will have simple objects that have to do simple tasks to empower the Net to a ubiquitous phase: to sense, to compute efficiently and to communicate with a small bandwidth to the next IP hop. Most connected objects will have one IP address, but locally will interoperate with multiple sensors and computing devices – which are to be cheap and simple to design. For those, the conventional nano-scale CMOS, at the current level of 65nm or below is more than sufficient. In fact the 45nm CMOS technology available today is too expensive for most system needs in ubiquitous communication. Energy transducing at µW level requires area, not area reduction. Smaller, in this case, does not mean better. With sensors integration on-chip this is often the case also. High performance analog sub-systems, with large signal-to-noise ratio, also do not scale in total silicon area as they are designed in more advanced CMOS.

4.5 Electronic Design Automation Tools

The quality of the SoCs design is directly dependent of the quality of the EDA (Electronic Design Automation) tools available. So, the challenge is to find out algorithms that can emulate the skills and strategies of experienced designers and cope with the restriction and features of new fabrication technologies. The variability of recent and future technologies demands new design tools sets, tuned to new design methodologies, which could provide reliable SoCs even using non-reliable components. Also to minimize power and delay there is a strong request to reduce at most the amount of transistors used to implement a function [6]. The reduction of the needed number of transistors to implement a function helps to reduce area, and doing this the average length of interconnections will also be reduced, and consequently the delay will also be reduced. But maybe the main advantage on reducing the number of transistors is the reduction on the static power consumption due to the leakage current [6]. The traditional standard cell approach is far away from an optimal physical design approach, as the number of available cells in a traditional cell library has no more than 150 different logic functions. If we put a limit of 4 stacked transistors in a CMOs circuit the number of possible logic functions goes to 3503 [7], several times more than the number of functions available in a traditional cell library. So, it is needed a tool that would be able to generate any kind of transistor network, even with different number of P and N transistors. ASTRAN [8] is a tool that can do it.

Also, in a cell library we find normally 3 different sizing for each cell. When doing the cell generation on the fly we can do any sizing we want. So, a cell is automatically customized to the location of the circuit where it will be inserted. The Physical Design at a Network of Transistors Level depends on the construction of an all-new physical design approach.

Another challenge is the search for efficient EDA tools to cope with the design of 3D chips.

5 Impacts on the Global Hardware Industry

The ICT hardware is produced in complex industries for the global IT market. The electronics industry is globally a 1.6 Trillion US dollars industry, in which the key in its supply chain are the semiconductor chip industry and the software industry. The semiconductor industry accounted for around US$ 273 Billion revenues in the 2007 calendar year.

The integrated circuits (ICs) are high tech intermediate industrial goods, essential for all electronics. The system drivers for the IC industry can be separated in the following categories: a) portable/consumer devices; b) networking and communication; c) medical electronics; d) office and departmental computing devices; e) automotive, and f) defense electronics. The ICT hardware is the most important driver for the semiconductor industry. The new market drivers for ICT are the devices for the ubiquitous, ambient-aware, permanently-on computing devices. Mostly of light computing load, but extreme mobility and energy autonomy. The intelligent objects of the future InterNet will require cheap, and yet powerful and communicating devices. These everlasting requirements mean that silicon circuits on planar wafers will not become economically unviable in the foreseeable future. Quite the contrary, the semiconductor industry will be a key enabler of the next generation computing – and in all spectrum of computing power. Uninformed is the confusion to be made with the trend to draw and fabricate nano-wires onto silicon substrates – the silicon manufacturing for CMOS transistors below 10nm is technically feasible, although such manufacturing is currently ruled out as being too costly. And not viable with photolithography tools that today use deep UV (ultraviolet) 193 nm light sources to fabricate 50nm device structures. Hence, the experts in technology presently assert that it may not be viable to assemble 10 Billion dollars fabrication lines for very high volume of silicon, but they do not contradict the fact that 45 nm to 180 nm CMOS nano-devices are economically the viable integration choice, now and into future generations. In this reasoning, the CMOS silicon technologies and their derivatives will be mainstream for an industry that reached 270 billion dollar yearly, and it is bound to increase.

On the systems design area, the impact of complex systems integration in silicon has already established a global economic paradigm for systems development: the design teams in the nano-electronics industry are increasingly global, and they require a tight integration of software embedding techniques and hardware design. The latter enabling the former. The main impacts for the industry in the future are:

a) Managing complex systems design of ever increasing complexity hardware in global, multi-national engineering teams of software and hardware developers. The industry goal is to manage the high Non-Recurring Engineering (NRE) expenses, as well as to develop products that reach high volume scale quickly. General computing/communication devices are by definition high volume in the global markets. Embedded software is essential to enable services and other country-specific features, while the chip devices will have to truly global enabler.

b) The arrangement of 16nm-22nm CMOS factories around inter-company alliances for manufacturing. The complexity and challenges of CMOS manufacturing are to be overcome only to the extent that the integration benefits override the competition and can financially offset the large investments for CMOS wafer fabs. Such alliances are growing since the inception of Sematech in the 1980´s, an organization that brings together development teams from tens of different leading semiconductor companies to develop the key technologies for the future of semiconductor manufacturing.

c) Design methodologies will have to incorporate "more-than-Moore" heterogeneous device design. Integrating optics, sensors, actuator, and the like will require more complex and diverse EDA tools, dealing with other domains, not just digital systems design.

d) Design methodologies to cope with the request of strong reduction on power consumption. The cost of transistor is being reduced more and more, but the cost of energy to work a transistor is more and more expensive, as well the mechanisms to do power dissipation.

e) The integration technologies of importance are both on-chip planar tooling, as well as multi-chip 3-D stacking with through-silicon vias. This system-in-package trend is to use silicon thinned-wafers with chips on top, similar to what a PC board does with copper. Hence, silicon will be replacing board layers, instead of being replaced by emerging devices.

f) The trend towards miniaturized components on a packaged 3-D system, of about 1 to 5 cm3, will be the mainstream in the 2020´s, or even earlier. This is a transitional technology that will not drive silicon out of the computing – it will instead thrive on it.

g) 3-D integration is a key technology that will further even more the divergence between manufacturing technologies for memory on-silicon, and manufacturing technologies for processors, sensors, actuators and RF front-end circuits.

6 Conclusions

This paper discussed the challenges for ICT hardware integration technologies. In our scenario we dismiss the "beyond silicon" jargon commonly used as a synonym for silicon technology full replacement. Future disrupting technologies will have to find compatibility with computing-on-silicon, 3-D stacking of dies or otherwise they will be ruled out as unviable by the leading hardware manufacturers. Transitional technologies are likely to emerge, in which at the nano-scale semiconductor materials other than silicon (Si) will be used. Si substrate will still hold submicron-scale devices. This is a reality today, with germanium 2-D ultra-thin layers (sub-10-nm thicknesses) as part of 20nm CMOS transistors. Future transitional technologies will include carbon on different forms and shapes (tubes or planes called graphenes), and even light-emitting devices with nano-particles. All being held by a silicon matrix. Transitional technologies will enable new systems integration on silicon, even electro-optics integration.

In this paper the authors proposed that: i) nano-scaled CMOS on silicon will remain the basic technology well into the 2020s, and will still be the key for electronics systems innovation; ii) non-silicon technologies that are compatible with the silicon substrate and can co-exist in the silicon fabrication line will be the winner technologies for the next massive hardware platform of commercial significance for general computing: heterogeneous system-in-package, with the most valuable general computing and memory still relying on silicon chips with complex 3-D integration between dies; iii) the CMOS technology evolution will diverge into two CMOS tiers: one technology for very dense memories, tera-scale bits on-the-same-chip, for main memory, and the other CMOS tier for multi-processors and x-level caches on a single chip. This latter CMOS tier will be used for programmable logic devices, which will continue to play a key role in computing systems design well into the future.

The architectures with over 1K or 10K processors per 3-D package (less than 1 to 3 cm3) will be the main high-end computing engines for servers in the 2020s. The issues that are relevant to the industry are: how to move forward in heterogeneous integration to create value and commercial opportunities in computer systems design; and how to create value and new technology jobs by fabricating the devices that embed ICT intelligence and bring to fruition the capacity to envision future ICT products. Not the least, industry has to produce them on the scale that the economics of this industry dictates, as envisioning is easy, making them is very challenging. In the 2020s and beyond, ICT will still be relying on silicon technology.

Acknowledgements. The authors acknowledge the support of CNPq and FINEP for their research in micro- and nano-electronics, as well as the PGMICRO and PPGC graduate students and faculty members at UFRGS Federal University. This work is being supported by CNPq through the Millennium Institute NAMITEC (Network of Excellence Centers) and by the current National Institute (INCT) on Nano-electronics, which has more than 15 Universities working in challenging aspects of micro and nano-circuits integration in Brazil.

References

[1] Kilby, J.: US Patent (1959)
[2] Brazilian Computer Society: Grand Challenges in Computer Science Research in Brazil 2006-2016, Brazil, pgs 25 (2006), http://www.sistemas.sbc.org.br (last accessed December 22,2008)
[3] International Roadmap Committee. The International Technology Roadmap for Semiconductors - 2009 (2009), http://www.itrs.net (last accessed January 18, 2010)
[4] Gartner Group (2008), http://www.eweek.com/c/a/Desktop...Chip-Revenue....Semiconductor-Industry (last accessed February 09, 2009)
[5] Hiroshi, I.: Future of CMOS Technology and Manufacturing. EEE DL talk at Federal University of Rio Grande do Sul, mimeo, p. 105 (2007)
[6] Reis, R.: Design Automation of Transistor Networks, a New Challenge. In: IEEE International Symposium on Circuits and Systems, ISCAS 2011, Rio de Janeiro, Brazil, May 15-19, pp. 2485–2488. IEEE Press, Los Alamitos (2011) ISBN: 978-1-4244-9472-9
[7] Detjens, E., et al.: Technology Mapping in MIS. In: IEEE ICCAD, pp. 116–119 (1987)
[8] Ziesemer, A., Lazzari, C., Reis, R.: Transistor Level Automatic Layout Generator for non-Complementary CMOS Cells. In: International Conference on Very Large Scale Integration, IFIP/CEDA VLSI-SoC 2007, pp. 116–121 (2007)

Thermal Modeling and Management of Liquid-Cooled 3D Stacked Architectures

Ayşe Kıvılcım Coşkun[1], José L. Ayala[2],
David Atienza[3], and Tajana Simunic Rosing[4]

[1] Boston University, Boston, MA 02215, USA
acoskun@bu.edu
[2] Complutense University of Madrid, Spain
jayala@fdi.ucm.es
[3] Ecole Polytechnique Fédérale de Lausanne (EPFL), Switzerland
david.atienza@epfl.ch
[4] University of California, San Diego, CA 92039, USA
tajana@ucsd.edu

Abstract. 3D stacked architectures are getting increasingly attractive as they improve yield, reduce interconnect power and latency, and enable integrating layers manufactured with different technologies on the same chip. However, 3D integration results in higher temperatures following the increase in thermal resistances. This chapter discusses thermal modeling and management of 3D systems with a particular focus on liquid cooling, which has emerged as a promising solution for addressing the high temperatures in 3D systems. We first introduce a framework that is capable of detailed thermal modeling of the interlayer structure containing microchannels and through-silicon-vias (TSVs). For energy-efficient liquid cooling, we describe a controller to adjust the liquid flow rate to meet the current chip temperature. We also discuss job scheduling techniques for balancing the temperature across the 3D system to maximize the cooling efficiency and to improve reliability.

1 Introduction

3D integration is a recently proposed design method for overcoming the limitations regarding the delay and power consumption of the interconnects. However, this increased level of integration also results in new limitations and design challenges, including the challenges related to higher temperatures. A *k-tier* 3D chip could potentially use k times as much current as a single 2D chip of the same footprint, while utilizing similar packaging technology due to cooling cost limitations. The implications of this observation are:

– The 3D stacked systems will likely consume more power than their 2D counterparts, and the heat generated as a result of the power consumption must be removed from the system. Unless the 3D chip design has been optimized with thermally-aware techniques, considering that the package characteristics of the 3D system are similar to those of 2D chips, on-chip temperatures for 3D chips will be higher than temperatures on 2D chips.

J. Becker, M. Johann, and R. Reis (Eds.): VLSI-SoC 2009, IFIP AICT 360, pp. 34–55, 2011.

- Stacking layers vertically increase the thermal resistances on a given unit. Therefore, it is more difficult to remove heat from the chip, especially for the layers that are further away from the cooling infrastructures. This situation further escalates the temperature-induced challenges.
- Elevated temperatures and large thermal gradients degrade performance and reliability of chips. Reliability issues in 3D stacks will also be aggravated because of the higher temperatures and presence of mechanical stress. Therefore, on-chip thermal management is a critical issue in 3D design.

Liquid cooling is a potential solution to address the high temperatures in 3D chips, due to the higher heat removal capability of liquids in comparison to air. Liquid cooling is performed by attaching a cold plate with built-in microchannels, and/or by fabricating microchannels between the layers of the 3D architecture. Then, a coolant fluid (i.e., water or other fluids) is pumped through the microchannels to remove the heat. The heat removal performance of this approach, called interlayer cooling [1], scales with the number of tiers. The flow rate of the pump can be altered dynamically, but as there is a single pump connected to the system, the flow rates among the channels are the same—assuming identical channel dimensions. One obvious way to set the flow rate is by matching it with the worst-case temperature. However, the pump power increases quadratically with the increase in flow rate [1], and its contribution to the overall system power is significant. Also, over-cooling may cause dynamic fluctuations in temperature, which degrade reliability and cooling efficiency. Through runtime system analysis and intelligent control of the flow rate, it is possible to determine the minimum flow rate to remove the heat and maintain a safe system temperature. In addition, by maintaining a target temperature value throughout the execution, we can minimize the temperature variations. Note that, while reducing the coolant flow rate, it is necessary to maintain the temperature at a level where the temperature-dependent leakage power does not revert the benefits achieved with lower-power pumping.

Current technology enables fabricating the infrastructures required for interlayer liquid cooling. IBM Zurich Research Laboratory has built a 3D chip with multiple microchannels that allow water flow (see Figure 1). The 50 μm channels between individual chip layers are able to cool with a rate of 180 $watt/cm^2$ per layer for a stack with a footprint of $4cm^2$ [2].

3D systems have an inherent temperature imbalance among the various processing units, due to the change in thermal resistance that is a function of the location of the unit. Cores located at different layers or at different coordinates across a layer may have significantly different rates for heating and cooling [3]. Therefore, even when we select the appropriate energy-efficient flow rate for the coolant in a 3D liquid-cooled system, large temperature gradients across the system may still exist. Conventional multicore schedulers, e.g., dynamic load balancing, do not consider such thermal imbalances. To address this issue, we discuss temperature-aware load balancing, which weighs each core's workload with the core's thermal properties and uses this weighted computation to balance the temperature. The highlights of this chapter are the following:

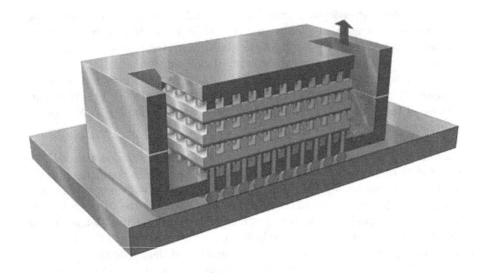

Fig. 1. 3D chip with microchannels for liquid cooling (by IBM)

- We show in detail how to model the effects of the liquid flow on temperature. Our model is based on the liquid cooling work of IBM [1]. The liquid cooling model (introduced in [4, 5]) includes a fine-grained computation of the heat spread and takes into account the effects of TSVs and microchannels. We use model parameters verified by finite element simulation, and integrate our modeling infrastructure in HotSpot [6] for ease of use.
- We describe a controller for adjusting the liquid flow rate dynamically to maintain a target temperature while minimizing the pump power consumption. Our controller forecasts maximum system temperature, and uses this forecast to proactively set the flow rate. This way, we avoid over- or under-cooling due to delays in reacting to the temperature changes.
- We integrate the controller with a job scheduler that computes the current workload of each core as a function of the core's thermal properties. The scheduler addresses the inherent thermal imbalances in multicore 3D systems and reduces the frequency of large thermal gradients.
- On the 2- and 4-layered 3D systems that we simulate, we see that our method achieves up to 30% reduction in cooling energy, and 12% reduction in system-level energy in comparison to setting the flow rate at the maximum value, while we maintain the target temperature. We also show that temperature-aware load balancing reduces the hot spots and gradients significantly better than load balancing or reactive thread migration.

The rest of this chapter starts with an overview of the prior art. Section 3 describes the thermal model for 3D systems with liquid cooling. In Section 4, we provide the details of the flow rate controller and job scheduler. The experimental results are in Section 5, and Section 6 concludes the chapter.

2 Related Work

2.1 Thermal Modeling and Management

Accurate thermal modeling is critical in the design and evaluation of systems and policies in 3D systems. There has been abundant work on design-time full-chip thermal models [7, 6, 8, 9]. However, existing studies do not provide flexibility on thermal package modeling. HotSpot [6] is an automated thermal model, which calculates transient temperature response given the physical and power consumption characteristics of the chip. To reduce simulation time even for large multicore systems, a thermal emulation framework for FPGAs is proposed in [10]. In such thermal models the typical packaging configuration is forced air convection with a heat sink and/or spreader.

In addition to simulation frameworks for thermal modeling, there are existing studies on runtime thermal characterization methods. For example [11, 12] provide insights into using on-chip temperature sensors in processors that contain integrated sensors, such as IBM POWER series processors. However, many of the hot spots can be missed as the number of sensors is limited. Another runtime thermal characterization method is IR thermal imaging [13, 14]. While this technique can capture the detailed thermal map in real-time, the limited sampling rate of the IR camera may filter out high-frequency transient thermal fluctuations.

Dynamic thermal management in response to thermal measurements in microprocessors has been first introduced by Brooks et al. [15], where the authors explore performance trade-offs among various dynamic thermal management mechanisms. Activity migration [16] and fetch toggling [6] are other examples of dynamic management techniques. Kumar et al. propose a hybrid method that combines clock gating and software thermal management [17]. The multicore thermal management method introduced by Donald et al. [18] combines distributed DVS with process migration; while Chaparro et al. [19] investigate thermal management techniques for multicore systems. For multicore systems, temperature-aware task scheduling [20] shows a lot of potential to achieve desirable thermal profiles at low performance cost. Li et al. [21] and Monchiero et al. [22] consider the thermal constraints in multicore systems at a detailed microarchitecture level with comprehensive architecture simulations for multi-programmed and multi-threaded workloads, respectively. For manycore architectures, Huang et al. [23] look at a heat-spreading floorplanning approach to increase the power envelope of symmetric manycore chips without running into thermal violations.

2.2 Design, Modeling, and Management of 3D Systems

The fabrication technology for manufacturing 3D systems determines many of the electrical, architectural, and thermal characteristics of the final stack. Various 3D fabrication technologies have been proposed in the recent years. For example, prior work [24, 25, 26] proposes diverse fabrication technologies. Two commonly used fabrication technologies are: die-bonding and Multi-Layer Buried Structures (MLBS). Die-bonding process employs conventional 2D fabrication processes and metal vias to bond the planar die vertically [27]. Figure 2 (a) shows a conventional planar IC modeled as five layers: metal layers (A), active silicon (B), bulk silicon (C), heat spreader (D) and heat sink (E). The heat spreader is attached to the bulk silicon with a thermal interface material. Figure 2 (b) shows a 2-die 3D IC built with two planar dies stacked with their metal layers face-to-face (F2F). In MLBS technology [28] it is possible to stack many heterogeneous dies to mix dissimilar process technologies such as high-speed CMOS with high-density DRAM [29, 30]. The MLBS approach (shown schematically in Figure 3) combines dual Damascene process for in-plane and out-plane interconnects, chemical-mechanical polishing of bondable roughness, and a critical low temperature layering step in order to achieve the three-dimensional structures.

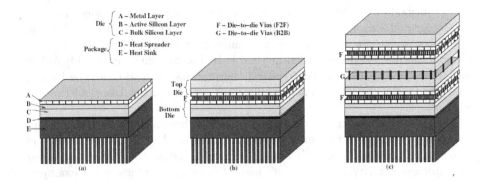

Fig. 2. Die-bonding process [31]

There are three different stacking topologies for interfacing multiple planar dies: face-to-face (F2F), face-to-back (F2B) and back-to-back (B2B). These topologies have different quality and pitch of the die-to-die (D2D) vias at the interfaces and thus influence the benefits obtained from building a 3D IC. For the 2-die 3D IC with the F2F topology shown in Figure 2 (b), D2D vias are etched and deposited on top of the metal layer of each of the planar dies using conventional metal etching technology. Therefore, the via pitch can be as dense as regular on-die interconnects, and the realizable pitch is only limited by the accuracy of aligning the two dies. The die-to-die via interface is densely populated since the vias are required as the physical bonding mechanism independent of whether they actually carry a signal. The bulk silicon layer of the top die is usually thinned down with chemical-mechanical polishing down allowing low impedance backside vias to be etched through, which provide I/O and power/ground connections.

Most of the prior work in thermal management of 3D systems addresses design stage optimization, such as thermal-aware floorplanning (e.g. [33]) and integrating thermal via planning in the 3D floorplanning process [34]. In [35], the authors

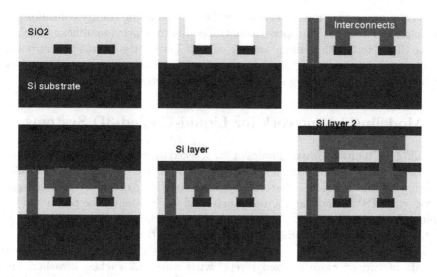

Fig. 3. MLBS process. [32]

evaluate several policies for task migration and DVS. A recent paper proposes a temperature-aware scheduling method specifically for air-cooled 3D systems [3]. This method takes into account the thermal heterogeneity among the different layers of the system.

The use of convection in microchannels to cool down high power density chips has been an active area of research since the initial work by Tuckerman and Pease [36]. Their liquid cooling system can remove 1000 W/cm^2; however, the volumetric flow rate and the pressure drop are large. More recent work shows how back-side liquid cold plates, such as staggered microchannel and distributed return jet plates, can handle up to 400 W/cm^2 in single-chip applications [37]. The heat removal capability of interlayer heat-transfer with pin-fin in-line structures for 3D chips is investigated in [1]. At a chip size of 1 cm^2 and a $\Delta T_{jmax-in}$ of 60 K, the heat-removal performance is shown to be more than 200 W/cm^2 at interconnect pitches bigger than 50 μm. Previous work in [38, 39] describes how to achieve variable flow rate for the coolant. Finally, in a recent work by Jang et al. [40], the authors evaluate the architectural effects (temperature, leakage, and reliability) of the direct interlayer cooling method for 3D integrated processors, where the dielectric coolant flows in-between individual dies. The evaluation shows that this liquid cooling scheme significantly reduces on-chip temperature under 350K, which completely eliminates thermal emergencies. The temperature reduction also leads to more than 10% leakage reduction of the 3D integrated processor.

Prior work on liquid-cooled 3D systems [4] evaluates existing thermal management policies on a 3D system with a fixed-flow rate setting, and also investigates the benefits of variable flow using a policy to increment/decrement the flow rate based on temperature measurements, without considering energy consumption. The follow-up work in [5] proposes a controller design to provide sufficient coolant flow to the system with minimal cooling energy. The runtime management policy combines this controller with a job scheduler to reduce thermal gradients, and further improves the cooling efficiency without affecting performance.

3   Modeling Framework for Liquid-Cooled 3D Systems

Modeling the temperature dynamics of 3D stacked architectures with liquid cooling consist of: (A) Forming the grid-level thermal R-C network, (B) Detailed modeling of the interlayer material between the tiers, including the through-silicon-vias (TSVs) and the microchannels, and (C) Modeling the pump and the coolant flow rate. We assume forced convective interlayer cooling with water [1] in this chapter, but the model can be extended to other coolants as well.

Figure 4 shows the 3D systems targeted in this chapter. A target system consists of two or more stacked layers (with cores, L2 caches, crossbar, and other units for memory control, buffering, etc.), and microchannels are built in between the vertical layers for liquid flow. The crossbar contains the TSVs that provide the connection between the layers. The microchannels, which are connected to an impeller pump (such as [41]), are distributed uniformly, and fluid flows through each channel at the same flow rate. The liquid flow rate provided by the pump can be dynamically altered at runtime. In the rest of this section, we provide the details of the thermal modeling infrastructure that we developed for the 3D system.

3.1   Grid-Level Thermal Model for 3D Systems with Liquid Cooling

Similar to thermal modeling in 2D chips, 3D thermal modeling is performed using an automated model that forms the R-C circuit for given grid dimensions. In this work, we utilize HotSpot v.4.2. [6], which includes 3D modeling capabilities. The existing model in HotSpot considers the interlayer material between two stacked layers as a layer with homogeneous thermal characteristics, represented by a thermal resistivity and a specific heat capacity value. The extension we have developed for the multi-layered thermal modeling provides a new interlayer material model to include the TSVs and the microchannels.

In a typical automated thermal model, the thermal resistance and capacitance values of the blocks or grid cells are computed initially at the start of the simulation, assuming that the system properties do not vary at runtime. To model the heterogeneous characteristics of the interlayer material including the TSVs and microchannels, we introduce two novelties: (1) As opposed to having a uniform thermal resistivity value of the layer, our infrastructure enables having various resistivity values for each grid cell, (2) The resistivity value of the cell can vary at runtime. Item (1) enables distinctly modeling TSVs, the microchannels, and

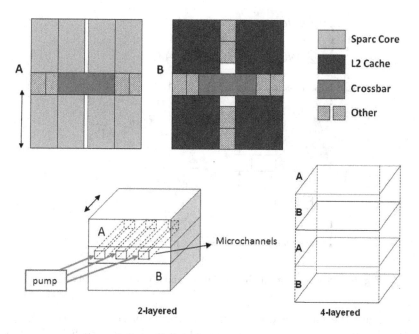

Fig. 4. Floorplans of the 3D Systems

the interlayer material, while item (2) enables modeling the liquid coolant and dynamically changing flow rate. Thus, the interlayer material is divided into a grid, where each grid cell except for the cells of the microchannels has a fixed thermal resistance value depending on the characteristics of the interface material and TSVs. The thermal resistivity of the microchannel cells is computed based on the liquid flow rate through the cell, and the characteristics of the liquid at runtime. We use grid cells of $100\mu m$ x $100\mu m$ in our experiments.

In a 3D system with liquid cooling, we compute the local junction temperature using a resistive network, as shown in Figure 5. In this figure, the thermal resistance of the wiring layers (R_{BEOL}), the thermal resistance of the silicon slab (R_{slab}), and the convective thermal resistance (R_{conv}) are combined to model the 3D stack. In the figure, the heat flux values ($\dot{q}$) represent the heat sources. This R-network can be solved to get the junction temperature (T_j). Note that the figure shows the heat sources and the resistances of only one layer, and heat will be dissipated to both opposing vertical directions (i.e., up and down) from the heat sources. For example, if there is another layer above the two heat-dissipating layers shown in the figure, $\dot{q}_1$ will also be dissipating heat towards the upper stack. Also, the network in Figure 5 is a simplification and it assumes isothermal channel walls; i.e., top and bottom of the microchannel have the same temperature.

The typical junction temperature (T_j) response at uniform chip heat flux and convective cooling is a sum of the following three components: (1) The thermal gradient due to conduction (ΔT_{cond}); (2) the coolant temperature, which

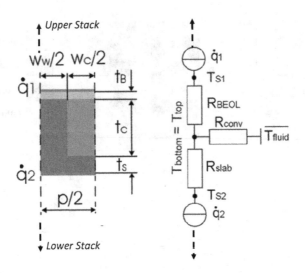

Fig. 5. Cross section of the 3D layers and the resistive network

increases along the channel due to the absorption of sensible heat (ΔT_{heat}); and (3) the convective (ΔT_{conv}) portion, which increases until fully developed hydrodynamic and thermal boundary layers have been reached [1]. The total temperature rise on the junction, ΔT_j, is computed as the following:

$$\Delta T_j = \Delta T_{cond} + \Delta T_{heat} + \Delta T_{conv} \tag{1}$$

Thermal gradient due to heat conduction through the BEOL layer, ΔT_{cond} is computed with Equations 2 and 3. Note that ΔT_{cond} is independent of the flow rate. Figure 5 demonstrates t_B, and k_{BEOL} is the conductivity of the wiring layer.

$$\Delta T_{cond} = R_{th-BEOL} \cdot \dot{q}_1 \tag{2}$$

$$R_{th-BEOL} = \frac{t_B}{k_{BEOL}} \tag{3}$$

Temperature change due to absorption of sensible heat is computed using Equations 4 and 5. A_{heater} is the area of the heater (i.e., total area consuming power), c_p is the heat capacity of the coolant, ρ is the density of the coolant, and $\dot{V}$ is the volumetric flow rate in the microchannel (in l/min). Equations 4 and 5 are valid for uniform power dissipation. For the general case, heat absorption in the fluid is calculated iteratively along the channel: $\Delta T_{heat}(n+1) = \sum_{i=1}^{n} \Delta T_{heat}(i)$, where n is the position along the channel.

$$\Delta T_{heat} = (\dot{q}_1 + \dot{q}_2) \cdot R_{th-heat} \tag{4}$$

$$R_{th-heat} = \frac{A_{heater}}{c_p \cdot \rho \cdot \dot{V}} \tag{5}$$

Finally, Equation 7 shows how to calculate ΔT_{conv}. Note that ΔT_{conv} is independent of flow rate in case of developed boundary layers. h is dependent on hydraulic diameter, Nusselt number, and conductivity of the fluid [1]. As ΔT_{conv} is not affected by the change in flow rate, we compute this parameter prior to simulation and use a constant value during experiments. Figure 5 demonstrates w_c, t_c, and p parameters on the cross-section of the 3D system.

$$\Delta T_{conv} = (\dot{q}_1 + \dot{q}_2) \cdot h_{eff} \tag{6}$$

$$h_{eff} = h\frac{2 \cdot (w_c + t_c)}{p} \tag{7}$$

The equations above give the ΔT_j for the unit cell shown in Figure 5; thus, we extend the computation to model multiple layers and multiple cells as well.

Table 1 lists the parameters used in the computations, and provides the values for the constants, which are taken from prior liquid cooling work [1]. Note that the flow rate $(\dot{V})$ range provided in the table is per cavity (i.e., the interlayer cavity consisting of all the microchannels in one layer), and this flow is further divided into the microchannels.

Table 1. Parameters for computing Equation 1

Parameter	Definition	Value
$R_{th-BEOL}$	Thermal resistance of wiring levels	Eqn.(3) 5.333 $(K \cdot mm^2)/W$
t_B	See Figure 5	$12\mu m$
k_{BEOL}	Conductivity of wiring levels	$2.25 W/(m \cdot K)$
$R_{th-heat}$	Effective thermal resistance	Eqn.(5)
A_{heater}	Heater area	Area of grid cell
c_p	Coolant heat capacity	$4183 J/(kg \cdot K)$
ρ	Coolant density	$998 kg/m^3$
$\dot{V}$	Volumetric flow rate	0.1-1 l/min per cavity
h	Heat transfer coefficient	$37132 W/(m^2 \cdot K)$
w_c	See Figure 5	$50\mu m$
t_c	See Figure 5	$100\mu m$
t_s	See Figure 5	$50\mu m$
p	See Figure 5	$100\mu m$

We compute the flow rate dependent components whenever the flow rate changes. Heat flux, $\dot{q}$ (W/cm^2), values change as the power consumption changes. Instead of reacting to every instant change in power consumption of the cores, we re-compute the $\dot{q}$ values periodically to reduce the simulation overhead.

Considering the dimensions and pitch requirements of microchannels and TSVs, we assume there are 65 microchannels in between each two layers (in each cavity), and there are cooling layers on the very top and the bottom of the stacks. Thus, there are 195 and 325 microchannels in the 2- and 4-layered systems, respectively.

In our target systems shown in Figure 4, we assume the TSVs are located within the crossbar. Placing the TSVs in the central section of the die provides an advantage on the thermal design as well, as TSVs reduce the temperature due to the low thermal resistivity of Cu. We assume there are **128 TSVs** within the crossbar block connecting each two layers. Feasible TSVs for microchannels of $100\mu m$ height and $100\mu m$ pitch have a minimal pitch of $100\mu m$ as well due to aspect ratio limits. We assume each TSV occupies a space of $50\mu m$x$50\mu m$, and the TSVs have a minimum spacing requirement of $100\mu m$.

Previous work has studied granularity and accuracy of TSV modeling [4]. The study shows that using a block-level granularity for TSVs, i.e., assigning a TSV density to each block based on the functionality of the unit, constitutes a reasonable trade-off between accuracy and simulation time. Thus, based on the TSV density of the crossbar, we compute the joint resistivity of that area combining the resistivity values of interlayer material and Cu. We do not alter the thermal resistivity values for the regions without TSVs or microchannels. We assume that the effect of the TSV insertion to the heat capacity of the interface material is negligible, which is a reasonable assumption considering the total area of TSVs constitutes a very small percentage of the total area of the material.

3.2   Modeling the Pump and Liquid Flow Rate

All the microchannels are connected to a pump to receive the coolant. We assume a 12V DC-pump, *Laing DDC* [41], which has suitable dimensions, flow rates, and power consumption for this type of liquid cooling. The power consumption of the pump across the *five* flow rate settings we use is shown in Figure 6 (right y-axis). The pressure drop for these flow rates changes between 300-600 mbar [41]. We assume that the total flow rate of the pump is equally distributed among the cavities, and among the microchannels. DC pumps typically have low efficiency. Also, the flow rate in the microchannels further decreases because the the pressure drop in the small microchannels is larger than its value in the pump output channel. In this work, we assume a global reduction in the flow rate by 50% to

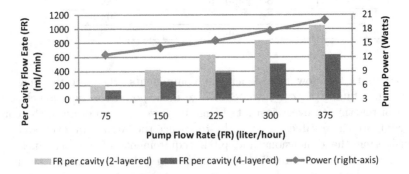

Fig. 6. Power consumption and flow rates of the pump (based on [41]). Per cavity flow rates reflect 50% efficiency assumption

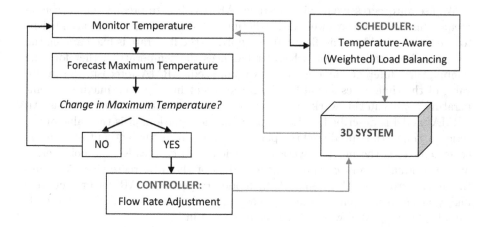

Fig. 7. Overview of the technique

account for the loss due to all of these factors. In Figure 6, we show the per cavity flow rates for the 2- and 4-layered 3D systems after applying the reduction factor.

4   Joint Flow Rate Control and Job Scheduling

This section provides the details of our energy-efficient thermal management technique for 3D systems with liquid cooling. The goals of our technique are: (1) Tuning the liquid flow rate to meet the heat removal demand of the current workload and reducing the energy consumption; (2) Minimizing the thermal imbalances across the chip to reduce the adverse effects of variations on reliability, performance, and cooling efficiency. To achieve these goals, we combine joint flow rate control with job scheduling. Figure 7 provides a flow chart of our method. We monitor the temperature at regular intervals for all the cores in the 3D system. Based on the forecasted change in maximum temperature, the controller is responsible for adjusting the coolant flow rate. The scheduler performs temperature-aware load balancing to also reduce the thermal gradients.

4.1   Temperature Monitoring and Forecasting

Monitoring temperature provides our technique with the ability to adapt the controller and job scheduler decisions. We assume each core has a thermal sensor. One way to utilize the thermal feedback is to react to temperature changes. A typical impeller pump like the one we use ([41]) takes around 250-300ms to complete the transition to a new flow rate. Due to the time delay in adjusting the flow rate, a reactive policy is likely to result in over-/under-cooling—the thermal time constant on a 3D system like ours is typically less than 100ms. Thus, for the liquid flow rate controller, we forecast temperature into the near future, and adjust the flow rate control on time to meet the heat removal requirement.

We use autoregressive moving average (ARMA) [42] to predict the *maximum temperature* for the next interval. Predicting maximum temperature is sufficient to select the suitable liquid flow rate to apply, as the flow rate is fixed among the channels. Note that our job scheduler balances the temperature, therefore the temperature difference among cores is minimized. ARMA forecasts the future value of the time-series signal based on the recent history (i.e., maximum temperature history in this work), therefore we do not require an offline analysis. An ARMA model is described by Equation 8. In the equation, y_t is the value of the series at time t (i.e., predicted temperature value), a_i is the lag-i auto-regressive coefficient, c_i is the moving average coefficient and e_t is called the noise, error or the residual. p and q represent the orders of the auto-regressive (AR) and the moving average (MA) parts of the model, respectively. ARMA prediction is highly accurate for temperature forecasting, and runtime adaptation methods can also be integrated with ARMA as discussed in [42].

$$y_t + \sum_{i=1}^{p}(a_i\, y_{t-i}) = e_t + \sum_{i=1}^{q}(c_i\, e_{t-i}) \tag{8}$$

The prediction is highly accurate because of the serial correlation within most workloads and the slow change in temperature due to the thermal time constants. Furthermore, the rate of change of maximum temperature is typically even slower, resulting in easier prediction. In our experiments, we use a sampling rate of 100ms, and predict 500ms into the future.

If the trend of the maximum temperature signal changes and the predictor cannot forecast accurately, we reconstruct the ARMA predictor, and use the existing model until the new one is ready. Such cases occur when the workload dramatically changes (e.g., day-time and night-time workload patterns for a server). To achieve fast and easy detection, we apply the sequential probability ratio test (SPRT) [43]. SPRT is a logarithmic likelihood test to decide whether the error between the predicted series and measured series is diverging from zero [43, 42]—i.e., if the predictor is no longer fitting the workload, the difference function of the two time series would increase. As the maximum temperature profile changes slowly, we need to update the ARMA predictor very infrequently.

4.2   Liquid Flow Rate Control

The input to the controller is the predicted maximum temperature, and the output is the flow rate for the next interval. Then, considering that we have discrete flow rate settings for the pump, we first analyze the effect of each flow rate for both 3D systems (2- and 4-layered).

Figure 8 shows which flow rate (per cavity) should be applied when the maximum temperature is T_{max} so that the temperature is guaranteed to cool below the target operating temperature of 80^oC. In this figure, the dashed lines show the discrete flow rate settings, while the triangular and circular shaped data points refer to minimum rate to maintain the desired temperatures.

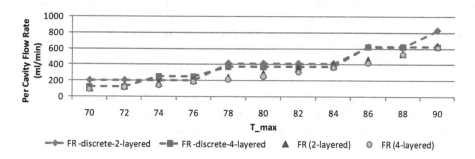

Fig. 8. Flow rate requirements to cool a given T_{max}

Based on this analysis, we see that for a given system and maximum temperature, we already know which flow rate setting is able to cool the system to the target temperature level. We set-up a look-up table indexed by temperature values, and each line holds a flow rate value. At runtime, depending on the maximum temperature prediction, we select the appropriate flow rate from the table. As the maximum temperature prediction is highly accurate (well below 1^oC), this way we can adjust the cooling system to meet the changes in the heat removal demand on time. To avoid rapid oscillations, once we switch to a higher flow rate setting, we do not decrease the flow rate until the predicted T_{max} is at least 2^oC lower than the boundary temperature between two flow rate settings. The runtime overhead of using a look-up table based controller is negligible, considering that the cost is only limited to a look-up from a small-sized table.

4.3 Job Scheduling

Our job scheduler is a temperature-aware version of load balancing. Dynamic load balancing is a common policy used in multicore schedulers today. While frequent load balancing eliminates contention and long thread waiting times in the queues, it does not consider the location of the cores. However, a core's thermal behavior is strongly correlated with where it is placed on the chip, and the power consumption of the neighboring units.

We assume short threads, which is a common scenario in server workloads running on multiprocessor systems [18, 20]. For instance, in real-life workloads running on the UltraSPARC T1, the thread length (i.e., continuous execution time without any interrupt) has been reported to vary between a few to several hundred milliseconds [20]. Thus, since we consider threads with short lengths and similar execution time, we use number of threads for computing the job queue length of each core. Note that, depending on the available information, our approach can be extended for other workload metrics such as instruction count per thread.

To address the thermal asymmetries of cores in a 3D system, we run *Weighted Load Balancing* [5]. Weighted load balancing does not change the priority and performance aware features of the load balancing algorithm, but only modifies how the queue lengths are computed. Each core has a queue to hold the incoming threads, and the weighted queue length of a core is computed as:

$$l^i{}_{weighted} = l^i{}_{queue} \cdot w^i{}_{thermal}(T(k)) \tag{9}$$

In the equation, $l^i{}_{queue}$ is the number of threads currently waiting in the queue of core i, and $w^i{}_{thermal}(T(k))$ is the thermal weight factor. This weight factor is a function of the current maximum temperature of the system. For a given set of temperature ranges, the weight factors for all the cores are computed in a pre-processing step and stored in the look-up table. For example, consider a 4-core system, where the average power values for the cores to achieve a balanced 75^oC are p_1, p_2, p_3, and p_4, and $p_1 = p_4 > p_2 = p_3$. This means cores 2 and 3 should run fewer number of threads per unit time to maintain a balanced temperature. Thus, we take the multiplicative inverse of the power values, normalize them, and use them as weight factors to balance temperature.

5   Experimental Results

The 3D multicore systems we use in our experiments are based on the 90nm UltraSPARC T1 (i.e., Niagara-1) processor [44]. The power consumption, area, and the floorplan of UltraSPARC T1 are available in [44]. UltraSPARC T1 has 8 multi-threaded cores, and a shared L2-cache for every two cores. Our simulations are carried out with 2-, and 4-layered stack architectures. We place cores and L2 caches of the UltraSPARC T1 on separate layers (see Figure 4). Separating core and memory layers is a preferred design scenario for shortening interconnections between the cores and their caches and achieving higher performance.

First, we gather workload characteristics of real applications on an Ultra-SPARC T1. We sample the utilization percentage for each hardware thread at every second using `mpstat`, and record half an hour long traces for each benchmark. Also, the length of user and kernel threads were recorded using `DTrace` [45]. We use various real-life benchmarks including web server, database management, and multimedia processing. The web server workload is generated by SLAMD [46] with 20 and 40 threads per client to achieve medium and high utilization, respectively. For database applications, we experiment with MySQL using `sysbench` for a table with 1 million rows and 100 threads. We also run the `gcc` compiler and the `gzip` compression/decompression benchmarks as samples of SPEC-like benchmarks. Finally, we run several instances of the `mplayer` (integer) benchmark with 640x272 video files as typical examples of multimedia processing. A detailed summary of the benchmarks workloads is shown in Table 2. The utilization ratios are averaged over all cores throughout the execution. We also record the cache misses and floating point (FP) instructions per 100K instructions using `cpustat`. The workload statistics collected on the UltraSPARC T1 are replicated for the 4-layered 16-core system.

Table 2. Workload characteristics

	Benchmark	Avg Util (%)	L2 I-Miss	L2 D-Miss	FP instr
1	Web-med	53.12	12.9	167.7	31.2
2	Web-high	92.87	67.6	288.7	31.2
3	Database	17.75	6.5	102.3	5.9
4	Web & DB	75.12	21.5	115.3	24.1
5	gcc	15.25	31.7	96.2	18.1
6	gzip	9	2	57	0.2
7	MPlayer	6.5	9.6	136	1
8	MPlayer&Web	26.62	9.1	66.8	29.9

The peak power consumption of SPARC is close to its average value [44]. Thus, we assume that the instantaneous dynamic power consumption is equal to the average power at each state (active, idle, sleep). The active state power is taken as 3 Watts [44]. The cache power consumption is 1.28W per each L2, as computed by CACTI [47] and verified by the values in [44]. We model the crossbar power consumption by scaling the average power value according to the number of active cores and the memory accesses. To account for the temperature effects on leakage power, we used the second-order polynomial model proposed in [48].

Many systems have power management capabilities to reduce the energy consumption. We implement Dynamic Power Management (DPM), especially to investigate the effect on thermal variations. We utilize a fixed timeout policy, which puts a core to sleep state if it has been idle longer than the timeout period (i.e., 200ms in our experiments). We set a sleep state power of 0.02 Watts, which is estimated based on sleep power of similar cores.

We use HotSpot Version 4.2 [6] as the thermal modeling tool. We use a sampling interval of 100 ms, and all simulations are initialized with steady state temperature values. The model parameters are provided in Table 3. Modeling methodology for the interlayer material to include TSVs and the microchannels has been described in Section 3. In our experiments, we compare air-cooled and liquid-cooled 3D systems. For the conventional system, we use the default characteristics of a modern CPU package in HotSpot.

We assume that each core has a temperature sensor, which is able to provide temperature readings at regular intervals (e.g., 100ms). Modern OSes have a multi-queue structure, where each CPU core is associated with a dispatch queue, and the job scheduler allocates the jobs to the cores according to the current policy. In our simulator, we implement a similar infrastructure, where the queues maintain the threads allocated to cores and execute them.

We compare our technique to other well-known policies in terms of temperature, energy, and performance. **Dynamic Load Balancing (LB)** balances the workload by moving threads from a core's queue to another if the difference in

Table 3. Thermal Model and Floorplan Parameters

Parameter	Value
Die Thickness (one stack)	$0.15mm$
Area per Core	$10mm^2$
Area per L2 Cache	$19mm^2$
Total Area of Each Layer	$115mm^2$
Convection Capacitance	140 J/K
Convection Resistance	0.1 K/W
Interlayer Material Thickness	0.02 mm
Interlayer Material Thickness (with channels)	0.4 mm
Interlayer Material Resistivity (without TSVs)	0.25 mK/W

queue lengths is over a threshold. LB does not have any thermal management features. **Reactive Migration** initially performs load balancing, but upon reaching a threshold temperature, which is set to 85^oC in this work, it moves the currently running thread from the hot core to a cool core. Our novel temperature-aware weighted load balancing method is denoted as **TALB**. We also compare liquid cooling systems with air cooling systems (denoted with *(Air)*). In the plots *Var* refers to variable flow rate and *Max* refers to with using a maximum (worst-case) flow rate.

Figure 9 shows the average percentage of time spent above the threshold across all the workloads, percentage of time spent above threshold for the hottest workload, and energy for the 2-layered 3D system. We demonstrate both the pump energy and the total chip energy in the plot. Note that, for the air-cooled system, there is also an additional energy cost due to the fans, which is beyond

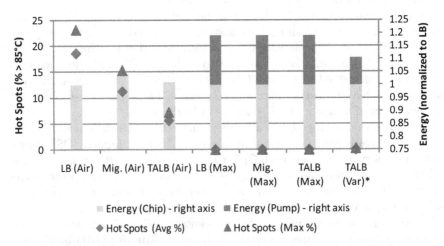

Fig. 9. Hot spots (left-axis) and energy (right-axis) for all the policies. (*) denotes our novel policy.

the focus of this work and not included in the plot. The energy consumption values are normalized with respect to the load balancing policy on a system with air cooling. We see that temperature-aware load balancing combined with liquid flow control achieves 10% energy savings on average in comparison to setting the worst-case flow rate. For low utilization workloads, such as `gzip` and `MPlayer`, the total energy savings (including both chip and pump energy) reach 12%, and the reduction in cooling energy exceeds 30%.

Figure 10 shows the average and maximum frequency of spatial and temporal variations in temperature, respectively, for all the policies. We evaluate the spatial gradients by computing the maximum difference in temperature among all the units at every sampling interval. Similarly, for thermal cycles, we keep a sliding history window for each core, and compute the cycles with magnitude larger than 20^oC. In the experiments in Figure 10, we run DPM in addition to the thermal management policy. Our weighed load balancing technique (TALB) is able to minimize both temporal and spatial thermal variations much more effectively than other policies.

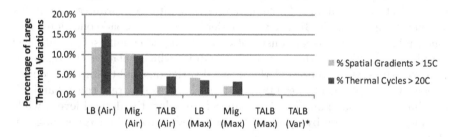

Fig. 10. Thermal variations (with DPM). (*) denotes our novel policy

Figure 11 compares the policies in terms of energy and performance, both for the air and liquid cooling systems. For the multicore 3D systems, we compute throughput as the performance metric. We define throughput as the number of threads completed per given time. As we run the same workloads in all experiments, when a policy delays execution of threads, the resulting throughput drops. Most policies we have run in this work have a similar throughput in comparison to default load balancing. Thread migration, however, reduces the throughput especially for high-utilization workloads because of the performance overhead of frequent temperature-triggered migrations. The overhead of migration disappears for the liquid cooled system, as the coolant flowing at the maximum rate is able to prevent all the hot spots, and therefore no temperature-triggered migrations occur. The figure shows that for 3D systems with liquid cooling, our technique is able to improve the energy savings without degrading performance.

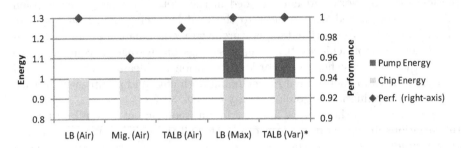

Fig. 11. Performance and Energy. (*) denotes our novel policy.

6   Conclusion

Liquid cooling is a promising solution to overcome the elevated thermal problems of 3D chips, but intelligent control of the coolant flow rate is needed to achieve energy-efficiency. In this chapter we have presented a novel controller that is able to select the minimum the coolant injection rate to guarantee a bounded maximum temperature in 3D MPSoCs under variable workload conditions. Our method minimizes the energy consumption of the liquid cooling subsystem. The controller is integrated with a novel job scheduler which balances the temperature across the system to prevent the thermal variations and to improve cooling efficiency. Our experimental results show that the joint flow rate control and job scheduling technique maintains the temperature below the desired levels, while reducing cooling energy by up to 30% and achieving overall energy savings up to 12%.

Acknowledgements. The authors would like to thank Thomas Brunschwiler and Bruno Michel at IBM Research GmbH, Zurich, Switzerland for their valuable contributions to the research that forms the basis of this chapter.

This research has been partially funded by the Nano-Tera.ch NTF Project CMOSAIC (ref. 123618), which is financed by the Swiss Confederation and scientifically evaluated by SNSF. This research has also been partially funded by Sun Microsystems, UC MICRO, Center for Networked Systems at UCSD, MARCO/DARPA GSRC, and NSF Greenlight.

References

[1] Brunschwiler, T., et al.: Interlayer cooling potential in vertically integrated packages. Microsyst. Technol. (2008)
[2] Gruener, W.: IBM Cools 3D Chips With Integrated Water Channels,
http://www.tomshardware.com/news/IBm-research,5604.html
[3] Coskun, A.K., Rosing, T.S., Ayala, J., Atienza, D., Leblebici, Y.: Dynamic thermal management in 3D multicore architectures. In: Design Automation and Test in Europe, DATE (2009)

[4] Coskun, A.K., Ayala, J., Atienza, D., Rosing, T.S.: Modeling and dynamic management of 3D multicore systems with liquid cooling. In: IFIP/IEEE International Conference on Very Large Scale Integration, VLSI-SoC (2009)

[5] Coskun, A.K., Atienza, D., Rosing, T.S., Brunschwiler, T., Michel, B.: Energy-efficient variable-flow liquid cooling in 3D stacked architectures. In: Design Automation and Test in Europe, DATE (2010)

[6] Skadron, K., Stan, M., Huang, W., Velusamy, S., Sankaranarayanan, K., Tarjan, D.: Temperature-aware microarchitecture. In: International Symposium on Computer Architecture, ISCA (2003)

[7] Li, P., Pileggi, L., Asheghi, M., Chandra, R.: IC thermal simulation and modeling via efficient multigrid-based approaches. IEEE Transactions on Computer-Aided Design of Integrated Circuits and Systems 25(9), 1763–1776 (2006)

[8] Wang, T.Y., Chen, C.: Thermal-ADI - a linear-time chip-level dynamic thermal-simulation algorithm based on alternating-direction-implicit (ADI) method. IEEE Transactions on Very Large Scale Integration (VLSI) Systems 11(4), 691–700 (2003)

[9] Yang, Y., Gu, Z., Zhu, C., Dick, R.P., Shang, L.: ISAC: Integrated space-and-time-adaptive chip-package thermal analysis. IEEE Transactions on Computer-Aided Design of Integrated Circuits and Systems 26(1), 86–99 (2007)

[10] Atienza, D., Valle, P.D., Paci, G., Poletti, F., Benini, L., Micheli, G.D., Mendias, J.M.: A fast HW/SW FPGA-based thermal emulation framework for multiprocessor system-on-chip. In: Design Automation Conference, DAC (2006)

[11] Lee, K.J., Skadron, K., Huang, W.: Analytical model for sensor placement on microprocessors. In: Proceedings of 2005 IEEE International Conference on Computer Design: VLSI in Computers and Processors, ICCD 2005, pp. 24–27 (October 2005)

[12] Mukherjee, R., Memik, S.O.: Systematic temperature sensor allocation and placement for microprocessors. In: DAC 2006: Proceedings of the 43rd Annual Design Automation Conference, pp. 542–547. ACM, New York (2006)

[13] Hamann, H.F., Weger, A., Lacey, J.A., Hu, Z., Bose, P., Cohen, E., Wakil, J.: Hotspot-limited microprocessors: Direct temperature and power distribution measurements. IEEE Journal of Solid-State Circuits 42(1), 56–65 (2007)

[14] Mesa-Martinez, F.J., Nayfach-Battilana, J., Renau, J.: Power model validation through thermal measurements. SIGARCH Comput. Archit. News 35(2), 302–311 (2007)

[15] Brooks, D., Martonosi, M.: Dynamic thermal management for high-performance microprocessors. In: International Symposium on High-Performance Computer Architecture (HPCA), pp. 171–182 (2001)

[16] Heo, S., Barr, K., Asanovic, K.: Reducing power density through activity migration. In: International Symposium on Low Power Electronics and Design (ISLPED), pp. 217–222 (2003)

[17] Kumar, A., Shang, L., Peh, L.S., Jha, N.K.: HybDTM: a coordinated hardware-software approach for dynamic thermal management. In: DAC, pp. 548–553 (2006)

[18] Donald, J., Martonosi, M.: Techniques for multicore thermal management: Classification and new exploration. In: International Symposium on Computer Architecture, ISCA (2006)

[19] Chaparro, P., Gonzalez, J., Magklis, G., Cai, Q., Gonzalez, A.: Understanding the thermal implications of multi-core architectures. IEEE Transactions on Parallel and Distributed Systems 18, 1055–1065 (2007)

[20] Coskun, A.K., Rosing, T.S., Whisnant, K.A., Gross, K.C.: Static and dynamic temperature-aware scheduling for multiprocessor socs. IEEE Transactions on VLSI 16(9), 1127–1140 (2008)

[21] Li, Y., Lee, B., Brooks, D., Hu, Z., Skadron, K.: Cmp design space exploration subject to physical constraints. In: The Twelfth International Symposium on High-Performance Computer Architecture, pp. 17–28 (February 2006)

[22] Monchiero, M., Canal, R., González, A.: Design space exploration for multicore architectures: a power/performance/thermal view. In: ICS 2006: Proceedings of the 20th Annual International Conference on Supercomputing, pp. 177–186. ACM, New York (2006)

[23] Huang, W., Stan, M.R., Sankaranarayanan, K., Ribando, R.J., Skadron, K.: Many-core design from a thermal perspective. In: 45th ACM/IEEE Design Automation Conference, DAC 2008, pp. 746–749 (June 2008)

[24] Topol, A.W., La Tulipe Jr, D.C., Shi, L., Frank, D.J., Bernstein, K., Steen, S.E., Kumar, A., Singco, G.U., Young, A.M., Guarini, K.W., Ieong, M.: Three-dimensional integrated circuits. IBM J. Res. Dev. 50(4/5), 491–506 (2006)

[25] Tezzaron: 3D IC industry summary, http://www.tezzaron.com/technology/3D_IC_Summary.html

[26] Samsung, http://www.samsung.com

[27] Reif, R., Fan, A., Chen, K.N., Das, S.: Fabrication technologies for three-dimensional integrated circuits. In: Proceedings of International Symposium on Quality Electronic Design, pp. 33–37 (2002)

[28] Tsai, Y.F., Xie, Y., Vijaykrishnan, N., Irwin, M.J.: Three-dimensional cache design exploration using 3dcacti. In: ICCD 2005: Proceedings of the 2005 International Conference on Computer Design, pp. 519–524. IEEE Computer Society, Washington, DC (2005)

[29] Loh, G.H.: 3d-stacked memory architectures for multi-core processors. In: ISCA 2008: Proceedings of the 35th International Symposium on Computer Architecture, pp. 453–464. IEEE Computer Society, Washington, DC (2008)

[30] Puttaswamy, K., Loh, G.: Implementing caches in a 3d technology for high performance processors. In: Proceedings of 2005 IEEE International Conference on Computer Design: VLSI in Computers and Processors, ICCD 2005, pp. 525–532 (October 2005)

[31] Puttaswamy, K., Loh, G.H.: Thermal analysis of a 3D die-stacked high-performance microprocessor. In: Proceedings of GLSVLSI (2006)

[32] Xue, L., Liu, C., Tiwari, S.: Multi-layers with buried structures (MLBS): an approach to three-dimensional integration. In: 2001 IEEE International SOI Conference, pp. 117–118 (2001)

[33] Healy, M., et al.: Multiobjective microarchitectural floorplanning for 2-D and 3-D ICs. IEEE Transactions on CAD 26(1) (January 2007)

[34] Li, Z., et al.: Integrating dynamic thermal via planning with 3D floorplanning algorithm. In: International Symposium on Physical Design (ISPD), pp. 178–185 (2006)

[35] Zhu, C., Gu, Z., Shang, L., Dick, R.P., Joseph, R.: Three-dimensional chip-multiprocessor run-time thermal management. IEEE Transactions on CAD 27(8), 1479–1492 (2008)

[36] Tuckerman, D.B., Pease, R.F.W.: High-performance heat sinking for VLSI. IEEE Electron Device Letters 5, 126–129 (1981)

[37] Brunschwiler, T., et al.: Direct liquid-jet impingement cooling with micron-sized nozzle array and distributed return architecture. In: ITHERM (2006)

[38] Bhunia, A., Boutros, K., Che, C.L.: High heat flux cooling solutions for thermal management of high power density gallium nitride HEMT. In: Inter Society Conference on Thermal Phenomena (2004)

[39] Lee, H., et al.: Package embedded heat exchanger for stacked multi-chip module. In: Transducers, Solid-State Sensors, Actuators and Microsystems (2003)

[40] Jang, H.B., Yoon, I., Kim, C.H., Shin, S., Chung, S.W.: The impact of liquid cooling on 3D multi-core processors. In: IEEE International Conference on Computer Design, ICCD (2009)

[41] Laing: 12 volt DC pumps datasheets,
http://www.lainginc.com/pdf/DDC3_LTI_USletter_BR23.pdf

[42] Coskun, A.K., Rosing, T., Gross, K.: Proactive temperature balancing for low-cost thermal management in mpsocs. In: International Conference on Computer-Aided Design (ICCAD), pp. 250–257 (2008)

[43] Gross, K.C., Humenik, K.E.: Sequential probability ratio test for nuclear plant component surveillance. Nuclear Technology 93(2), 131–137 (1991)

[44] Leon, A., et al.: A power-efficient high-throughput 32-thread SPARC processor. In: International Solid-State Circuits Conference, ISSCC (2006)

[45] McDougall, R., Mauro, J., Gregg, B.: Solaris Performance and Tools. Sun Microsystems Press (2006)

[46] SLAMD: Distributed Load Engine, www.slamd.com

[47] Tarjan, D., Thoziyoor, S., Jouppi, N.P.: CACTI 4.0. Technical Report HPL-2006-86, HP Laboratories Palo Alto (2006)

[48] Su, H., et al.: Full-chip leakage estimation considering power supply and temperature variations. In: International Symposium on Low Power Electronics and Design, ISLPED (2003)

Performance and Energy Evaluation of Memory Organizations in NoC-Based MPSoCs under Latency and Task Migration

Gustavo Girão, Daniel Barcelos, and Flávio Rech Wagner

Federal University of Rio Grande do Sul,
Institute of Informatics,
Porto Alegre, RS, Brazil
{ggbsilva,danielb,flavio}@inf.ufrgs.br

Abstract. This chapter presents a study on the performance and energy consumption arising from distinct memory organizations in an NoC-based MPSoC environment. This evaluation considers three sets of experiments. The first one evaluates the performance and energy efficiency of four different memory organizations in a situation where a single application is executed. In the second experiment, a traffic generator is responsible for the injection of synthetic traffic into the system, simulating the impact of the parallel execution of additional applications and increasing the latency of the NoC. Results show that, with a low NoC latency, the distributed memory presents better results for applications with low amount of data to be transferred. On the other hand, results suggest that shared and distributed shared memories present the best results for applications with high data transferring needs. In the second set of experiments, with higher NoC latency, for applications with low communication bandwidth requirements, a memory organization that is physically centralized and logically shared (called nDMA) is shown to have a smooth performance degradation when additional traffic rises up to 20% of the network capacity (22% degradation for an application demanding high communication, and 34% degradation for a low communication one). In contrast, a distributed memory model presents 2% of degradation in an application with high communication requirements, when traffic rises up to 20% of the network capacity, and reaches 19% of degradation in low communication ones. Shared and distributed shared memory models are shown to present lower tolerance to high latencies. A third set of experiments evaluates the performance of the four memory organization models in a situation of task migration, when a new application is launched and its tasks must be distributed among several nodes. Results show that the shared memory and distributed shared memory models have a better performance and energy savings than the distributed memory model in this situation. In addition, the nDMA memory model presents a smaller overhead when compared to the shared memory models and tends to reduce the traffic in the migration process due to the concentration of all memory modules in a single node of the network.

Keywords: Multiprocessor-System-on-Chip, Network-on-chip, Memory Organization, Cache Coherence, Task Migration, Performance and Energy Evaluation.

J. Becker, M. Johann, and R. Reis (Eds.): VLSI-SoC 2009, IFIP AICT 360, pp. 56–80, 2011.

1 Introduction

Nowadays, embedded systems have become very complex. This complexity has many reasons, but the most evident one is the use of such devices for general purpose computing, leading to the execution of many different and complex applications. However, even with higher performance requirements, low power design is still a very desirable goal in portable devices [1].

To support processing requirements and also meet stringent constraints in terms of area and memory, as well as low energy consumption and low power dissipation, a solution using several cores in a single chip is widely adopted. This architecture is known as Multiprocessor System-on-Chip (MPSoC). This scenario usually implies a communication bandwidth between cores that demands a more efficient communication mechanism than a single bus [2]. With this concern in mind, the concept of Network-on-Chip (NoC) has been created.

Considering an MPSoC scenario, memory organization plays a key role since it is not only a major performance bottleneck but also represents a significant component in terms of energy consumption. In addition, memory organization is closely related to the communication model adopted in the application development. For instance, when using a shared memory organization, the communication mechanism usually adopted is the memory itself and, therefore, the memory organization becomes even more important.

Realizing that NoCs are communication structures with high scalability, it is not hard to imagine a situation with dozens or hundreds of processing elements and memory nodes, running a large number of applications concurrently. In this scenario, it is of great interest the evaluation of the behavior of different memory organizations when the network latency increases due to the large number of components and applications in the system. In addition, the memory model also impacts the system performance when a new application is dynamically launched and a task migration mechanism is applied such that a new task allocation is found which better meets system requirements, especially real-time and energy constraints.

This chapter presents a study on the performance and energy consumption arising from distinct memory organizations in an NoC-based MPSoC environment. This evaluation considers three sets of experiments, running on a virtual platform. The first one evaluates the performance and energy efficiency of four different memory organizations in a situation where a single application is executed. In the second set of experiments, a traffic generator is responsible for the injection of synthetic traffic into the system, simulating the impact of the parallel execution of additional applications and increasing the latency of the NoC.

The following memory organizations have been implemented in the virtual platform and evaluated in the experiments: (i) distributed memory, where processors have their local private memories; (ii) shared memory, with a single memory component in a dedicated node on the NoC that is accessed by all processors; (iii) distributed shared memory, composed by several physically distributed memory nodes that share the same address space; and, finally, (iv) a physically shared but logically distributed memory, whose communication model resembles a DMA communication protocol and is thus called nDMA.

Experiments show that, considering the communication requirements of an application, the results of performance and energy consumption may widely vary. For applications with high communication demands, the distributed memory model presents the highest tolerance to communication latency in most situations. However, for applications with low communication workload, the distributed memory model seems to present a larger degradation when NoC latency increases. Also, the nDMA model presents better results as the communication workload decreases. Experiments with the distributed memory model present a variation from 2% to 19% of performance reduction when traffic load rises from 10% to 20%, when using applications with high communication workload and low communication workload, respectively. On the other hand, the nDMA model shows a variation of performance reduction from 22% to 33% in the same situations, which represents a lower relative degradation if compared to the distributed memory model. On the other hand, the shared and distributed shared memory models present low tolerance to high latencies due to the use of a remote memory for communication among tasks.

A third set of experiments show that the shared memory and distributed shared memory models have a better performance and energy savings than the distributed memory model in a task migration situation. In addition, the nDMA memory model presents a smaller overhead when compared to the shared memory models and tends to reduce the traffic in the migration process due to the concentration of all memory modules in a single node of the network.

The remaining of this chapter is organized as follows. Section 2 discusses related work. Section 3 presents the virtual platform used to implement the experiments. Section 4 presents the experimental setup. In Sections 5 and 6, results for experiments with and without additional synthetic traffic, respectively, are presented. Finally, Section 7 draws conclusions and introduces future work.

2 Related Work

Several works regarding memory hierarchy in multiprocessor systems have been developed. However, the majority of these works only consider the use of busses instead of NoCs as communication mechanisms. In such systems, the massive communication parallelism may lead to different side effects due to the memory hierarchy.

Marescaux et al. [3] show a comparison between caches and scratchpads in an NoC-based MPSoC using a distributed shared memory model. In this environment, the use of six DSPs with local L1 caches and a shared L2 cache is considered. Experiments with two NoCs with different QoS methods are presented. The results show that scratchpads have a better performance than caches. However, these experiments do not consider a cache coherence mechanism in hardware. In this case, the adoption of a software coherence conservative approach that invalidates shared data on every access might have led to unnecessary invalidations.

Monchinero et al. [4] explore the use of a distributed shared memory in an NoC-based MPSoC. The platform presents private L1 caches for each core and a shared L2 cache. Each processor has its own address space but there are also several banks of a distributed shared memory. A hardware MMU manages the shared data allocated to each processor. It is shown that by increasing the number of distributed shared banks the performance also increases but only up to some point where the NoC size leads to a greater latency. It is also shown that the energy consumption drops as the number of distributed shared banks increases.

Enright-Jerger et al. [5] propose a new cache coherence solution for multi-core architectures. The Virtual Tree Coherence (VTC) relies on a virtually ordered interconnection that keeps track of sharers of a coarse grain region. The protocol works in such a way that a virtual tree of nodes that share some region is established and each access to this shared region by any of these nodes leads to a message request to the root node of this virtual tree. The root node requests the data to the node that currently owns them. This request is performed as a multicast message, similarly to conventional snoop implementations. However, those multicast message requests are performed in a tree-like fashion in order to decrease the latency on the network, when compared to a multicast based on sequential unicast messages. The VTC solution is compared to a directory-based protocol and to a greedy-order protocol extended onto an unordered interconnect. VTC presented results 25% and 11% better, respectively, concerning performance. Nonetheless, this work does not present results about energy consumption of those cache coherence solutions.

Although the works presented in this section deal with memory organizations in an NoC-based MPSoC environment, none of them considers a high latency situation.

3 The SIMPLE Virtual Platform

Aiming at an accurate evaluation of the tolerance of memory models to a high latency scenario, four distinct memory models were implemented in the SIMPLE (Simple Multiprocessor Platform Environment) virtual platform. SIMPLE is a SystemC, cycle-accurate virtual platform that emulates an NoC-based MPSoC.

In SIMPLE, each Processing Element (PE) is a multi-cycle Java processor that is a hardware implementation of the Java Virtual Machine [6]. Each instruction takes from 3 to 14 cycles (not including a possible cache miss). To generate the Java bytecodes, a compiler that follows the JVM specification is used. This compiler generates the contents of both the instruction memory and data memory customized for the application. These memories are used as inputs for the simulation in SIMPLE.

The NoC used in SIMPLE [7] implements a wormhole packet switching to reduce energy consumption. It also uses XY routing to avoid deadlock situations and a handshake control flow. Additionally, each router has five bi-directional ports with input buffer size of four phits. The phit size is four bytes.

As already mentioned, the simulator supports distinct memory organizations (distributed memory, shared memory, distributed shared memory, and nDMA memory) and cache configurations, regarding size, replacement policy, associativity, and block size.

For the distributed memory model, each router of the NoC is attached to a PE that, in turn, is attached to private memories (instruction and data). In this configuration, there are no caches and the communication mechanism uses message passing. Figure 1a depicts an example of this configuration.

The second model is a shared memory. Here, each router is attached to a PE or to a global Data Memory (the placement of each resource in the network is also configurable). Each PE has its own private data cache, while instruction memories are still local. In such environment there is a cache coherence problem. To solve this problem, SIMPLE adopts a directory-based cache coherence solution [8]. This solution centralizes the memory access requests on an entity (the directory) that, based on the state of the block (if it is dirty or clean), makes decisions that could lead to invalidation or write-back requests if the block is dirty. The flowcharts for read and write operations are presented in Figures 2 and 3, respectively. The shared memory in SIMPLE has a hardware-implemented directory, and each request from a cache to the memory is responded by it. This shared memory environment is shown in Figure 1b.

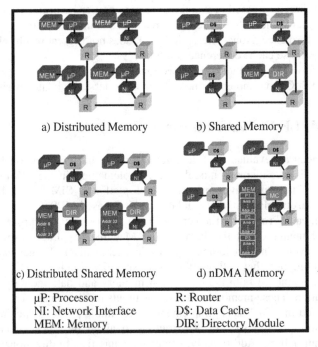

a) Distributed Memory   b) Shared Memory

c) Distributed Shared Memory   d) nDMA Memory

µP: Processor	R: Router
NI: Network Interface	D$: Data Cache
MEM: Memory	DIR: Directory Module

Fig. 1. Memory models available in SIMPLE

The third memory configuration is a distributed shared memory, represented in Figure 1c. In this situation, there can be more than one shared data memory module. However, all of these modules share the same address space. This means that, if a memory module ends with the address N, then some other module in the system begins with the address N + 1. In this scenario, there are also private data caches for each PE and all global memory modules have their own directory module to maintain coherence.

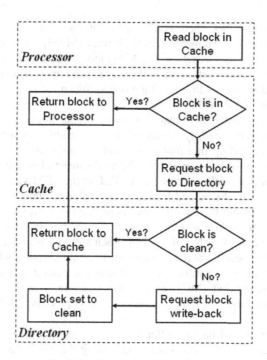

Fig. 2. Read operation using directory

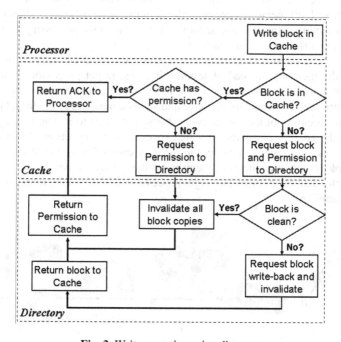

Fig. 3. Write operation using directory

For each router on the NoC there is a Network Interface. In routers with a PE there is also a component called Memory Access Handler (MAH) that receives the signal from the processor when it needs data. The MAH module acts as an interface between the cache and the network interface when there is a cache miss. It creates a message to be sent to the directory module requesting a block. When the data are ready they are sent to the PE by the MAH module.

In both shared and distributed shared memory organizations the communication between the PEs is performed by means of shared variables protected by mutexes. The operations down and up in a mutex are made through test-and-set and test-and-reset operations, respectively, supported by the hardware (caches and directory).

The fourth memory model available in SIMPLE is the nDMA organization, which implements a physically shared and logically distributed memory model, as depicted in Figure 1d. In this model the data memory is placed in an exclusive node, as in the shared memory model. This memory node, however, has N banks, each of them storing the memory data of each of the N PEs. Each memory bank has its own address space, and no PE can access the data of another PE. In addition, each PE has private data caches. When there is a miss, the cache sends a request to the memory node, where a Memory Controller (MC) receives the message, identifies the PEs that is requesting data, and, based on that, accesses the memory bank that hold its memory data.

A direct consequence of having different address spaces is that the most intuitive communication method to be used is message passing. Message passing is essentially implemented sending data from a processor (from its own memory, to be more precise) to another one through the physical communication mechanism. However, in the nDMA model, all memories are centralized in the same node, and, therefore, there is no need to send data through the network. Hence, the message passing method must be modified to work in such environment.

Basically, the processor that wishes to send a message must send a copy request message to the memory (instead of sending it to the target processor) informing an address source and the amount of bytes to be copied. In the memory node, the memory controller identifies this message and sends a message to the target processor informing the intention of the source processor to send data to it. The target processor replies with the address destination for that specific communication. When this reply message arrives at the memory node, the memory controller starts copying from one memory bank (containing the data memory of the source processor) to another one (containing the data memory of the target processor). Figure 4 illustrates this message passing mechanism.

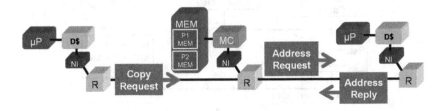

Fig. 4. nDMA message passing mechanism.

Since the memory node needs to be, at some level, programmed by the source processor to copy bytes from one address to another, the memory controller works similarly to a DMA, and, therefore, this memory organization is called nDMA (standing for NoC DMA).

Considering that each processor has its own private data cache, at the moment of sending the copy request the source processor must perform a forced write-back operation of the blocks inside the range of data that it is trying to send. However, the cache performs this write-back operation only on the blocks that have been modified. In a similar way, the target processor must also perform forced write-back operations on the blocks inside the range of the target addresses for that message, before the data are exchanged. Furthermore, the cache of the target processor must invalidate the blocks modified by the data exchange. These are the only moments during the entire communication process when data are exchanged through the network.

4 Experimental Setup

The experiments consider four applications: a matrix multiplication, a motion estimation algorithm, a Mergesort algorithm, and a JPEG encoder.

The Matrix Multiplication was parallelized in such a way that each processor multiplies a subset of lines of matrix A by a subset of lines of matrix B. Each matrix used in simulations has 32 x 32 elements.

In the Motion Estimation, every PE searches a macroblock (a subset of an image) in a different part of the reference image. In the simulations, a macroblock of 8x8 pixels and an image in QCIF format (176x144 pixels) have been used.

For the Mergesort, the parallelism took advantage of its divide-and-conquer nature. Initially, each PE performs the Mergesort on a subset of the vector. Afterwards, one PE is responsible for assembling the whole vector, using the subsets already ordered by the various PEs.

A JPEG encoder can be seen as a three step algorithm. The first two steps (2-D DCT and Quantization) can be performed in parallel for different parts of the image. However, the third step (Entropy coding) can only be correctly performed with the whole image. Based on that, this parallel approach divides an image of 32x16 pixels in eight 8x8 blocks, and each PE is responsible for executing the first two steps on an equal amount of those eight blocks. At the end of those steps, each PE sends the resulting blocks to a master PE, which performs the final step with the complete image.

Considering the data inputs for the applications described above, Figure 5 represents their communication workload regarding different numbers of processors. Based on this chart, it is expected that the Motion Estimation algorithm will generate a larger amount of data exchanges.

Three kinds of experiments were performed. The first one evaluates the different memory organizations on an environment executing only a single parallelized application, with no addition of synthetic traffic. The second set of experiments investigates the behavior of the same memory organizations with the addition of different synthetic traffics, thus simulating the execution of several concurrent applications. Experiments have been performed for different numbers of processors and for different cache sizes. The third set evaluates the overhead in the system caused by a task migration. The task migration mechanism adopted in the experiments is quite simple. It is performed in three distinct steps that are performed sequentially by the processor were the task is located. The three steps correspond to the transmission (and proper receiving) of program code and data memory contents. Of course, the transmission of the data memory is not required when the shared data model is used. Also, because of the fact that the experiments assume a scenario where the tasks are recently created, there is no meaningful stack contents and therefore no need to migrate it.

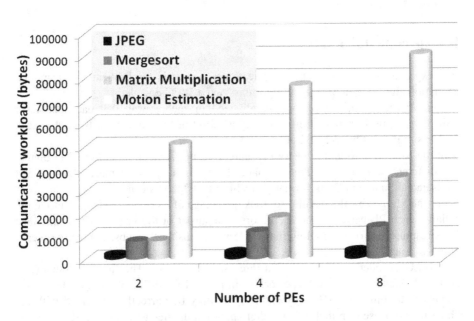

Fig. 5. Communication workload

Experiments evaluate two characteristics: performance, measured by the total execution time of each application, and the overall dynamic energy spent, including processors, network, and memories. For the energy of the processors, a cycle-accurate power simulator [9] is used. For the network (including buffers, arbiter, crossbar, and links), the Orion library [10] is applied, and for the memory and caches the Cacti tool [11] is used. In all simulations, the processors and the NoC operate at 100 Mhz and the technology considered was 0.18μm. At this technology node, the static energy consumption is negligible.

5 Experiments without Synthetic Traffic

5.1 Performance

Concerning performance, Figures 6 thru 9 show the overall execution time of each application, measured in millions of cycles. For each memory organization, there are three columns representing different cache sizes – 256, 512, and 1024 bytes in the Motion Estimation, Mergesort, and JPEG simulations, and 1024, 2048, and 4096 bytes for the Matrix Multiplication.

For applications with low communication workload (such as Matrix Multiplication, Mergesort, and JPEG), the distributed memory model presents better results than all other models. As for the Motion Estimation algorithm, the chart shown in Figure 6 indicates that the distributed memory does not present an overall result better than the other organizations. This is due to the fact that this algorithm requires a large number of data exchanges between processors, as depicted in Figure 5.

The nDMA memory presents very similar results if compared to the other two shared memory models. For the Mergesort and JPEG application (Figures 8 and 9, respectively), the nDMA presents even better results, especially considering more realistic MPSoC sizes, as with eight PEs. Considering the other applications (like the Matrix Multiplication depicted in Figure 7), the distributed shared memory shows a slightly superior performance, especially with eight processors. This enhanced performance is due to the parallel memory accesses performed by the several PEs. However, this advantage does not increase proportionally to the number of memory modules because not all of the modules have the same access profile. This means that some module may concentrate more accesses than others, and, hence, the performance speed up of this solution is not so high.

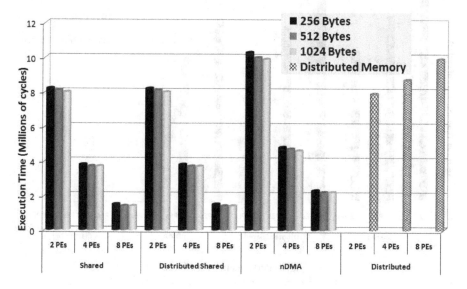

Fig. 6. Performance for Motion Estimation

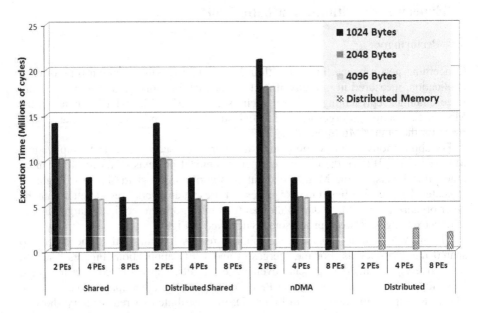

Fig. 7. Performance for Matrix Multiplication

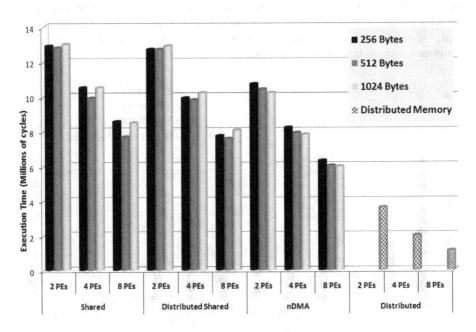

Fig. 8. Performance for Mergesort

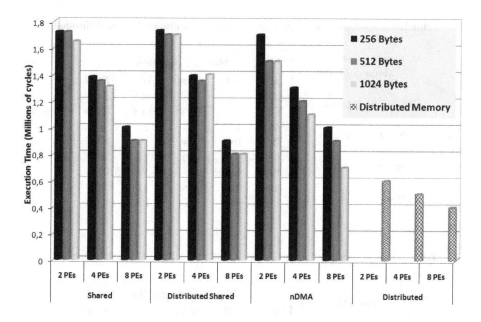

Fig. 9. Performance for JPEG

5.2 Energy Consumption

Concerning dynamic energy, Tables 1 thru 4 show the consumption for the four applications. For each application, there are four columns representing the energy consumption (considering an average between the cache sizes) for the Processors, Caches, Memories, and NoC for eight PEs.

Analyzing the energy consumption difference between the nDMA solution and the other two shared memory organizations, it is possible to see that the NoC consumption is much different. This behavior is a consequence of the fact that the nDMA memory uses small control messages for communication and does not need cache coherence messages. The use of a cache coherence solution in the shared and distributed shared memories also leads to invalidations that increase the memory accesses (in order to retrieve the block again) and the cache accesses. Therefore, the energy consumption of those components is also higher.

As depicted, in the distributed memory model the processor consumption is the major responsible for the energy consumption in the system. The NoC and sometimes also the memory energy are negligible in this environment. The memory energy is more significant in the Motion Estimation simulation due to the amount of data to be manipulated.

Table 1. Energy consumption (mJ) without synthetic traffic for Motion Estimation

Memory Model	Motion Estimation				
	μP	D$	Mem	NoC	Total
Distributed Memory	3180 87%	--	452 12%	4 0.1%	3634 100%
Shared Memory	668 79%	137 16%	13 2%	25 3%	843 100%
Distr. Shared Memory	667 80%	136 16%	10 1%	24 3%	837 100%
nDMA	866 75%	183 16%	96 8%	12 1%	1157 100%

Table 2. Energy consumption (mJ) without synthetic traffic for Motion Estimation

Memory Model	Matrix Multiplication				
	μP	D$	Mem	NoC	Total
Distributed Memory	288 54%	--	243 45%	2 0.5%	533 100%
Shared Memory	919 41%	1214 54%	21 1%	103 4%	2257 100%
Distr. Shared Memory	919 41%	1214 54%	14 0.6%	83 4%	2230 100%
nDMA	1342 44%	1628 54%	38 1%	24 1%	3032 100%

Table 3. Energy consumption (mJ) without synthetic traffic for Mergesort

Memory Model	Mergesort				
	μP	D$	Mem	NoC	Total
Distributed Memory	408 70%	--	173 29%	2 0.5%	583 100%
Shared Memory	1260 54%	479 20%	122 5%	472 21%	2333 100%
Distr. Shared Memory	1264 56%	484 21%	60 3%	440 20%	2244 100%
nDMA	866 73%	238 20%	45 4%	42 3%	1191 100%

Table 4. Energy consumption (mJ) without synthetic traffic for JPEG

Memory Model	JPEG				
	μP	D$	Mem	NoC	Total
Distributed Memory	48	--	27	1	76
	63%		36%	1%	100%
Shared Memory	98	27	10	45	180
	54%	15%	6%	25%	100%
Distr. Shared Memory	99	28	8	43	178
	56%	16%	4%	24%	100%
nDMA	129	31	5	3	168
	77%	18%	3%	2%	100%

For the two shared memory organizations and the nDMA model, the processor also plays a key role in the overall energy consumption. However, in the case of Matrix Multiplication, because of the larger caches, these components present a very significant energy consumption as well. In fact, for the shared memory organizations, the cache energy increases in a non-linear fashion as the cache size increases. As opposed to the increase of the cache sizes, the NoC energy decreases, and, except for the smallest cache size, one can say that the NoC is not a key factor in this case. The same can be said about the memory.

As an overall analysis, the energy consumption results tend to follow the performance results, and, therefore, the distributed memory presents better results for the low communication workload applications (Matrix Multiplication, Mergesort, and JPEG) and worst results for the Motion Estimation.

6   Experiments with Synthetic Traffic

The physical communication mechanism of a multiprocessor system directly affects the memory model adopted. This is due to the fact that the memory model leads to a certain communication model, which, in turn, is influenced by the physical communication mechanism. Based on that, this study tries to emulate an environment with high latency and quantify its impact on the system for different memory models.

In order to emulate such environment, a traffic generator was developed. The general idea is to create a synthetic traffic to increase the latency of the communication mechanism, thus emulating the parallel execution of several applications that generate communications among the various processors.

The Traffic Generator is placed inside the network interface (which is present in every node of the system), as depicted in Figure 10, and a state machine coordinates the inclusion of a traffic package in the Send Buffer. In addition, making use of an identifier in the header of the package, the traffic generator analyzes the incoming packages in the Receive Buffer to exclude any synthetic traffic package. This avoids the resource associated to the Network Interface (PE or a memory) from reading and processing it.

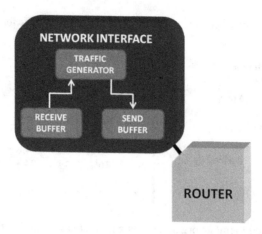

Fig. 10. Traffic Generator

The traffic generator woks in a very simple fashion. At every period (previously configured), it creates a 10-byte package to be sent to a destination node determined through a round-robin sequence of all routers in the system, one at a time. Each traffic package has a 10-byte size in order to guarantee that the network interface is able to send a package in only one cycle.

With this round-robin system, at every 10 cycles router 0 in the system sends a synthetic traffic packet to router 1, router 1 sends a packet to router 2, and so on. In the next period, router 0 sends a packet to router 2, router 1 sends a packet to router 3, and so on. Therefore, at a certain time, each router sends a synthetic traffic packet to a different destination. On the other hand, when these packets arrive at their final destinations, the Traffic Generator removes them from the Receive Buffer.

The experiments use 10% and 20% traffic loads, meaning that at every 10 cycles or 5 cycles, respectively, each router in the system sends a 10-byte traffic packet to a different router. Results indicate by how much the performance decreases (or the energy consumption increases), when the traffic load increases from 10% to 20%.

This Traffic Generator creates a traffic that is uniformly distributed both in time and in space. As future work, more complex generators (as in [12, 13]) will be used, to assess the possible influence of the traffic model on the experimental results.

6.1 Performance

Considering the summarized results of reduction in performance depicted in Table 5, it is possible to see how the increase in the latency impacts the performance.

Although the distributed memory presents better results when compared to the other memory models, it is very clear how much the higher latency impacts the performance as the communication workload of an application increases. In the Motion Estimation application, a higher latency only affects the distributed memory results in 2%. However, when an application with less communication workload (the JPEG) is executed, the impact of a higher latency reaches up to 19%.

The shared memory and distributed shared memory models seem to suffer less from this communication workload variation, although, in absolute numbers, the overall decrease of performance is higher than in any other memory model. On the other hand, the nDMA model suffers less as the latency increases, and its absolute results are in the middle between the shared memory models and the distributed one. This is mainly due to the necessity of accessing a remote memory even though small control messages are used.

These results suggest that a higher latency in the NoC affects much more the distributed memory model than the other models, as the communication workload of an application decreases. Furthermore, the nDMA model seems to have results with less variation as the communication workload of an application decreases.

Table 5. Impact of NoC latency on performance

Application	Motion Estimation	Matrix Multiplication	Mergesort	JPEG
Distributed Memory	2%	4%	6%	19%
Shared Memory	29%	40%	40%	44%
Dist. Shared Memory	33%	48%	49%	55%
nDMA	22%	33%	33%	33%

Note: values in the table indicate how much the performance is reduced when traffic load increases from 10% to 20%.

6.2 Energy Consumption

Again, the pattern present on the performance results also appears in the dynamic energy consumption. These results suggest that applications with high communication requirements seem to have a smaller reduction in the energy consumption as the latency increases.

In the same way as for the performance results, it is possible to see that a higher latency impacts the energy consumption of the memory models differently, depending on the communication workload characteristics of the various applications. Results in Table 6 show that the distributed memory model seems to suffer more in a high latency situation if the communication workload of the application is low. Again, the shared memory and distributed memory organizations seem to suffer more than other models, whereas the nDMA model presents a graceful degradation if the communication workload of the application is low.

Table 6. Impact of NoC latency on energy consumption

Application	Motion Estimation	Matrix Multiplication	Mergesort	JPEG
Distributed Memory	1%	10%	14%	32%
Shared Memory	25%	50%	65%	67%
Dist. Shared Memory	44%	70%	77%	79%
nDMA	15%	24%	24%	24%

Note: values in the table indicate how much the energy consumption increases when traffic load increases from 10% to 20%.

7 Experiments with Task Migration

This section presents experimental results regarding the impact of the distinct memory models on task migration, considering the performance on the migration execution and the dynamic energy spent on it. Experiments quantify the task migration overhead in each model. Since all memory models consider that each PE has its own private instruction memory, all of them demand the transmission of program code during task migration, as well as of data memory, depending on the model. The experiments consider a worst case scenario, corresponding to the creation of a new application with N tasks in a single node and the following migration of these tasks to other nodes. Considering that N represents the number of processors, each processor has exactly one new task assigned to it after the migration. In this case, the new task has no data on the stack and therefore, it is not necessary to migrate its contents.

7.1 Performance Results

According to the performance results presented in Figures 11 thru 14, the distributed memory model presents worst results in all cases. This was already expected due to the fact that the distributed memory model demands the migration of the whole data memory. This situation does not happen in the case of shared and distributed shared memories. In the case of the nDMA model, due to the fact that it is essentially a shared memory model, in a sense that all data (from all processors) is located in a single node, the copy can be made simultaneously to the program code migration. In addition, in the nDMA memory model there is no traffic overhead for the data memory transfer during migration.

However, these are not the only factors responsible for the worse performance of the distributed memory model. Another factor is the size of the code, which, in the case of distributed memory, is usually higher than in other models. This is due to the fact that communication needs to be completely explicit in the code. The programmer has to describe the copying of data to sending buffers and the reading of data from receiving buffers, as well as calls for these functions. This procedure is less intense in the case of the nDMA memory model, which, although not requiring the transmission of the contents of the data memory, works by sending explicit messages to control communication between the processing elements. On the other hand, the shared memory and distributed shared memory models present the best performance in all cases. The fact that only the application code contents is copied is not the single reason for that, but also the simplicity of the code in the shared memory models.

Despite the better results of the shared and distributed shared memory models, it is important to note that the migration of the contents of the caches was not taken into account in these experiments. Therefore, a loss of performance may be expected during the initial stages of task execution after its migration in these cases, due to a considerable amount of compulsory cache misses. This case has not been considered in the experiments since the migration occurs at the time of the creation of the task and so the caches contain virtually no information relevant to that task. However, if one takes into account a migration during the execution of this task, the compulsory

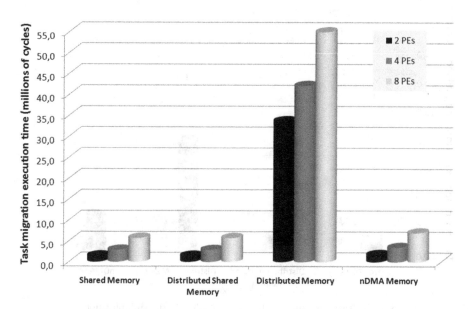

Fig. 11. Task migration performance for the Motion Estimation

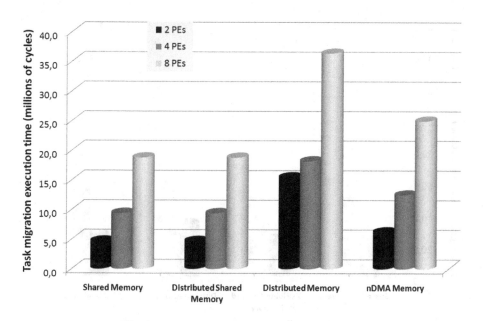

Fig. 12. Task migration performance for the JPEG

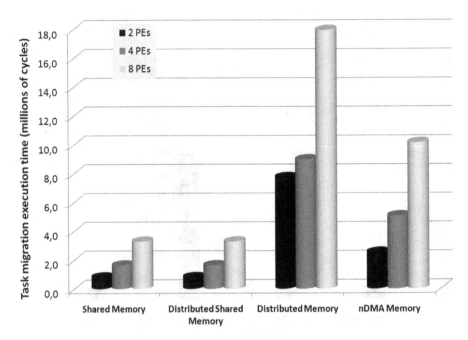

Fig. 13. Task migration performance for the Matrix Multiplication

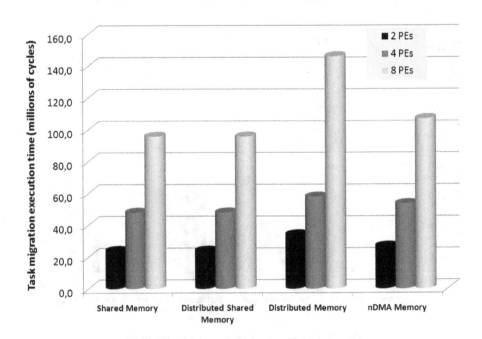

Fig. 14. Task migration performance for the Mergesort

cache misses will occur. This is a situation whose outcome depends on the point in time within the execution of the task in which the decision is taken to perform the migration. This choice is a function of the task allocation algorithm and was not considered in the experiments, which evaluate only the mechanism of task migration itself.

7.2 Energy Consumption Results

Regarding the dynamic energy consumption, results shown in Figures 15 thru 18 demonstrate the same pattern presented in the previous performance results.

Among the components of the system, it is noticeable that the NoC has an extremely low energy consumption during the migration process when compared to the energy consumption of processors and memory. In particular, the migration process appears to be very expensive for the processor that needs to execute the whole process of sending and receiving messages and perform the routines of reading and writing on program and data memories (in the case of distributed memory).

Again, the results point to a worse result for the distributed memory, due to the reasons already discussed in the previous section. The shared and distributed shared memories are the most efficient ones, given the smaller size of code to be read and written in memory (thus reducing the number of memory accesses). This also reduces the execution time of the processor performing this task, which leads to a lower power consumption.

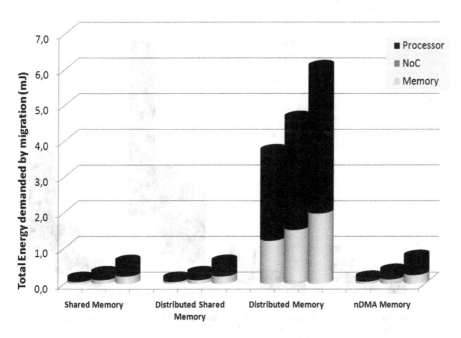

Fig. 15. Task migration energy consumption of the Motion Estimation

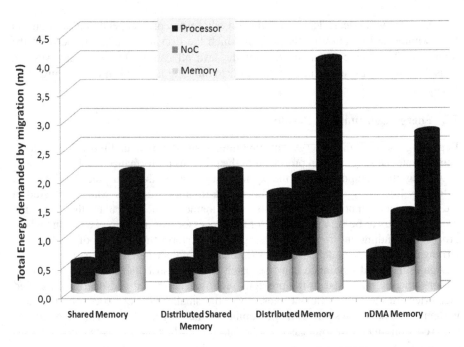

Fig. 16. Task migration energy consumption of the JPEG

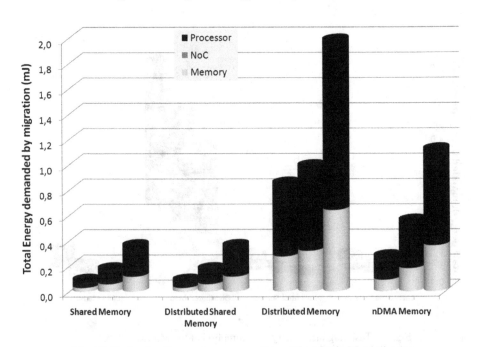

Fig. 17. Task migration energy consumption of the Matrix Multiplication

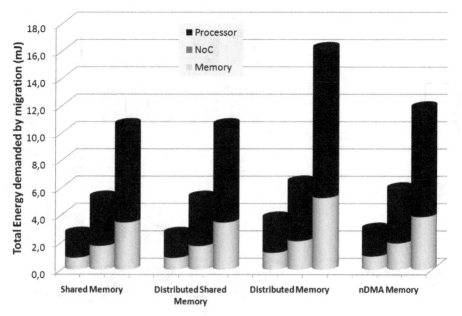

Fig. 18. Task migration energy consumption of the Mergesort

8 Conclusions and Future Work

This chapter presented a study on the tolerance of different memory organization models under high latency NoC scenarios and also the impact of these memory models in a task migration situation. The experiments considered not only different memory models and traffic loads but also different numbers of processors and cache sizes and various applications with different bandwidth requirements.

The experiments suggest that the distributed memory model presents a higher tolerance to communication latency in most situations. The nDMA model also presents some tolerance and presents better results as the communication workload increases. The high level of communication requirements on shared and distributed shared memory leads to the worst results as the synthetic traffic increases. This is due to the fact that not only network communication is required to retrieve application data but also the communication among tasks is performed through a remote memory.

Regarding dynamic energy consumption, it is possible to conclude that the most affected component of an MPSoC based on a high latency NoC is the NoC itself, while other components such as memory and cache are not affected, due to the fact that the number of accesses does not change and thus neither the dynamic energy consumption.

Although the distributed memory model presents better results in most situations, there is a pattern that shows that, for applications with low communication workload, it suffers more with higher latencies on the NoC. On the other hand, the nDMA memory model presents results with lower degradation as the communication workload of an application is low.

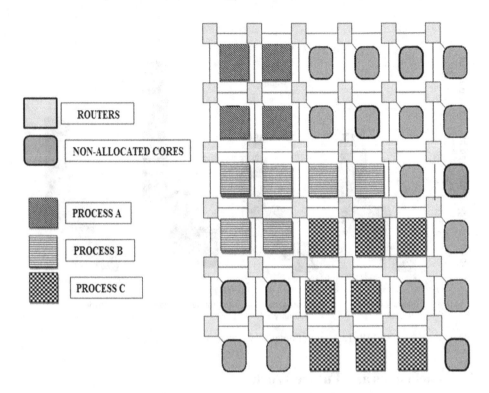

ROUTERS

NON-ALLOCATED CORES

PROCESS A

PROCESS B

PROCESS C

Fig. 19. Cluster allocation in a large MPSoC

The experimental results also suggest that the distributed memory model is the one in which the task migration is more expensive. These experimental results were expected due to the simple fact that the distributed memory needs to send task data explicitly through the network, which is not true for the other models. In the case of shared and distributed shared memories the fact of having a global memory limits the amount of information to be transferred in a migration to the program memory. In the case of the model nDMA the situation is very similar. The difference occurs because the data memory copy is performed locally on the node where the memory banks are located, making it a quicker process, independent of the network. Another factor that explains why the shared and distributed shared memories obtain better results is the fact that the application code in such cases is simpler than in the distributed memory model, where all communication must be specified explicitly.

Future work includes more experiments considering other applications and synthetic traffics with more complex distributions, as well as the proposal and evaluation of an optimized task migration model for each memory organization, also considering high latency situations. The evaluation of the static energy consumption for more recent technology nodes must also be considered.

An ongoing work will propose a cluster scenario for an MPSoC with dozens or even hundreds of processors. According to the results presented in this chapter, it was possible to see that different applications have distinct memory hierarchy demands, and, therefore, an MPSoC with different memory organization solutions in the same chip, in order to address the needs of different applications running concurrently, makes sense. The ongoing work relies on these observations to build a system with multiple clusters on the NoC, where each cluster may have a distinct memory organization. Thus, it is possible to take advantage of parallelism at application and task level. Figure 19 gives an insight on how this MPSoC could be. In the figure, there are three applications allocated in the MPSoC and the processors running tasks from the same application build a single cluster. As the parallelism of an application changes during the execution [14], the task allocation can be dynamic, making the cluster size also dynamically modifiable, thus favoring another application that may need more processing or memory resources.

Each of these clusters makes use of a memory organization that provides a better performance for the task (or set of tasks) being performed on it. To accomplish the communication between clusters it is necessary to provide a component that builds a bridge between the memory models. This component could be centralized, so that all inter-cluster communication would be sent to a single component in the system. Another solution would provide components for inter-cluster communication within each cluster, in a manner similar to a router, but at a higher level of abstraction. These components would have to perform communication in accordance to the memory organization adopted by the cluster (message passing, shared variable, etc).

In addition, as future MPSoCs tend to provide adaptability, the memory hierarchy can be also dynamic in a sense that each memory node (i.e. a node that holds a general memory structure) can be configurable in terms of a distinct memory organization. Hence, the memory node can become a cache or a main memory, leading to a shared memory or to a distributed memory model, respectively. In order to do that, it is also required a software layer to identify the application needs.

Another objective of this future work is the support of consistency of data between different models of memory organization, as proposed in [15]. This problem can be seen as a more expanded version of the problem of consistent caches. However, in this case it is intended to maintain consistency between the memory hierarchies of several clusters. Again the solution to this problem is likely to be centralized, creating a template directory that keeps a record of the location of all data in the system. An alternative solution is the adoption of a hierarchical system of directories. In this case, each cluster contains a directory that centralizes data consistency for the cluster itself and responds directly to a central directory that maintains the consistency of data at a macro level.

References

1. Marwedel, P.: Embedded System Design. Kluwer Academic Publishers, Dordrecht (2003)
2. Lee, H.G., Chang, N., Ogras, U.Y., Marculescu, R.: On-Chip Communication Architechture Exploration: a Quantitative Exploration of Point-to-Point, Bus and Network-on-chip Architectures. ACM Transactions on Design Automation of Eletronic Systems 12, 21–40 (2007)
3. Marescaux, T., Brockmeyer, E., Corporaal, H.: The Impact of Higher Communication Layers on NoC Supported MPSoCs. In: Proceedings of the First International Symposium on Networks-on-Chip, pp. 107–116 (May 2007)

4. Monchiero, M., Palermo, G., Silvano, C., Villa, O.: Exploration of Distributed Shared Memory Architectures for NoC-based Multiprocessors. In: Proceedings of the International Conference on Embedded Computer Systems: Architectures, pp. 144–151 (July 2006)
5. Enright-Jerger, N., Peh, L.-S., Lipasti, M.: Virtual Tree Coherence: Leveraging Regions and In-Network Multicast Trees for Scalable Cache Coherence. In: Proceedings of 41st International Symposium on Microarchitecture (MICRO), Lake Como, Italy (November 2008)
6. Ito, S.A., Carro, L., Jacobi, R.P.: Making Java Work for Microcontroller Applications. IEEE Design & Test of Computers 18, 100–110 (2001)
7. Zeferino, C.A., Kreutz, M.E., Susin, A.A.: RASoC: a Router Soft-core for Networks-on-Chip. In: Proceedings of Design, Automation and Test in Europe Conference and Exhibition, pp. 198–203. IEEE Computer Society, Washington, DC (2004)
8. Girão, G., de Oliveira, B.C., Soares, R., Silva, I.S.: Cache Coherency Communication Cost in a NoC-based MPSoC Platform. In: Proceedings of 20th Symposium on Integrated Circuits and Systems Design, Rio de Janeiro, pp. 288–293. ACM, New York (2007)
9. Beck Filho, A.C.S., Mattos, J.C.B., Wagner, F.R., Carro, L.: CACO-PS: a General purpose Cycle-accurate Configurable Power Simulator. In: Proceedings of 16th Symposium on Integrated Circuits and Systems Design, São Paulo, pp. 349–354. IEEE Computer Society, Los Alamitos (2003)
10. Wang, H.-S., Zhu, X., Peh, L.-S., Malik, S.: Orion: a Power-Performance Simulator for Interconnection Networks. In: Proceedings of 35th International Symposium on Microarchitecture (MICRO), pp. 294–305 (November 2002)
11. Wilton, S., Jouppi, N.: Cacti: An Enhanced Cache Access and Cycle Time Model. IEEE Journal of Solid State Circuits 31(5), 677–688 (1996)
12. Carara, E., Mello, A., Moraes, F.: Communication Models in Networks-on-Chip. In: Proceedings of 18h International Workshop on Rapid System Prototyping, pp. 57–60 (June 2007)
13. Mahadevan, S., Angiolini, F., Storgaard, M., Olsen, R.G., Sparso, J., Madsen, J.: A Network Traffic Generator Model for Fast Network-on-Chip Simulation. In: Proceedings of the Design, Automation and Test in Europe Conference, pp. 780–785 (June 2005)
14. Kumar, R., Farkas, K.I., Jouppi, N.P., Ranganathan, P., Tullsen, D.M.: Single-ISA Heterogeneous Multi-Core Architectures: The Potential for Processor Power Reduction. In: Proceedings of 36th International Symposium on Microarchitecture (MICRO), San Diego, USA (December 2003)
15. Dutt, N.: Memory-aware NoC Exploration and Design. In: Proceedings of the Design, Automation and Test in Europe, vol. 1, pp. 1128–1129. IEEE, Munich (2008)

Crosstalk Fault Tolerant NoC: Design and Evaluation

Alzemiro H. Lucas, Alexandre M. Amory, and Fernando G. Moraes

Faculdade de Informática - Pontifícia Universidade Católica do Rio Grande do Sul (PUCRS)
Av. Ipiranga, 6681 - prédio 32 - Porto Alegre - Brazil - CEP 90619-900
{alzemiro.silva,alexandre.amory,fernando.moraes}@pucrs.br

Abstract. The innovations on integrated circuit fabrics are continuously reducing components size, which increases the logic density of systems-on-chip (SoC), but also affect the reliability of these components. Chip-level global buses are especially subject to crosstalk faults, which can lead to increased delay and glitches. This paper evaluates different crosstalk fault tolerant approaches for Networks-on-chip (NoCs) links such that the network can maintain the original network performance even in the presence of errors. Three different approaches are presented and evaluated in terms of area overhead, packet latency, power consumption, and residual fault coverage. Results demonstrate that the use of CRC coding at each link is preferred when minimal area and power overhead are the main goals. However, each one of the methods presented here has its own advantages and can be applied depending on the application.

Keywords: fault tolerance, reliability, Networks-on-Chip (NoCs), error correction and detection.

1 Introduction

NoCs has emerged as a candidate solution to interconnect IPs in complex SoCs, due to its scalability and parallelism, compared to bus architectures. A NoC can be defined as a set of routers responsible to transmit data on the intra-chip domain, exploiting methods used in general networks, decoupling communication from computation, enabling the creation of protocols to grant reliability and quality of service.

Besides the communication infrastructure, an important SoC design challenge is the degradation of the signal integrity on long wires. Coupling capacitances tends to increase with the reduced components size. Faster clocks and lower operation voltage makes the delay induced by crosstalk effects even more critical, being the major source of errors in nanoscale technologies [1]. Another noise sources that can produce data errors [2] are electromagnetic interference, radiation-induced charge injection, and source noise.

Compared to buses, NoCs provide more opportunities to implement fault tolerance techniques for intra-chip communication. For instance, a NoC has multiple paths for any pair of modules, which can be exploited to improve the fault tolerance of the communication by using adaptive routing algorithms. Techniques based on codification for error detection/correction can also be applied for NoCs. Other approaches include place and route techniques to avoid routing of bus lines in

J. Becker, M. Johann, and R. Reis (Eds.): VLSI-SoC 2009, IFIP AICT 360, pp. 81–93, 2011.

parallel, changes in the geometrical shape of bus lines and addition of shielding lines between two adjacent signal lines. However, those techniques require advanced knowledge on electric layout design, and they are executed later in the design flow.

Considering these issues, bus encoding techniques represents a good tradeoff between implementation costs and design time to minimize crosstalk effects [3], and it is a technology independent mechanism to increase reliability on intra-chip communication. Even though, designers should carefully choose the codification technique, taking into account that the ideal codification should have minimal area overhead while delivering the desired reliability [3], due to strict performance and power constraints of NoC architectures.

This paper evaluates error recovery mechanisms to increase the reliability of NoC links, making it resilient against crosstalk faults. As a design constraint, the evaluated mechanisms must be able to keep the NoC performance (latency, throughput, and bandwidth) in case of errors. Additional design constraints include low area overhead, high fault coverage, and minimum delay.

This paper is organized as follows. Section 2 presents related work in fault tolerance for NoCs. Section 3 presents the design of the crosstalk fault tolerant NoCs. Section 3 reports the fault modeling used to simulate and validate the network. The fault tolerant NoCs are evaluated and compared in Section 4. Finally, Section 5 concludes this paper.

2   Related Work

Several types of faults and fault tolerance techniques can be applied to NoCs. Faults can be classified, according to the fault *duration*, as a transient or permanent fault, or according to the *moment* the fault is detected, as an on-line (self-checking) or off-line approach.

The types of fault tolerant solutions for NoCs range from adaptive routing algorithms (used to find alternative paths for communication), coding techniques (use redundancy codes to detect and/or correct bit flips), retransmission in case of faults detected, and a combination of those techniques. The retransmission approach can be further classified according to the place where the retransmission takes place: router-to-router or end-to-end.

This paper focuses on on-line self-checking fault-tolerance techniques for transient faults on NoC links, employing coding techniques and router-to-router retransmission. Our goal is to evaluate different implementations, comparing metrics as silicon area, latency, and power consumption. Although one of the presented architectures can detect some faults in the router, our primary goal is to protect NoC links. Other fault-tolerance techniques that deviate from our focus, as adaptive routing, are not mentioned. Table 1 summarizes the related work.

Zimmer [4] proposes a fault model notation, where faults can occurs simultaneously in multiple wires, during multiple clock cycles. This fault model is used to evaluate coding techniques on NoC buses. The goal of this work is to present an accurate model to simulate the occurrence of faults in wide data bit buses and to show the reduction of residual faults when the bus is protected with coding techniques using single error correction and a double error detection (two bits coverage).

Table 1. Comparison of related work

Reference	Method	Implementation/ Evaluation	Metrics	Types of Faults
ZIM03	- CRC/Hamming on links - Fault Model - QoS	Implementation	- Residual error rate	Transient
BER04	- Source CRC - Switch-to-switch retransmission	Implementation	Not presented	Transient
VEL04	- Parity/Hamming on links - QoS	Implementation	- Latency - Power	Transient
MUR05	- End-to-end retransmission - Switch-to-switch retransmission: -Flit level and packet level - Correction + Detection	Evaluation	- Latency - Power - Residual error rate	Transient
GRE07	- End-to-end retransmission - Switch-to-switch retransmission: -Flit level and packet level - Retransmission with and without priority	Evaluation	- Message arrival probability - Average detection time - Average correction time	Transient
Proposed work	- CRC/Hamming on links - Source CRC - Switch-to-switch retransmission/ correction	Implementation/ Evaluation	- Latency - Area Overhead - Power - Residual error rate	Transient

Bertozzi [5] presents a NoC architecture with pipelined links, pipelined arbitration and switching within the routers. The goal of this architecture is to provide high-speed operation and reliable communication. To achieve reliable communication, this architecture provides error control using CRC codes on links.

Vellanki [6] addresses a NoC architecture with Quality of Service (QoS) and error control techniques. This paper presents the evaluation of the proposed architecture, considering latency and power dissipation metrics. The two QoS methods addressed in this work are guaranteed throughput and best effort, and the error control techniques include single error detection and retransmission, and single error correction.

Murali [7] explores different error recovery methods for NoCs, evaluating for each one the energy, error protection, and latency overhead. The methods include end-to-end error detection, router-to-router error detection, at either at the flit-level and at the packet-level, and a hybrid scheme with correction of single errors and detection of multiple errors. This paper shown that packet storage is responsible for the major part of the energy consumption, thus the end-to-end error detection and retransmission has the higher cost in energy efficiency. Using the hybrid scheme, it is possible to reduce the energy overhead at lower error rates. Small errors are corrected and retransmissions are avoided. However, in the presence of multiple errors its efficiency is lower than error detection and retransmission schemes.

Grecu [8] proposed new metrics for performance evaluation of fault tolerant NoC architectures. The metrics proposed in this paper includes detection latency, recovery latency and message arrival probability. These metrics were analyzed in a simple simulation scenario taking into account retransmission with and without priority. The author states that these metrics can better estimate the quality of a particular fault tolerant implementation than just performance metrics such as latency, throughput, and power consumption.

The contribution of this work is the development, validation, and analysis of error detection and recovery techniques for NoCs. Compared to [5] and [7] this work presents 3 different solutions to apply fault tolerance on NoCs, considering the implementation feasibility of each technique, concerning area overhead, power consumption and residual fault analysis.

3   Crosstalk Fault Tolerant NoC Architectures

This paper presents three different strategies for fault tolerance on NoC links. All methods use as reference design the Hermes NoC [9]. Hermes is a configurable infrastructure, specified in VHDL at RT level, aiming to implement low area overhead packet switching NoCs. Routers have up to five bi-directional ports and each input port stores received data on a FIFO buffer. It uses the XY routing algorithm and a centralized round-robin arbitration grants access to incoming packets. The Hermes NoC architecture has been configured as a 8x8 2-D mesh network, flit size equal to 16 bits, 8-flit buffer depth, without virtual channels.

Two coding techniques are used for error detection/correction: CRC and Hamming.

CRC codification is adopted for error detection, due its small complexity on logic implementation, and small parity delay calculation when using a parallel architecture to generate N parity bits per clock cycle. The designed CRC circuit encodes 16 bits (flit width) per clock cycle and generates four parity bits. Using this approach, 93.75% of all possible 16-bit error patterns can be detected [10].

Sequential and combinational designs may be used to implement the CRC circuitry. The combinational design has been chosen because it does not add latency to the network, and the extra delay of the combinational logic is considered small. Considering the polynomial generator is $g = 1+X+X^4$, the resulting combinational circuit for the CRC encoder is presented below:

$$
\begin{aligned}
p_0 &= r_{15} \oplus r_{11} \oplus r_8 \oplus r_7 \oplus r_5 \oplus r_3 \oplus r_2 \oplus r_1 \oplus r_0 \\
p_1 &= r_{12} \oplus r_9 \oplus r_8 \oplus r_6 \oplus r_4 \oplus r_3 \oplus r_2 \oplus r_1 \\
p_2 &= r_{13} \oplus r_{10} \oplus r_9 \oplus r_7 \oplus r_5 \oplus r_4 \oplus r_3 \oplus r_2 \\
p_3 &= r_{15} \oplus r_{14} \oplus r_{10} \oplus r_7 \oplus r_6 \oplus r_4 \oplus r_2 \oplus r_1 \oplus r_0
\end{aligned}
\tag{1}
$$

The decoder uses the same circuit of the encoder and compares the received parity bits with the bits generated locally by this encoder. If the values of received parity bits are different from the calculated bits, the decoder signals an error.

The second coding technique used in this work is the Hamming code, which enables the correction of flits with error in one bit at most. The Hamming coder and decoder are based on the function *hamgen()* provided by Matlab. The following equations define the Hamming encoder:

$$
\begin{aligned}
p_0 &= r_{15} \oplus r_{12} \oplus r_{10} \oplus r_9 \oplus r_6 \oplus r_5 \oplus r_4 \oplus r_3 \oplus r_2 \\
p_1 &= r_{14} \oplus r_{11} \oplus r_9 \oplus r_8 \oplus r_5 \oplus r_4 \oplus r_3 \oplus r_2 \oplus r_1 \\
p_2 &= r_{15} \oplus r_{13} \oplus r_{12} \oplus r_9 \oplus r_8 \oplus r_7 \oplus r_6 \oplus r_5 \oplus r_1 \oplus r_0 \\
p_3 &= r_{14} \oplus r_{12} \oplus r_{11} \oplus r_8 \oplus r_7 \oplus r_6 \oplus r_5 \oplus r_4 \oplus r_0 \\
p_4 &= r_{13} \oplus r_{11} \oplus r_{10} \oplus r_7 \oplus r_6 \oplus r_5 \oplus r_4 \oplus r_3
\end{aligned}
\tag{2}
$$

The Hamming decoder has a similar design plus an additional logic to correct the erroneous bit indicated by the syndrome.

3.1 NoC with Link CRC

Figure 1 illustrates the first fault tolerant architecture implemented, which protects only the NoC links. This strategy provides router-to-router flit-level error detection and retransmission. This figure represents two adjacent routers, the sender and the receiver routers, and a link between them. Modifications compared to the non-fault tolerant design are in grey. It includes a CRC encoder at the sender, a CRC decoder and an error flip-flop at the receiver, additional signals *crc_in* and *error_out* in the link, and slight modifications in the input buffers.

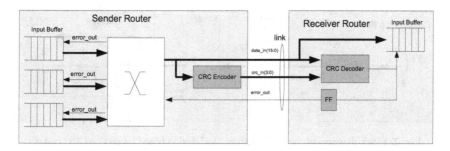

Fig. 1. Block diagram of the fault tolerant NoC design based on CRC for links

When the sender sends a flit to the receiver, it encodes the CRC in parallel due to its combinational logic. The CRC is sent through the *crc_in* signal to the receiver, which decodes it and test for faults. If there is no fault, the flit (not the CRC) is stored in the receiver buffer. If some fault arrives, the flit is not stored into the buffer, and an error is signaled, through the *error_out* signal, back to the sender, which retransmits the last flit. This approach enables error recovery in one clock cycle.

The benefit of this approach is that the buffers and the buses width inside the router remain unchanged, saving silicon area. Only the external router interface receives new signals for error detection and recovery. The impact in silicon area, power, and delay is smaller. There is no impact on the latency when the network has no faults. Under a faulty condition the latency is incremented by one clock cycle only, which is an advantage compared to an approach based on end-to-end retransmission. This approach also provides the following additional advantages:

- It is not necessary to store full packets at each router, enabling the use of wormhole packet switching, reducing area, power and latency compared to store-and-forward or virtual cut- through;

- This method is faster compared to full packet retransmissions, since once an error is detected, the flit can be retransmitted in the next clock cycle;

- Error detection occurs before routing decision, making the network resilient against misrouting due to header flit errors;

- Flits to be retransmitted are available at the sender routers buffers, inducing smaller area overhead.

3.2 NoC With Source CRC

This section presents the second fault tolerant NoC architecture, which is illustrated in Figure 2. This figure illustrates a path from the source router to a given router located in the path to the destination router. Modifications compared to the non-fault tolerant design are in grey. It includes a CRC encoder at the sender node, a CRC decoder and an error flip-flop at the receivers (intermediate routers and destination node), additional signals *crc_in* and *error_out* in the links, and a slight modification in the input buffers.

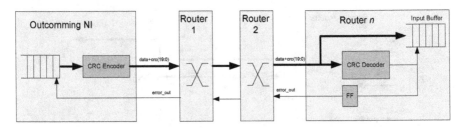

Fig. 2. Block diagram of the fault tolerant NoC design based on source CRC coder

The main modification compared to the design in Section 3.1 is that the CRC encoder is located only at the Network Interface (NI) of the module connected on the router local port. The CRC bits became part of the flit, increasing the width of all buffers of the network, as well as the internal buses of the routers, so that the CRC bits are carried through the network as part of the packet. As can be seen, the *data_out* signal have now 20 bit instead of 16 as the previous network, because this signal includes the *crc_out* signal, presented before in Figure 1.

This network has the advantage of using four less CRC modules at each router (local port does not have CRC). On the other hand, it increases the buffer width, which increases the silicon area, the power consumption, and the delay of routers. This approach uses the same mechanism to recover the corrupted data from the input buffers at the previous router, thus, this network presents the same latency as the previous network to retransmit corrupted flits (one clock cycle).

Another advantage of this approach is that it can not only protect the links, but also protect certain internal logic of the router. It is possible to detect transient or even permanent faults in certain internal modules of the routers like the buffers and the crossbar, however, it cannot detect faults in most of the router control logic. Another limitation is that, if the fault is a bit-flip in a buffer, the error cannot be recovered. Therefore, other techniques for fault tolerance should be adopted.

3.3 NoC Hamming on Links

Figure 3 presents a simplified structure of the network with Hamming code on links. This figure represents two adjacent routers (sender and receiver) where the link has been changed to carry Hamming parity bits. The sender has a combinational Hamming encoder at the output ports and the receiver has a combinational Hamming decoder at the input ports. Unlike the previous networks, none of the internal modules of the routers were changed.

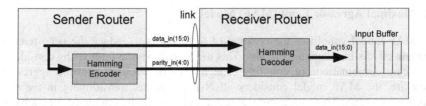

Fig. 3. Block diagram of the fault tolerant NoC design based on Hamming code

The incoming flits of the receiver are first decoded and then saved in to the buffer. If there is a single fault the Hamming decoder corrects it transparently, without need of flit retransmission, thus, unlike the previous networks, this approach does not add latency to the network in a faulty situation. Note that there is no error signal from the receiver to the sender like the previous networks.

4 Fault Modeling and Fault Injection

This section describes the strategy used to simulate the network and the fault injection technique used to evaluation the implemented error recovery mechanism.

4.1 Croasstalk Effects

Crosstalk effect is observed at each interaction of two adjacent wires running long distances in parallel. Each wire has its load capacitance and resistance, and each pair of wires has its cross-coupled capacitance that causes interferences during switch activity. Table 2 depicts the delay ratio factor g for a bus wire as a function of simultaneous transitions on neighboring lines [11].

Symbols ↑, ↓ and – represent positive transition, negative transition and no transition respectively. The factor r is a relation between inter-wire capacitance and the relative capacitance of the wire and the ground signal. In a usual situation, where these capacitances are the same, the r factor is 1. Thus, in the worst-case scenario, where both neighbors transit on the opposite direction of the victim wire, the delay factor g is 5. Consequently, the wire delay can vary over 500% between the worst and the best case, just as a function of the direction of the transitions on neighboring wires 11.

Table 2. Relation between transition directions and the delay factor g

bit k-1	bit k	bit k+1	Factor g
↑	↑	↑	1
↑	↑	–	$1+r$
↑	↑	↓	$1+2r$
–	↑	–	$1+2r$
–	↑	↓	$1+3r$
↓	↑	↓	$1+4r$

4.2 Maximal Agressor Fault (MAF) Model

The MAF model simplifies the creation of test vectors to induce the occurrence of crosstalk effects in integrated circuits. This model reduces the fault set by considering worst-case combinations of coupling capacitances between all possible aggressors. Therefore, the MAF model considers all N-1 aggressors transitioning in the same direction as a fault. This model considers that only one fault is modeled for each error on a victim line Y_i, and only one set of transitions can excite that fault. Figure 4 shows the necessary transitions to excite four types of fault for a victim wire Y_i according the MAF model.

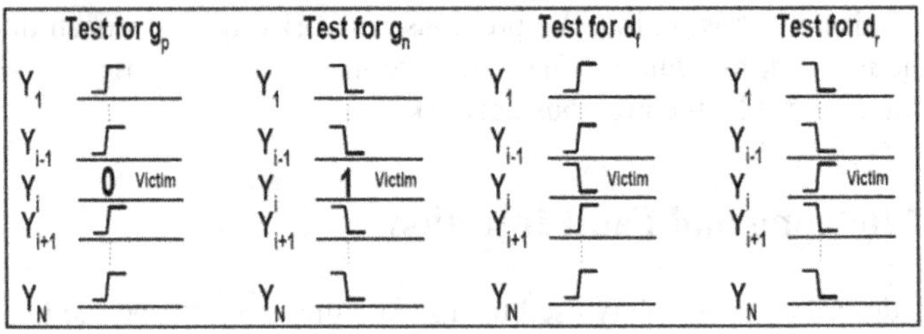

Fig. 4. Required transitions for MAF model 1

The fault model has four error conditions for each N-line wide set of interconnects to be tested: (*i*) g_p: positive glitch error; (*ii*) g_n: negative glitch error; (*iii*) d_f: falling delay error; (*iv*) d_r: rising delay error.

4.3 Saboteur Module

A module named *saboteur* is developed to control the fault injection during the simulation process. This module is responsible for monitoring the data transmitted in each channel of the network, and according to its patterns, changes the value of some data bits to simulate the crosstalk effect. The Maximal Aggressor Fault (MAF) model, described in [1], is used as a reference for the implementation of the saboteur module.

Each NoC link is connected to a saboteur module as illustrated in Figure 5. Besides fault injection, each saboteur module counts the amount of data transmitted in the link during a full simulation and the amount of errors injected on each link, enabling to generate statistics related to the fault injection on each channel.

In this work, it is considered every 5 bits in parallel, on each 16 bits data buses, to check MAF model conditions. If one of them is meet, the victim value changes. This module can also be parameterized to check individual conditions of MAF model as shown in Section 4.2. The amount of errors injected into the network allows the validation of the architecture. Note that the fault injection considers worst-case situations, and in real circuits, the rate of errors due to crosstalk is smaller, since not all true MAF conditions generate faults.

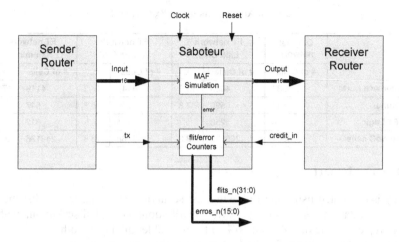

Fig. 5. Saboteur located between two routers

5 Results

This section presents area, power, latency and residual fault analysis, comparing the reference NoC to fault tolerant NoCs developed in this work.

5.1 Area Overhead

Four networks have been implemented and synthesized using Cadence Encounter RTL Compiler (0.35um standard cells library) to evaluate the silicon area. Table 3 shows the results for a router with 5 ports and for an 8x8 network.

The total standard cell area increased 13.3% for the FT NOC with CRC in the links. This area overhead is due to the addition of CRC encoders and decoders at each router port.

The area overhead of the NoC with CRC computed at the source router is 16.8%. The area overhead for this NoC comes from the increased buffer size (*flit* + CRC bits). As previously mentioned, this network can also provide some protection to transient faults on internal modules of the routers, justifying its use in designs where router fault tolerance is required.

The network with Hamming on links presented an area overhead of 16.4% compared to the original network. This overhead is due to the higher complexity of the Hamming decoding circuitry. The advantage of this technique is the error correction without retransmission, not interfering in the network latency in the presence of faults.

In conclusion, these results point out that a more complex code would probably not be an affordable fault tolerance technique for a NoC similar to Hermes. Perhaps, more complex NoCs could afford complex codes.

Table 3. Area results for an 8x8 network

	Original network	FT network Link CRC		FT network Source CRC		FT network Hamming	
	# of Cells	# of Cells	%	# of Cells	%	# of Cells	%
Router w/ 5 ports	3537	4025	13.8	4145	17.2	4149	17.3
- Buffer	547	590	7.8	630	15.3	547	0
- FT Logic	0	256	-	144	-	612	-
Total NoC cells	208864	236672	13.3	243968	16.8	243136	16.4

5.2 Latency Impact

Latency is evaluated using the following test scenario: (*i*) spatial traffic distribution: random destination; (*ii*) temporal traffic distribution: normal distribution, with an average injection rate of 20% and 10% of the available link bandwidth.

Table 4 presents results for the first scenario, with an average injection rate equal to 20% of the available link bandwidth. Each router sends 100 48-flits packets, resulting in 6,400 transmitted packets. Two error injection rates are adopted: 0.0717% (1,181 injected errors) and 2.03% (33,323 injected errors). As expected, both CRC architectures do not add extra latency in the absence of faults, and present the same average latency. The average latency increases 1.8% and 13% for a 1,181 and 33,323 injected faults, respectively. The network with Hamming code does not add extra latency for error protection, however with higher error injection rates some faults are not corrected (residual faults).

The first scenario corresponds to a worst-case situation, since in practice with this injection rate the network is congested. An injection rate of 10% of the available bandwidth, second simulation scenario, corresponds to a more realistic NoC traffic behavior. In this simulation, each router sends 200 48-flits packets, resulting in 12,800 transmitted packets. Two error injection rates are adopted: 0.113% (3,689 injected errors) and 2.23% (72,392 injected errors). The results presented in Table 5 shows smaller latency values, due to the smaller congestion inside the network (such average value is near to the minimal latency value, 70 clock cycles). The average latency is in practice the same, with or without error injection at lower injection rates.

Table 4. Average latency, in clock cycles, for an injection rate equal to 20%

Network	Transmitted Packets	Injected Errors	Average Packet Latency
Original	6,400	0	839.39
Link CRC	6,400	0	839.30
		1,181	854.77
		33,323	948.47
Source CRC	6,400	0	839.30
		1,181	854.77
		33,323	948.47
Hamming	6.400	1,181	839.39
		33,323	839.39

Table 5. Average latency, in clock cycles, for an injection rate equal to 10%

Network	Transmitted Packets	Injected Errors	Average Packet Latency
Original	12,800	0	101.08
Link CRC	12,800	0	101.08
	12,800	3,689	101.11
	12.800	72.392	101.77

Table 6. Latency of packets with and without fault recovery

Packet ID	Latency with fault recovery	Latency without fault recovery	Difference (clk cycles)
11767	351	299	52
6800	298	297	1
968	291	278	13

Table 6 shows the latency for some individual packets (worst, best and typical case), in clock cycles, for packets with retransmitted flits (simulation with injection rate equal to 10%). The worst-case latency overhead is 17%. It is important to note that this is a worst-case scenario, where the same crosstalk fault is repeated and recovered at each link in the path between the source and target router.

5.3 Residual Fault Analysis

This section shows the effectiveness of both methods to protect the network against crosstalk faults. To analyze residual faults using CRC and Hamming codes, the saboteur module is parameterized to inject faults varying the number of MAF model conditions to increase the error injection rate. The simulated scenario considers a 5x5 network, with each IP sending 200 packets to a random destination, using 15% of the link available bandwidth. Table 7 shows the results of these simulations.

As expected, the CRC coding presents a lower residual fault rate, since its fault coverage is higher than the Hamming code. When all conditions of the MAF model are verified, a 2.32% and 0.08% residual fault rate is observed for the Hamming and CRC codes respectively.

Table 7. Residual fault analysis

MAF Conditions	Transmitted flits	Injected errors	CRC Residual Faults		Hamming Residual Faults	
d_r	806,021	341	0	0%	0	0%
d_r, d_f	808,716	444	0	0%	0	0%
d_r, d_f, g_n	794,816	896	0	0%	0	0%
d_r, d_f, g_n, g_p	809,575	16,727	14	0.08%	389	2.32%

5.4 Power Consuption

The power consumption is measured using VCD analysis, with Synopsys Prime Time tool. The network is synthesized with the TSMC25 library, and simulated to generate the VCD files. To generate the VCD files we used a mapped 5x5 network, with the same traffic scenario used to evaluate residual faults.

Table 8 shows the average power consumption for routers at different locations of the network (routers at the borders of the network may have 3 or 4 ports, and the central router has 5 ports). The power of the entire NoC is roughly the sum of the power of each router.

Table 8. Power consumption overhead for the proposed architectures

	Original network (mW)	Link CRC (mW)	%	Source CRC (mW)	%	Hamming (mW)	%
3-port router	4.80	4.88	1.6	5.90	18.6	5.02	4.4
4-port router	6.34	6.46	1.9	7.82	18.9	6.70	5.4
5-port router	7.88	8.04	2.0	9.74	19.1	8.31	5.2
5x5 NoC	166.20	169.37	1.9	205.01	18.9	175.72	5.4

The power consumption overhead of the network with CRC coding on links is small (1.9%), compared to the original network. On the other hand, the power consumption overhead of the network with source CRC reaches 18.9%, since the buffer size increases (more 4 bits to store CRC values), confirming that most of the NoC power consumption is due to the buffers. The network with hamming on links presented 5.4% power consumption overhead due to increased logic and the additional parity bit, but it can be considered an acceptable cost for this implementation.

6 Conclusions and Future Work

The goal of this paper was to evaluate different crosstalk fault tolerant methods for network links such that the network can maintain the original network performance even in the presence of errors. Among the three evaluated architectures, the CRC applied at each link is the recommend method to protect the network against crosstalk effects. The *source CRC* penalizes area and power. On the other hand, the *source CRC* may protect some internal router components, since data transmitted through the router is protected. The assumed advantage of the Hamming codification, no required retransmission, presented a smaller fault coverage and higher area overhead compared to CRC, however it can be an interesting alternative for some applications, where a small number of data errors can be tolerated and the latency needs to be minimal.

It is possible to enumerate the following future works: (*i*) explore a *source Hamming* architecture, verifying the feasibility to use it for internal router protection; (*ii*) develop new methods to protect the router, minimizing the use of classical redundant approaches (TMR); (*iii*) evaluate and propose adaptive routing algorithms for faulty routers.

Acknoledgements. This research is supported partially by CNPq (*Brazilian Research Agency*), projects 300774/2006-0, 471134/2007-4 and by CAPES PNPD project 02388/09-0.

References

1. Cuviello, M., et al.: Fault Modeling and Simulation for Crosstalk in System-on-Chip Interconnects. In: IEEE/ACM Int. Conf. on Computer-Aided Design (ICCAD 1999), pp. 297–303 (1999)
2. Tang, H.H.K., Rodbell, K.P.: Single-event upsets in microelectronics fundamental physics and issues. Materials Research Society Bulletin 28, 111–116 (2003)
3. Bertozzi, D.: The Data-Link Layer in NoC Design. In: Micheli, G., Benini, L. (eds.) Networks on Chips: Technology and Tools, p. 408. Morgan Kaufmann, San Francisco (2006)
4. Zimmer, H., Jantsch, A.: A Fault Model Notation and Error-Control Scheme for Switch-to-Switch Buses in a Network-on-Chip. In: Hardware/Software Codesign and System Synthesis (CODES+ISSS 2003), pp. 188–193 (2003)
5. Bertozzi, D., Benini, L.: Xpipes: A Network-on-chip Architecture for Gigascale Systems-on-Chip. IEEE Circuits and Systems Magazine 4(2), 18–31 (2004)
6. Vellanki, P., et al.: Quality-of-Service and Error Control Techniques for Network-on-Chip Architectures. In: Great Lakes Symposium on VLSI (GLSVLSI 2004), pp. 45–50 (2004)
7. Murali, S., et al.: Analysis of Error Recovery Schemes for Networks on Chips. IEEE Design and Test of Computers 22(5), 434–442 (2005)
8. Grecu, C., et al.: Essential Fault-Tolerance Metrics for NoC Infrastructures. In: IEEE International On-Line Testing Symposium (IOLTS 2007), pp. 37–42 (2007)
9. Moraes, F., et al.: HERMES: an Infrastructure for Low Area Overhead Packet-switching Networks on Chip. Integration, the VLSI Journal 38, 69–93 (2004)
10. Koopman, P., Chakravarty, T.: Cyclic redundancy code (CRC) polynomial selection for ebedded systems. In: The International Conference on Dependable Systems and Networks, pp. 1–10 (2004)
11. Rabaey, J.: Digital Integrated Circuits. Prentice Hall, Englewood Cliffs (2003)

From Assertion-Based Verification to Assertion-Based Synthesis

Yann Oddos, Katell Morin-Allory, and Dominique Borrione

TIMA Laboratory (CNRS/Grenoble-INP/UJF),
46 Av. Félix Viallet, 38031 Grenoble CEDEX, France
{yann.oddos,katell.morin-allory,dominique.borrione}@imag.fr
http://tima.imag.fr

Abstract. We propose a linear complexity approach to achieve automatic synthesis of designs from temporal specifications. It uses concepts from the Assertion-Based Verification. Each property is turned into a component combining classical monitor and generator features: the extended-generator. We connect them with specific components to obtain a design that is correct by construction. It shortens the design flow by removing implementation and functional verification steps. Our approach synthesizes circuits specified by hundreds of temporal properties in a few seconds. Complex examples (*i.e.* **conmax-ip** and GenBuf) show the efficiency of the approach.

Keywords: Assertion Based Verification, Assertion Based Synthesis, PSL, LTL, High-level Automatic Synthesis, Monitors, Generators.

1 Introduction

To guarantee the correct functionality of a System On Chip is a daunting challenge. Over the past few years, design methods have started from higher description levels, and have been supported by more efficient CAD tools. In contrast, validation methods suffer from a growing lag, costing an increasing part of the overall design time.

Among all the proposed methods, the ABV [FKL03] (Assertion Based Verification) is widely used for its efficiency, both for static or dynamic verification, and is applicable all along the design flow. Within this framework, two kinds of temporal properties are of special interest:

- **Assertions** describe the correct behaviors of the design. They can be turned into monitors which check if the corresponding property is violated.
- **Assumptions** constrain the inputs produced by the environment to comply with the expected communication protocol of the Design Under Verification (DUV). They can be turned into generators which provide an executable model for this environment.

Two IEEE standards are mainly used to write temporal properties : PSL (Property Specification Language) [FWMG05] and SVA (SystemVerilog Assertions) [SMB+05]. In the following, all the properties are written in PSL, but our method applies to SVA as well.

J. Becker, M. Johann, and R. Reis (Eds.): VLSI-SoC 2009, IFIP AICT 360, pp. 94–117, 2011.

In our approach, we use the simple subset of PSL (denoted PSL_{simple}). It conforms to the notion of monotonic advancement of time and ensures that formulas within this subset can be used easily in dynamic verification: simulation, emulation etc...

As an example, consider the following PSL property **P1**:

Property **P1** : always($Start \rightarrow Req$ until Ack)

Property **P1** states: for each cycle where $Start$ is '1', a request Req should be produced and maintained active (Req='1') as long as the acknowledge signal Ack is not active (Ack='0').

The trace on Figure 1 satisfies property **P1**. Signal $Start$ is active at cycle ♯1 and Req is fixed to '1' during the same cycle. Then Req remains active up to ♯7. At ♯8, signal Ack takes value '1'. After this cycle, all the constraints have been satisfied and the trace complies with **P1**.

In the case of an unbounded trace, the property should be permanently valid due to the presence of the **always** operator. Each cycle when $Start$ is active should initiate a time sequence where Req is active at least up to the cycle when Ack is '1'.

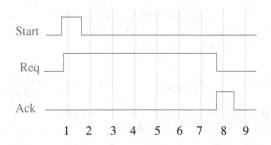

Fig. 1. A trace satisfying property P1

Figure 2 shows this retriggering of the property evaluation due to successive activations of $Start$. Although not necessarily what one would expect, the trace of Figure 2 also satisfies property P1.

We have developed the Horus project which aims at providing methodologies and tools for efficiently supporting property-based design all along the design flow. With respect to previous works and existing CAD software, Horus exhibits new and competitive advantages:

- The monitors and generators are built in a modular way, so that modules for sub-properties can be reused in more complex ones.
- The modular construction is very efficient: it takes a fraction of a second for dozens of complex properties.
- The method for building the monitors and the generators has been proven correct with the PVS theorem prover [MAB06].

Another promising research domain is the automatic synthesis from temporal specifications. It consists in automatically transforming a temporal specification into an HDL description which is correct by construction. Figure 3 depicts a typical design flow where

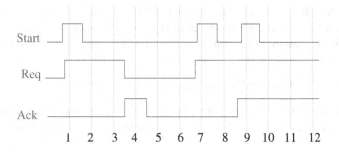

Fig. 2. Trace with several activations of *Start*

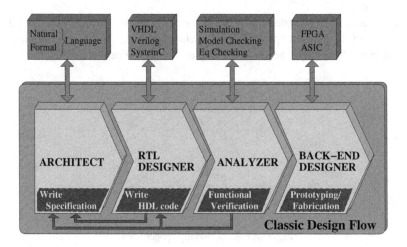

Fig. 3. Design flow including the functional verification of a hand-coded RTL design

the hand-coded design has to be verified to guarantee that the realized functionnality complies with the specification.

As shown on Figure 4, the main advantage of automatic synthesis is the elimination of the implementation and functional verification steps from the design flow.

The problem of the automatic synthesis was first formulated by Church in 1982 by the following question: "Given a specification, is there a realization satisfying it?". Unfortunately, this problem has a solution triply exponential, resulting in three major limitations:

- explosion of the memory size
- explosion of the synthesis time.
- the resulting design is too complex and not efficient (huge area and low frequency).

Up to now, all the proposed methods that have been explored reduce the complexity by constraining the type of properties or designs that can be processed. It results in exponential or polynomial complexities that still limit the approach to simple case studies.

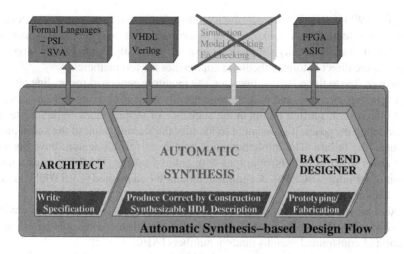

Fig. 4. Design flow with automatic synthesis of the RTL from formal properties

Whereas linear complexity approaches are available for Boolean specifications, no such methods exist for complex temporal specifications.

We use concepts of Assertion-Based Verification and the property synthesis approach developed for Horus to define the method SyntHorus. It has a linear complexity approach regarding the specification and automatically synthesizes a temporal specification written in PSL_{simple} into a correct by construction HDL description.

We turn assertions and assumptions into a new kind of hardware components mixing monitors and generators: the extended-generators. They are the basic components of the synthesized design and have been proved correct with respect to the PSL semantics. Combined with specific components called Solvers, the resulting circuit provides the final design corresponding to a given specification.

The SyntHorus tool can process complex specifications, composed with hundreds of properties, and produces the final circuit in a few seconds. The size of the circuit is proportional to the size of the specification.

2 State of the Art

2.1 Assertion-Based Verification

Many static verifiers, and the main commercial RTL simulators support PSL [CVK04]. The European funded project "PROSYD" has published methodologies for the use of PSL, and developed tools around PSL [PRO]. Notably, the RAT prototype, based on SAT and bounded model checking, helps verify property consistency [BCE+04].

The first industrial implementation of monitors is IBM FoCs [IBM]. The result of FoCs is a cycle accurate simulation process that may be turned into a synthesizable component with minor edition.

In the context of model checking, the usual technique translates a LTL formula into a non-deterministic automaton that recognizes all the acceptable sequences of values [DGV99, GO01]. The transformation into a deterministic automaton, needed for a hardware implementation, is exponential in the number of non-deterministic decision states [ST03]. A syntactically simple PSL formula can easily expand into a large LTL formula, so the direct automata theoretic approaches are too inefficient.

Moreover, due to the `always` operator, the monitors generated for on-line observation must be retriggerable, and may be concurrently evaluating several instances of the property for several starting points in the sequence of signal values. When a property fails, for debug purposes, it is essential to identify the starting point of the subsequence that caused the failure. The implementation principles for this feature have been described either in terms of control graphs with colored tokens [MAB07], or as a multiplication of monitors [BCZ06]. A similar automata-based method [CRST06] is used in model checking.

Another aspect is the use of properties to specify constraints on the design environment. Most industrial simulators provide software test vector generators based on the generation of constrained pseudo-random numbers [ABC$^+$].

Among the static methods, Calamé [Cal05] builds the product of the design automaton and the property automaton to extract test vectors that may lead to a wrong execution. Another approach is based on slicing [YJC04]: the design is cut between registers to extract constraints and produce test vectors for each slice, which are then composed to get the test vector for the whole component. All these techniques are difficult to use due to the complexity of their algorithms.

More efficient approaches rely on the property formulas, not the design under verification, to generate test vectors. The concept of "cando objects" [SNBE07] is technically very different, and oriented towards model checking rather than on-line execution; in particular, they do not support arbitrary repetition ('+' and '*') operators.

2.2 Automatic Synthesis from Specifications

A large body of research was devoted to the synthesis of combinatorial operators from untimed mathematical relations. We shall not discuss them, since the target of our work is the synthesis of control-type sequential circuits, where the successive occurrence of events is an essential aspect of the circuit behavior.

The specification of such sequences with regular expressions is not new [FU82, SB94]. These pioneer works use different kinds of BDDs (Free-BDDs and Reduced-Ordered BDDs respectively) to support the synthesis process. The use of BDD-based algorithms leads to the so called "state explosion problem" which confines the application to simple designs.

Other specification methods have been proposed, focusing on communication protocols. From BNF grammars, Öberg synthesizes controllers using a directed acyclic graph representation [Obe99]. Alternatively, Müller [SM02] defined a dedicated SystemC library to describe the specifications and uses automata-based methods to build the final design.

Aziz et al. use logical S1S formulas (second order properties on naturals) to perform automatic synthesis of sequential designs [ABBSV00]. Despite the application of a variety of optimization techniques to reduce the complexity during the creation of the design, the automata-based approach cannot apply to complex designs.

Taking as input a specification in a standard assertion language is a more recent concern. Bloem et al. [BGJ+07] defined a "Generalized Reactivity(1)" subset of PSL from which properties are translated to automata; game theory algorithms are applied to compute all the correct behaviors of the design under all admissible interactions with the environment. The method is more powerful than the preceding ones. It is polynomial in N^3, where N is the sequential complexity of the specification.

Eveking et al. [SOSE08] aim at generating verification-friendly circuits. This method takes as input ITL, a proprietary dialect of interval temporal logic defined by OneSpin Solutions. It is similar to the PSL simple subset, limited to finite traces. In contrast to our approach, non deterministic behaviors assume additional inputs fed by an external random source, and consistency is checked statically during the construction.

Our main objective is to quickly generate efficient circuits from complex sets of properties. Instead of using an automata based approach, or restricting the application to a specific type of designs, we use a modular construction. The complexity is then encapsulated in different levels of basic components. The overall synthesis method was proved to correctly generate circuits that comply with the PSL semantics.

3   Assertion-Based Verification

3.1   Monitors

A monitor is a synchronous design detecting dynamically all the violations of a given temporal property. We detail here the last release of our approach used to synthesize properties into hardware monitors. It is based on the principles described in [MAB06].

The monitor synthesis is based on a library of primitive components, and an interconnection scheme directed by the syntax tree of the property. In particular, there is one primitive monitor for each FL operator of PSL. We have defined two types of primitive monitors: connectors and watchers. The first one is used to start the verification of a sub-property. The watcher is used to raise any violation of the property.

The sets of connectors and watchers are given Table 1. The watcher mnt_Signal is used to observe a simple signal.

Primitive monitors have a generic interface depicted Figure 5. It takes as input two synchronization signals *Clk* and *Reset_n*, a *Start* activation signal, and the ports *expr* and *cond* for the observed operands. The output ports are: *trigger* and *pending* for a connector; *pending* and *valid* for a watcher.

Table 1. Primitive PSL monitors

Watchers	mnt_Signal, ↔, eventually!,never, next_e, next_event_e, before
Connectors	→, and, or, always, next!, next_a, next_event, next_event_a, until

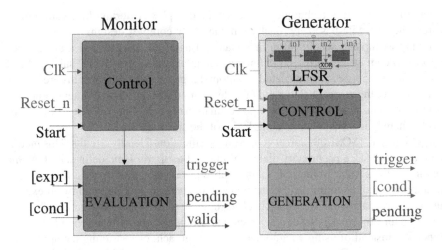

Fig. 5. Architectures and Interfaces for primitives monitors and generators

The overall monitor is built by post-fixed left to right recursive descent of the property syntax tree. For each node of type connector, its Boolean operand, if any, is connected to input *cond*. The output *trigger* is connected to input *Start* of its FL operand. For the watcher type node, its Boolean operands are directly connected to the inputs *expr* and *cond* of the current monitor. Its output *valid* is the *valid* output of the global monitor.

Figure 6 gives the syntax tree of Property P1 defined in section 1:

Property **P1** : always(*Start* → *Req* until *Ack*)

The corresponding monitor for P1 is given Figure 7. The couple of signals (*valid*, *pending*) gives the current state of the property at any cycle: failed, holds, holds strongly or pending.

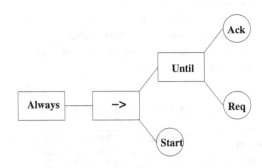

Fig. 6. Tree Structure of PSL Property P1

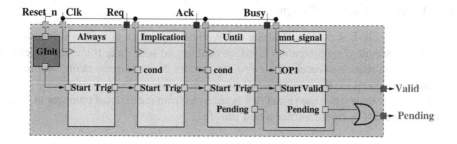

Fig. 7. Monitor for the PSL property P1

3.2 Generators

A generator is a synchronous design producing sequences of signals complying with a given temporal property. Their synthesis follows the same global principle as for the monitors: the overall generator is built as an interconnection of primitive generators, based on the syntax tree of the property [OMAB06].

Primitive generators are divided into all the connectors (associated to all PSL operators) and the single type of producer to generate signal values: gnt_Signal.

The interface of primitive generators (Fig 5) includes:

- the inputs Clk, $Reset\_n$, $Start$: same meaning as for monitors.
- the outputs $trigger$ and $cond$ used to launch the left and right operand (for connectors).
- the output $pending$, to indicate if the current value on $trigger$ and $cond$ are constrained or may be randomly assigned.

Since many sequences of signals can comply with the same property, we need the generators to be able to cover the space of correct traces. To achieve this goal, the gnt_Signal embeds a random number generator (based on a Linear Feedback Shift Register or a Cellular Automaton). By default, the outputs of an inactive complex generator are fixed to '0'. It is possible to produce random values by switching the generic parameter RANDOM to 1. If $pending$ is inactive, the values on $trigger$ and $cond$ are not constrained and produced by the random block.

4 From Assertion-Based Verification to Assertion-Based Synthesis

A design specification involves signals to be monitored (inputs of the design), and to be generated (outputs of the design). It is necessary to make a clear distinction between these two kinds of signals, directly into the specification. PSL has been designed for functional verification and not for the synthesis of temporal specifications. It does not provide this distinction at the specification level. We have to adapt PSL for specification synthesis.

Moreover, as a generated signal can be driven by several sources (*i.e* a signal generated in different properties), a resolution mechanism has to be designed to solve the value of multi-source signals.

4.1 Example: The CDT Design

The controller CDT is used to illustrate our synthesis approach of temporal specifications. It is a simple communication interface enabling to send data. If the controller is idle and a data request is received on *Req*, it transfers the value present on *Cmd* to an external component via the output port *Data*.

The transfer ends when the signal *Ack* is received from the external component. The controller needs 4 cycles to initiate a new transfer.

4.2 Annotations of PSL Properties

We have chosen to annotate each signal *sig* using the following convention:

- sig_m: signal *sig* is monitored
- sig_g: signal *sig* is generated

Consider the following specification Spec_cdt for the CDT design:

- inputs=$\{Init,Req,Ack,Cmd\}$, outputs=$\{Data,Busy,Send\}$
- **F0** : always($Init_m \rightarrow$ (!$Send_g$ && !$Busy_g$ && $Data_g$="0000"));
- **F1** : always(!$Init_m$ && Req_m)$\rightarrow$ (($Send_g$ && $Data_g=Cmd_m$)until Ack_m);
- **F2** : always((!$Init_m$ && $Send_m$)$\rightarrow$ next_a[1:4]($Busy_g$));

Property F0 states that during the initialization (signal *Init* active), all the output signals are fixed to '0' (*Send*, *Busy* and *Data*).

The two following properties are used when the design is not being initialized.

Property F1: if a request is submitted, the value *Cmd* is passed on output *Data* until the transfer is ended by receiving '1' on input *Ack*. Meanwhile the signal *Send* is maintained to '1' until the reception of *Ack*. It notifies the external component that the transfer is currently being processed.

Property F2: for each request, the interface is busy during 4 consecutive cycles and cannot receive any other request.

In our examples, properties only deal with input and output ports of the design. This is not a limitation. In other cases, internal signals may be used as well.

A signal that is annotated "g" in several properties, or several times in a single property, is called *duplicated*. For instance, signals *Send*, *Busy* and *Data* are duplicated in Spec_cdt.

In the current status of our development, the annotation of signals is partially automated and may have to be complemented by the designer.

4.3 Consistency of the Specification

Before engaging into the process of producing an implementation, it is a pre-requisite that the specification be proven to be consistent. Two concepts must be distinguished:

Inconsistency. A set of properties is inconsistent if the set of value traces for which they are satisfied is empty. As an example, the following two properties are inconsistent:

- assert always ($a_m \wedge c_g$)
- assert always ($a_m \wedge !c_g$)

Tools such as RAT (Requirement Analysis Tool) [BCE$^+$04] or the method on which Cando objects are built [SNBE07] detect inconsistencies statically.

We shall call consistent a set of properties such that, whatever the input combination, all the outputs always can be given a valid value.

Realizability. It may happen that one, two or more properties are satisfied under some constraints on the input signals, and exhibit inconsistencies otherwise. Take the following example:

- assert always ($a_m \Rightarrow c_g$)
- assert always ($b_m \Rightarrow !c_g$)

If a and b have different values, the specification is realizable. But if signals a and b are both active at a given cycle, c is constrained to contradictory values.

Overcoming this problem is done by adding assumptions to the specification. In the above example, the following assumption is added: assume never (a and b).

Synthesizing the specification. In our approach, the specification is analyzed using RAT. *Assume* properties may be added in the process to produce realizable specifications.

Methods described in pre-existing works statically enumerate all the possible responses of the design under all the possible actions of the environment, and hard-code all the responses directly in the design. In contrast, our technique relies on the use of special purpose "solver" components that compute the output values on the fly.

5 Assertion-Based Synthesis

5.1 The Extended-Generator

An extended-generator component is a combination of a monitor and a generator. The basic principle is to produce a predefined sequence of signals (generator part) when a special sequence is recognized (monitor part).

Primitive extended-generator. Only binary operators OPb can have both a monitored and a generated operand. Such operator has two corresponding primitive extended-generators: OPb$_{mg}$ and OPb$_{gm}$ which respectively (monitor, generate) and (generate, monitor) the left and right operands.

We impose the following restriction for the PSL properties: *a monitored operand of an extended-generator must be Boolean.* This limitation is just the adjustment of the PSL simple subset in the context of the extended-generators. To clarify the problem met in the monitoring of an FL operand, consider the following example:

Property P2: ($sig_m \rightarrow$ (next[4]A_m) until B_g)

Assume that sig is '1' at cycle 0 and the production of signal B='1' is planned at cycle t. For all cycles $j<t$, the sub-property next[4]A_m must be verified. The verification will complete at cycle $t+3$. It is then impossible to ensure at cycle t that the extended-generator always fulfills the corresponding property.

The monitoring of an FL property that requires a knowledge of the future to produce signals at the present cycle is contrary to the principles of the PSL simple subset. Our restriction applies these principles in the new context introduced by the extended-generators, which combines the observation and generation concepts.

It follows that all the binary operators have at least one Boolean operand. This avoids all the potential ambiguities concerning the choice of a primitive extended-generator (OPb_{mg} or OPb_{gm}). As an example, it is possible to use $\mathsf{until}gm$ since the right operand is Boolean, but not $\mathsf{until}mg$ as the left operand can be a FL property.

Primitive extended-generators have the same interface as the generators (*cf.* Figure 8). The only difference lies in the port *cond* which is an input for the extended-generators. All the extended-generators are connectors. Their architecture is based on the monitors.

Extended Generator

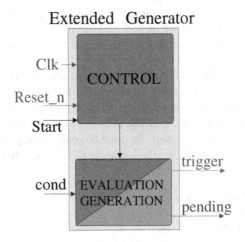

Fig. 8. Primitive Extended Generator Interface

Complex extended-generator. While a primitive extended-generator matches a *binary PSL operator*, the complex extended-generator corresponds to a PSL *property*. It is composed of three kinds of primitive components: monitors, generators and extended-generators.

This feature raises the issue of using the appropriate primitive, and justifies the need for property annotation discussed in section 4. The property (A until B) can be turned into a monitor (A and B observed), a generator (A and B produced) or an extended-generator(A produced, B observed). All these ambiguities are solved by annotating the property before building the complex extended-generator.

A complex extended-generator has a generic interface taking as inputs the observed and synchronization signals, and providing on its outputs the generated and associated *pending* signals.

Building the complex extended-generator is performed in two steps, based on the syntax tree.

Step1 - Selection of primitive components: A node of the syntax tree that has generators or extended-generators as operands is defined as a generator. If it has one operand of type generator and one of type monitor, it is an extended-generator. Two monitored operands produce a primitive monitor.

Step2 - Interconnection: The interconnection scheme is the same as the one used for the monitors. All the basic elements are producers gnt_Signal. The extended-generator for property F1 is given Figure 9.

F1 : always(!$Init_m$ && Req_m)→ (($Send_g$ && $Data_g$=Cmd_m)until Ack_m);

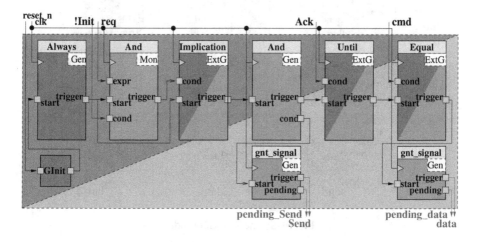

Fig. 9. Complex Extended Generator Architecture for F1

5.2 Building the Final Design

One extended-generator is produced for each property of the specification. The elaboration of the final design is achieved by connecting the duplicated signals to *Solvers*, one for each duplicated signal. As shown on Figure 10, properties F0 and F1 have one duplication of signal *Send*, which is input to component Solver$_{send}$. The correct final value for *Send* is produced as output.

A solver has two input ports *SIG* and *PENDING* (N bits each). *SIG* takes the N duplications $sig(i)$ of *sig*. *PENDING* takes the corresponding N duplications $pending(i)$ indicating if $sig(i)$ is constrained. The resolved value for *sig* is provided on the output port *Val*.

Consider a consistent specification. If *PENDING* is all zeros, *SIG* is not constrained, and *Val* is set to 0 (or to a random value if mode RANDOM is active). Otherwise, *SIG* is constrained and all the constrained values are known to be identical. The first one is assigned to *Val*.

If the consistency of the specification has not been verified, an enhanced release of the Solvers is required. In this situation, it may happen that two duplications sig(i) and sig(j) take different values. The Solver has an extra output port *Err* used to dynamically notify this inconsistency.

Once the extended-generators have been interconnected to the Solvers, the resulting design is encapsulated into a top-level entity that takes as inputs signals *Clk* and *Reset_n* and all the observed external signals. The outputs are the generated external signals. Figure 10 gives the structure of the final design obtained for the specification Spec_cdt defined in section 4.

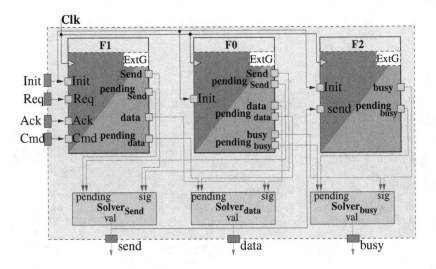

Fig. 10. Synthesized Spec_cdt

5.3 Verification of the Approach

The initial verification of the synthesized circuits has been performed by model-checking on a set of test cases: we used RuleBase Parallel Edition [HIL04] to check that all the properties listed in the specification hold on the circuit synthesized from them.

Then, the overall construction scheme has been proved correct using the PVS theorem prover following the method described in [MAB06].

6 Case Study: Wishbone Crossbar Controller

6.1 A Crossbar Bus and the Wishbone Specification

A crossbar switch is a bus-based architecture allowing to connect M masters to N slaves simultaneously. It enables parallel communications and enhances the whole system performances.

In this chapter, we illustrate the application of Horus on a Wishbone compliant cross-bar [Her02]. The Wishbone specification defines a generic interface and a communication protocol for the insertion of predefined IPs in a design. This context appears particularly appropriate for demonstrating the use of Horus.

Figure 11 illustrates the generic interfaces of master and slave components. For each signal *sig* that connects a master to a slave (directly or through a switch), we denote M_sig_o the output port of the master and S_sig_i the input port of the slave connected to it, S_sig_o and M_sig_i in the other direction. For readability M^j (S^j) denotes the j-th master (or slave). In the actual PSL properties, the indices are macro-generated as constant values, and part of standard identifiers.

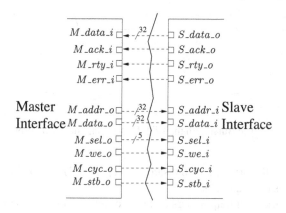

Fig. 11. Interfaces for **Wishbone** Master and Slave components

The communication between a master and a slave is based on a hand-shake protocol. To initiate the communication and hold the bus during the transfer, the master asserts a signal *cyc* (cycle valid). To transfer data, it asserts the signal *stb* (strobe) and indicates the write/read operation with signal *we* (write enable). Both signals remain '1' until the slave sets either *ack*, *busy*, or *err* (transfer error).

In the last two cases, the master has to retry (*rty*). Signals *data* and *addr* represent the data being sent and the address where it must be read or written. The four most significant bits of *addr* represent the address of the slave. Since data is transferred through a 32-bit bus, signal *sel* indicates where the valid data is expected. This protocol is clock (*clk*) and reset (*reset*) synchonized.

Figure 12 illustrates a write burst. At cycle ♯1, the master asks for a transfer by asserting M_cyc_o that remains asserted until the end of the communication (at ♯7). At cycle ♯2, data is ready to be written (M_stb_o is asserted and M_we_o is set to '1'), ports M_data_o and M_addr_o are valid. The request is acknowledged at cycle ♯2 allowing a new request at cycle ♯3 which is acknowledged too. At cycle ♯4, the bus communication is maintained (M_cyc_o is '1') but no data is transferred: a wait state has been inserted by the master. At cycle ♯5, the master makes a new request, but the slave does not acknowledge it immediately: it has inserted a wait cycle. The request is acknowledged on the next cycle. At cycle ♯7, all control signals are negated.

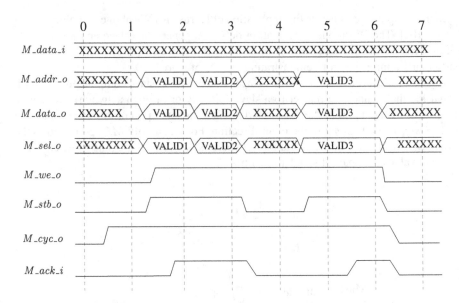

Fig. 12. Write Burst with the **Wishbone** Communication Protocol

For a read burst, the principle is the same, except that M_we_o keeps value '0' and M_data_i receives the read data.

Two more remarks will help understand the communication protocol. When a slave is being used, its S_cyc_i port is asserted: this signal is observed to test if it is busy. Furthermore, a controller ensures the exclusive interconnection between a master and a slave on a Wishbone crossbar switch.

The conmax-ip controller: The conmax-ip controller [Uss02] allows the communications between up to 8 masters and up to 16 slaves on a crossbar switch with up to 4 levels of priority. The four most significant bits on M_addr_o address the slave. The selection of the master that will own a slave is based on two rules:

- **Priorities:** Each master has a priority that is stored in an internal register CONF of the controller. The master i priority is given by CONF[2i..2i-1]. At each cycle, the master with the greatest priority gets the slave.
- **Round-Robin:** Among masters of equal priority, a round-robin policy is applied.

6.2 Assertion-Based Verification with Horus

The Horus flow. The Horus software is based on two parts: the core implemented in C and the graphic interface implemented in Java. The core implements a PSL parser, generates the VHDL description of the property. It is approximately 10000 lines long.

The Horus environment helps the user build an instrumented design to ease debugging: it can synthesize monitors and generators, connect them to the design under test

(DUT) and adds a device to snoop the signals of interest. It comes with the VHDL flavor. The Horus system has a friendly graphical user interface for the generation of the instrumented design in 4 steps.

Step 1 - Design selection: The DUT, with its hierarchy, is retrieved.

Step 2 - Generators and Monitors synthesis: Select properties or property files, define new properties, select target HDL language, synthesize monitor or generator (verification IP).

Step 3 - Signal interconnection: The user connects the monitors and the generators to the design. All the signals and variables involved in the DUT are accessible in a hierarchical way. The user needs only select the signals to be connected to each verification IP.

Step 4 - Generation: The design instrumented with the verification IPs is generated. When internal signals are monitored, the initial design is slightly modified to make these signals accessible to the monitors.

The outputs of the verification IPs are fed to an instance of a generic analyzer; this component stores the monitors outputs and sends a global status report on its serial outputs. It also incorporates counters for performance analysis.

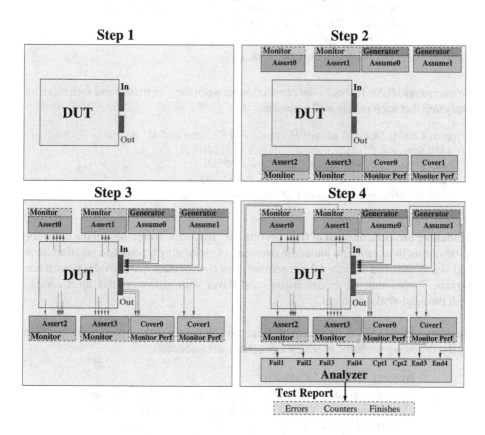

Fig. 13. Instrumentation of a design with Horus

The instrumented design has a generic interface defined for an Avalon or a Wishbone bus. If the FPGA platform is based on such a bus, the user can directly synthesize and prototype the instrumented design on it.

Monitors: Many aspects of the conmax-ip have been verified with the Horus platform. A brief overview is given.

Property Reset_Mj For all masters, signals M_cyc_o and M_stb_o must be negated as long as *Reset* is asserted (*c.f.* [Her02], rule 3.20):

Property Reset_Mj:assert always($Reset \rightarrow$ (not $M^j\_cyc\_o$ and not $M^j\_stb\_o$) until not $Reset$);

Property PrioMj_Mk Assume two masters M^j and M^k have priorities p_j and p_k such that $p_k > p_j$. If M^j and M^k request the same slave simultaneously, M^k will own it first.

Property PrioMj_Mk:assert always($M^j\_cyc\_o$ and $M^k\_cyc\_o$
and $CONF[2k..2k-1] > CONF[2j..2j-1]$
and $M^j\_addr\_o[0..3] = M^k\_addr\_o[0..3]$)
$\rightarrow$ ($M^k\_ack\_i$ before $M^j\_ack\_i$);

Property LinkMj_Sk It checks the connection between the j-th master and k-th slave by analyzing that each port is well connected.

Property LinkMj_Sk:assert always($M^j\_cyc\_o$ and $S^k\_cyc\_i$ and $M^j\_addr\_o = S^k\_addr\_i$)
$\rightarrow$ ($M^j\_data\_o = S^k\_data\_i$ and $M^j\_data\_i = S^k\_data\_o$
and $M^j\_sel\_o = S^k\_sel\_i$ and $M^j\_stb\_o = S^k\_stb\_i$
and $M^j\_we\_o = S^k\_we\_i$ and $M^j\_ack\_i = S^k\_ack\_o$
and $M^j\_err\_i = S^k\_err\_o$ and $M^j\_rty\_i = S^k\_rty\_o$);

Modelling the environment of the conmax-ip: To test the correctness of the conmax-ip controller in isolation, without the overhead of simulating a complete set of masters and slaves, we need to embed the controller in an environment that provides correct test signals. To this aim, we model masters and slaves with generators that must comply with the hand-shake protocol.

Property WriteMj_Sk: A write request from the j-th master to the k-th slave is specified by the following property, to which a generator is associated:

Property WriteMj_Sk:assume(
($M^j\_cyc\_o$ and $M^j\_we\_o$ and $M^j\_sel\_o$ and $M^j\_stb\_o$and
$M^j_data_o = $ VAL_DATA and $M^j_addr_o = $ VAL_ADDR_k)
until_ $M^j\_ack\_i$)

Since we are interested in the communication action, but not in the particular data value being written, the value VAL_DATA that is displayed on the port $M^i\_data\_o$ is a randomly computed constant. The four most significant bits of VAL_ADDR are fixed to select the j-th slave. This property is a simplified model of a master, it does not take into account signals $M^i\_rty\_i$ and $M^i\_err\_i$ (they are not mandatory). These signals would be present in a more realistic model. This property involves the acknowledgment input signal $M^i\_ack\_i$ that stops the constrained generation.

Property GenLaunch. The scenario GenLaunch illustrates the request of three masters numbered 0, 1, 2 to the same slave numbered 1. Master 0 first makes a request; then between 16 to 32 cycles later, masters 1 and 2 simultaneously make their request. This scenario is modeled using a property that generates the start signals for three instances of master generators (according to the previously discussed property), and one slave. These different start signals are denoted $start\_WriteM0\_S1$, $start\_WriteM1\_S1$, $start\_WriteM2\_S1$.

> assume eventually! ($start\_WriteM0\_S1$
> $\rightarrow$ next_e[16..32]($start\_WriteM1\_S2$ and $start\_WriteM2\_S2$));

A large number of scenarios of various complexity have been written, and implemented with generators, in order to have a realistic self-directed test environment. Modeling test scenarios for requests (i.e. read, burst, ...) is also performed with assumed properties, from which generators are produced.

For a slave, the most elaborate action is the response to a read request: signal S_ack_o is raised and the data is displayed on S_data_o. The following property expresses this behavior, at some initial (triggering) time.

assume next_e[1..8]($S^j\_ack\_o$ and $S^j\_data\_o = DATA$));

The generator for property Read_Sj must be triggered each time the slave receives a read request: its start signal is connected to the VHDL expression not $S^j\_we\_i$ and $S^j\_cyc\_i$.

Performance analysis. Monitors can be used to perform measurements on the behavior of the system. To this aim, the Horus platform is instrumented to analyze the monitor outputs, and count the number of times when a monitor has been triggered, and the number of times when a failure has been found.

On the wishbone switch, and assuming that it is embedded in a real environment, it may be useful to test on line the number of times the signal M_err_i of a slave is asserted, or how often a slave is requested simultaneously by several masters.

Property CountError. The following property is used to count the number of transfers ending with an error:

Property CountError: assert never ($M^0\_err\_i$ or ... or $M^7\_err\_i$);

Property ColliMj_Sk. The property allows to know the number of times when more than one master asks for the same slave:

Property ColliMj_Sk: assert never $(S^j\_cyc\_i$ and $S^k\_cyc\_i$ and $S^j\_addr\_i =$ $S^k\_addr\_i)$;

6.3 Assertion-Based Synthesis with SyntHorus

SYNTHORUS The SyntHorus tool aims at providing an environment to support automatic synthesis of HDL descriptions from PSL specifications, within the framework described here. It represents 5000 lines of C source code and has been tested on a laptop equipped with a dual core processor and 2Go of RAM. The SyntHorus process flow is depicted Figure 14.

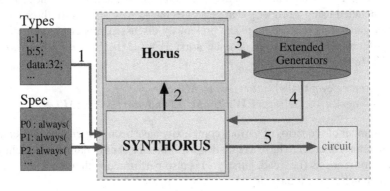

Fig. 14. The SyntHorus Tool

The idea consists in specifying control parts with PSL and synthesizing them with SyntHorus to guarantee their functionnality, while operative parts must be validated with other suitable methods.

SyntHorus takes as inputs the annotated specification file and a description for all the signals involved in the specification (input, output, internal and type). It is interfaced with HORUS, which produces the extended-generators. Afterwards SyntHorus interconnects all these components, adding Solvers if necessary. Finally it encapsulates the result in a global enclosing component that constitutes synthesized design.

We fed SyntHorus with various complex specifications containing hundreds of properties. For 700 properties, it produces an HDL description of 2,7 Mb within 16 seconds.

Synthesis Results. All syntheses have been done with Quartus7.0 for a CycloneII EP2C35F672C6 FPGA-based platform. The synthesis optimization option "balanced" has been used.

CDT Synthesis. The annotation was complete for the Spec_cdt specification.

Table 2 gives the synthesis results for the CDT built by SyntHorus. The original hand-coded design has 18 LCs, 6 FFs and a maximum frequency of 420Mhz. The design obtained from SyntHorus is slightly bigger than the original one.

In the following examples, we shall see that the efficiency of a SyntHorus design is greatly affected by the number of embedded solvers.

Table 2. CDT produced by SyntHorus

SyntHorus	LCs	FFs	Freq. (Mhz)
F0$_{cdt}$	1	0	-
F1$_{cdt}$	3	2	-
F2$_{cdt}$	6	6	-
Solvers	11	0	-
CDT	**21**	**8**	**420,17**

GenBuf Controller. Our first complex case study is the GenBuf controller described in [BGJ$^+$07]. GenBuf can connect N data senders to 2 data receivers.

Communications between senders and receivers use the handshake protocol. A round-robin algorithm schedules the data transfers through the controller. The annotated specification is not given here for space reasons, but can be found on our web page [Odd09].

Figure 15 shows the area used by different instantiations of GenBuf containing a number of slaves ranging from 1 up to 10, for the method of [BGJ$^+$07] (higher fast growing curve) and our tool SyntHorus (bottom two curves). The area of the circuit produced by our approach grows linearly with the number of senders (actually with the number of properties in the specification). In contrast, the best automata-based method, that hardcode the enumeration of the correct behaviors of the circuits, has a polynomial complexity on $0(N^3)$ [BGJ$^+$07].

In addition to producing efficient circuits, the construction time is also very small: a dozen seconds to build GenBuf for 60 senders, compared to hours reported in [BGJ$^+$07]. Again, this is explained by the fact that no enumerative state space traversal is involved in our construction. For SyntHorus, frequency results are good.

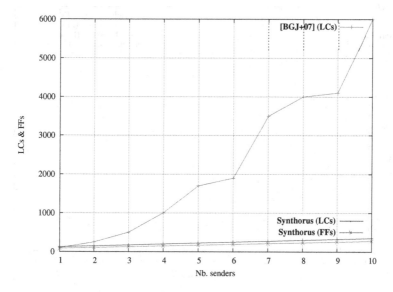

Fig. 15. GenBuf Synthesis Results : Method [BGJ$^+$07]/SYNTHORUS Method

CONMAX-IP The conmax-ip annotated specification represents dozens of complex temporal properties. It can be found on the following web page [Odd09].

The following property Master1ToSlave2 is an example of the used properties:

Master1ToSlave2: assert always((
  $(M^1\_cyc\_i_m$ and $M^1\_addr\_i_m=$"0010") and
  $(not(M^0\_cyc\_i_m)$ or $M^0\_addr\_i_m/=$"0010") and
  $not(S^2\_cyc\_o_m))\Rightarrow$ next[1]((
    $S^2\_addr\_o_g=M^1\_addr\_i_m$ and
    $(S^2\_data\_o_g=M^1\_data\_i_m$ and $S^2\_cyc\_o_g=M^1\_cyc\_i_m$)and
    $(S^2\_sel\_o_g=M^1\_sel\_i_m$ and $S^2\_we\_o_g=M^1\_we\_i_m)$ and
    $(S^2\_stb\_o_g=M^1\_stb\_i_m$ and $M^1\_data\_o_g=S^2\_data\_i_m)$ and
    $(M^1\_ack\_o_g=S^2\_ack\_i_m$ and $M^1\_rty\_o_g=S^2\_rty\_i_m$ and $M^1\_err\_o_g=S^2\_err\_i_m)$
  until $(M^1\_ack\_o_m$ or $M^1\_rty\_o_m$ or $M^1\_err\_o_c)));$

This property models the connection between the first master and the second slave when no other masters are trying to access the second slave. The connection is performed by connecting each port of the master to the corresponding port of the slave interface. The connection is maintained until the transfer is ended by the reception of one of the three following signals: $M^1\_ack\_o_m$ (transfer succeeded) or $M^1\_rty\_o_m$ (transfer aborted because slave was busy) or $M^1\_err\_o_c$ (transfer error).

Figure 16 compares the synthesis results obtained for the conmax-ip originally designed by hand and by SyntHorus. Results are given for 4 masters using 2 priority levels, connected to a number of slaves varying between 1 and 16.

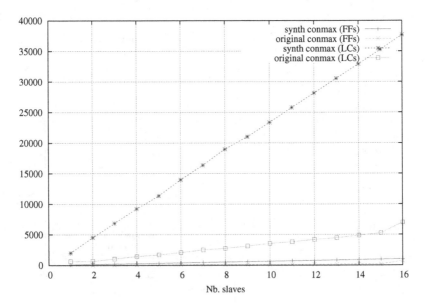

Fig. 16. Synthesis Results: Original/SyntHorus Conmax-ip

LCs overhead is clearly visible and remains linear when the number of slaves increases. The main part of this overhead is due to the use of the Solvers. Notice that the FFs overhead is noticeably less important.

If the specification contains just a few duplicated signals, then the resulting design is efficient and its complexity is slightly higher than the same hand-coded design. If there are lots of duplicated signals a significant overhead is introduced by SyntHorus. The designer should consider rewriting the specification to minimize the number of duplications.

7 Conclusion

A method to efficiently synthesize a test-bench from temporal properties has been presented. On one hand, the stimuli generation is carried out by hardware components synthesized from assumptions: the generators. On the other hand, monitors support the verification of the DUT behavior by on-line verifying that it complies with the corresponding assertions.

By annotating PSL signals and developing a new kind of hardware component called extended-generator, we went beyond Assertion-Based Verification to produce a correct-by-construction module (at RTL) from its temporal specification. This "Assertion-Based Synthesis" starts from a more abstract, formal and declarative specification than the conventional "High-level Synthesis" that takes as inputs an algorithmic specification. Assertion-Based Synthesis is best suited for control circuits.

The modularity of the approach encapsulates the high complexity of the specification into a hierarchy of verified components. The formal proof of the whole approach guarantees that the final circuit is correct by construction.

SyntHorus is a prototype tool that implements our Assertion-Based Synthesis method. It takes as input PSL specifications and produces a RTL design in VHDL. To the best of our knowledge, ours is the first approach with a linear complexity, able to process the full simple subset of PSL. Compared to the state of the art previous approaches, the resulting designs are very efficient (*i.e* small and fast). Despite the fact that they are in general less efficient than the same hand coded designs, the automatically-synthesized designs can still be used as a golden model. Our method has a distinct advantage: it can be used to produce a reference model, correct by construction, from the very first logic and temporal specifications. More efficient hand-coded designs can then be proved correct, by conventional equivalence checking with the reference produced by SyntHorus. Otherwise, the design produced by SyntHorus can be directly taped-out.

Currently, annotating the specification is not fully automated. While it is obvious to annotate the input ports with "m", output ports may occur as "m" and "g" in different properties (e.g. signal *Send* in Spec_cdt). More work remains to be done to complement the set of annotation rules we developed so far.

References

[ABBSV00]   Aziz, A., Balarin, F., Brayton, R.-K., Sangiovanni-Vincentelli, A.-L.: Sequential synthesis using S1S. IEEE Trans. on CAD of Integrated Circuits and Systems 19(10), 1149–1162 (2000)

[ABC⁺]   Anderson, T., Bergeron, J., Cerny, E., Hunter, A., Nightingale, A.: Systemverilog reference verification methodology: Introduction. EE Times, March 27 (2006)

[BCE⁺04]   Bloem, R., Cavada, R., Eisner, C., Pill, I., Roveri, M., Semprini, S.: Manual for property simulation and assurance tool (deliverable 1.2/4-5). Technical report, PROSYD Project (January 2004)

[BCZ06]   Boulé, M., Chenard, J.-S., Zilic, Z.: Adding debug enhancements to assertion checkers for hardware emulation and silicon debug. In: Proceedings of the 24th International Conference on Computer Design, ICCD 2006 (October 2006)

[BGJ⁺07]   Bloem, R., Galler, S., Jobstman, B., Piterman, N., Pnueli, A., Weiglhofer, M.: Specify, compile, run: Hardware from PSL. Electronic Notes in Theoretical Computer Science (ENTCS) 190 (2007)

[Cal05]   Calamé, J.R.: Specification-based test generation with TGV. Technical Report R0508, Centrum voor Wiskunde en Informatica (May 2005)

[CRST06]   Cimatti, A., Roveri, M., Semprini, S., Tonetta, S.: From PSL to NBA: a Modular Symbolic Encoding. In: Proceedings of IEEE Formal Methods for Computer Aided Design, FMCAD 2006, November 11-12, pp. 125–133 (2006)

[CVK04]   Cohen, B., Venkataramanan, S., Kumari, A.: Using PSL/Sugar for Formal and Dynamic Verification. VhdlCohen Publishing (2004)

[DGV99]   Daniele, M., Giunchiglia, F., Vardi, M.: Improved Automata Generation for Linear Temporal Logic. In: Halbwachs, N., Peled, D.A. (eds.) CAV 1999. LNCS, vol. 1633, pp. 249–260. Springer, Heidelberg (1999)

[FKL03]   Foster, H., Krolnik, A., Lacey, D.: Assertion-Based Design. Kluwer Academic Publishers, Dordrecht (2003)

[FU82]   Floyd, R.-W., Ullman, J.D.: The compilation of regular expressions into integrated circuits. J. ACM 29(3), 603–622 (1982)

[FWMG05]   Foster, H., Wolfshal, Y., Marschner, E., IEEE 1850 Work Group: IEEE standard for property specification language PSL. pub-IEEE-STD, pub-IEEE-STD:adr (October 2005)

[GO01]   Gastin, P., Oddoux, D.: Fast LTL to Büchi automata translation. In: Berry, G., Comon, H., Finkel, A. (eds.) CAV 2001. LNCS, vol. 2102, p. 53. Springer, Heidelberg (2001)

[Her02]   Herveille, R.: WISHBONE system-on-chip (SoC) interconnection architecture for portable IP cores. Technical report (September 2002), http://www.opencores.org/projects.cgi/web/wishbone/wbspec_b3.pdf

[HIL04]   Haifa-IBM-Laboratories. RuleBase Parallel Edition. IBM (November 2004)

[IBM]   IBM. PSL/Sugar-based Verification Tools. Web page, http://www.haifa.il.ibm.com/projects/verification/sugar/tools.html

[MAB06]   Morin-Allory, K., Borrione, D.: Proven correct monitors from PSL specifications. In: DATE 2006 (January 2006)

[MAB07]   Morin-Allory, K., Borrione, D.: On-line monitoring of properties built on regular expressions sequences. In: Vachoux, A. (ed.) Applications of Specification and Design Languages for SoCs. Springer, Heidelberg (2007)

[Öbe99]   Öberg, J.: ProGram: A Grammar-Based Method for Specification and Hardware Synthesis of Communication Protocols. PhD thesis, Royal Institue of Technologoy - Department of Electronics, Eletronic System Design, Sweden (1999)

[Odd09]   Oddos, Y.: PSL Specification for the WISHBONE Interconnect Matrix IP Core
             (2009), http://tima.imag.fr/vds/horus/synthorus_specs/
[OMAB06]   Oddos, Y., Morin-Allory, K., Borrione, D.: On-line test vector generation from
             temporal constraints written in PSL. In: Proc. VLSI SoC 2006 (2006)
[PRO]   PROSYD. Tools and techniques for property verification. Web page, http://
             www.prosyd.org/twiki/view/Public/DeliverablePageWP3
[SB94]   Seawright, A., Brewer, F.: Clairvoyant: A synthesis system for production-based
             specification. IEEE Trans. on VLSI, 172–185 (June 1994)
[SM02]   Siegmund, R., Müller, D.: Automatic synthesis of communication controller hard-
             ware from protocol specifications. IEEE Design & Test of Computers 19(4), 84–
             95 (2002)
[SMB+05]   Srouji, J., Mehta, S., Brophy, D., Pieper, K., Sutherland, S., IEEE 1800 Work
             Group: IEEE Standard for SystemVerilog - Unified Hardware Design, Specifica-
             tion, and Verification Language. pub-IEEE-STD, pub-IEEE-STD:adr (November
             2005)
[SNBE07]   Schickel, M., Nimbler, V., Braun, M., Eveking, H.: An Efficient Synthesis Method
             for Property-Based Design in Formal Verification: On Consistency and Com-
             pleteness of Property-Sets. In: Advances in Design and Specification Languages
             for Embedded Systems, pp. 179–196. Springer, Netherlands (2007), 978-1-4020-
             6149-3
[SOSE08]   Schickel, M., Oberkönig, M., Schweikert, M., Eveking, H.: A case-study in
             property-based synthesis: Generating a cache controller from property-set. In:
             Villar, E. (ed.) Embedded Systems Specification and Design Languages, pp. 271–
             275. Springer, Netherlands (2008)
[ST03]   Sebastiani, R., Tonetta, S.: More Deterministic vs Smaller Büchi Automata for
             Efficient LTL Model Checking. In: Geist, D., Tronci, E. (eds.) CHARME 2003.
             LNCS, vol. 2860, pp. 126–140. Springer, Heidelberg (2003)
[Uss02]   Usselman, R.: WISHBONE Interconnect Matrix IP Core (2002), http://www.
             opencores.org/projects.cgi/web/wb_conmax/overview
[YJC04]   Yen, C., Jou, J., Chen, K.: A divide-and-conquer-based algorithm for automatic
             simulation vector generation. IEEE Design & Test of Computers 21(2), 111–120
             (2004)

Power Macro-Modeling Using an Iterative LS-SVM Method

António Gusmão, Luis Miguel Silveira, and José Monteiro

INESC-ID / IST, TU Lisbon, Lisboa, Portugal
{antoniog,lms,jcm}@algos.inesc-id.pt

Abstract. We investigate the use of support vector machines (SVMs) to determine simpler and better fit power macromodels of functional units for high-level power estimation. The basic approach is first to obtain the power consumption of the module for a large number of points in the input signal space. Least-Squares SVMs are then used to compute the best model to fit this set of points. We have performed extensive experiments in order to determine the best parameters for the kernels.

We propose a new method for power macromodeling of functional units for high-level power estimation based on Least-Squares Support Vector Machines (LS-SVM). Our method improves the already good modeling capabilities of the basic LS-SVM method in two ways. First, a modified norm is used that is able to take into account the weight of each input for global power consumption in the computation of the kernels. Second, an iterative method is proposed where new data-points are selectively added as support-vectors to increase the generalization of the model.

The macromodels obtained compare favorably with those obtained using industry standard table models, providing not only excellent accuracy on average (close to 1% error), but more importantly, thanks to our proposed modified kernels, we were able to reduce the maximum error to values close to 10%.

Keywords: Power Estimation, Macromodel, SVM, Pruning, Norm.

1   Introduction

Electronic systems have become pervasive in our daily lives, work environments and even our social habits. Their design and verification prior to fabrication are challenging tasks due to inherent size and complexity. Rising costs of design and market pressure for fast delivery of error-free systems drive the need for reliable verification. A common approach towards easing the design process and enabling verification is to replace large and complex design blocks by smaller, more abstract macromodels that accurately represent relevant characteristics of the system. The resulting macromodeled system can then be verified and design exploration can be accomplished, leading to better, more efficient designs, with lower costs and added features.

J. Becker, M. Johann, and R. Reis (Eds.): VLSI-SoC 2009, IFIP AICT 360, pp. 118–134, 2011.

Power consumption has become one of the most important parameters in the design of VLSI circuits and accurate power estimation a requisite of any design exploration framework and verification environment. Many high-level power estimation tools have been proposed before to enable the evaluation of different architectures at early stage of design [8]. The general approach is to use power macromodels for each functional unit. These macromodels are obtained in a pre-characterization phase, stored in a library for later use and represent the power dissipation of the unit as a function of its input statistics.

Kernel methods provide a powerful and unified framework for pattern discovery, motivating algorithms that can act on general types of data and look for general types of relations (e.g. rankings, classifications, regressions, clusters) [16]. The application areas range from neural networks and pattern recognition to machine learning and data mining. In this paper, we investigate the use of learning algorithms, in particular support vector machines (SVMs), to determine simpler and better fit power macromodels. The basic approach is first to obtain the power consumption of the module for a large number of points in the input signal space. Least-Squares SVMs (LS-SVM) are then used to compute the best model to fit these set of points. The statistics for each of the module's output signals can be computed in a similar manner, thus providing a means of propagating the switching probabilities through the circuit. We have performed extensive experiments in order to analyze the possible kernels which are the basis of the SVM formulation and to determine the best parameters for these kernels.

Our proposed methodology improves the already good modeling capabilities of the basic LS-SVM method in two ways. In general, kernels treat every dimension uniformly. In the problem at hand, each input to the functional module defines a dimension for the kernel (although not necessarily so after optimizations, as discussed in Section 5.4). It is well-known that not all inputs have the same impact on the power consumption of a module. We propose a modification to the basic RBF kernel that takes into account a measure of the contribution of each input for the power consumption in the computation of the kernels. Secondly, an iterative method is proposed where new data-points are selectively added as support-vectors to better generalize the model

We present results that confirm the excellent modeling capabilities of the kernel-based methods. The macromodels obtained provide not only excellent accuracy on average (all below 2% average error and close to 1% on average), but, more importantly, thanks to our modified kernels, we were able to reduce the maximum error to values close to 10%. As we will show, such low error rates compare favorably with those obtained using standard table-based models.

The paper is organized as follows. In Section 2, we review previous work on power analysis techniques at the RT level and provide some background on kernel methods. Section 3 discusses the kernel parameters and their set up. The proposed optimization techniques, namely the modified norm and the iterative process, are described in Section 4. The implementation details of the power macromodeling process are described in Section 5. We present our results in Section 6 and draw conclusions and future work in Section 7.

2   Related Work

2.1   Power Macro-Modeling

There has been a fair amount of work on generating models for power dissipation at higher levels of abstraction. Top-down approaches have been proposed in [9] and [10]. They are both based on the concept of entropy and their focus is to derive implementation-independent measures of the signal activity in the circuit. A number of assumptions are made in both [9] and [10] on how to propagate the entropy of the inputs through the circuits. These methods can be very efficient, though given all the required approximations and the fact that they ignore issues such as glitching implies that these techniques are not very accurate.

Our method follows a bottom-up approach (for a survey, see [8]), where the model is obtained from an actual circuit implementation. This offers the best level of accuracy. These methods build their models from data points that consist of a power value for the circuit, under some input conditions. From this set of data points, different strategies exist for generating a model that not only fits these data points, but offers the best possible generalization ability.

Lookup tables have been successfully proposed [3]. N-dimensional tables have been used, where each dimension represents an input parameter. Several strategies exist for reducing the number of dimensions and for interpolating among table points. Alternatively, regression can be used to compute the coefficients of an expression [1,2,11,17]. A combination of both of these methods has also been proposed [3]. Models for specialized functions, such as arithmetic units, use different expressions for different inputs, namely depending on whether they correspond to the most or the least significant bits [6,7]. Using models tailored to specialized functions, however, requires very specific knowledge of the problem which restricts the applicability of the technique. Table interpolation or regression implicitly assumes a polynomial or spline representation and may require a large number of coefficients if the underlying surface is somewhat nonlinear. SVMs are quite useful in such a context as they can readily adapt to the data at hand, even if it exhibits strong nonlinearities. Therefore, much sparser approximants can be used while retaining or even improving on the accuracy.

We believe the model we propose, based on LS-SVMs, is more robust than previously proposed approaches: it is generic, systematic, and uses an underlying methodology with properties that have been proven both theoretically and in practice in many different fields. Our results demonstrate just that.

2.2   LS-SVMs

Consider a general problem where we are given N input/output data points, $\{\mathbf{x}_k, z_k\}_{k=1}^{N} \in \mathbb{R}^p \times \mathbb{R}$. These data points follow an unknown function $z(\mathbf{x}) = m(\mathbf{x}) + e(\mathbf{x})$, where $m(\mathbf{x})$ is the target function we wish to estimate and $e(\mathbf{x})$ is a sampling error. Support Vector Machines (SVMs) are a method of obtaining $y(\mathbf{x})$, an estimate of $m(\mathbf{x})$, from the given data set, referred to as training set. SVMs achieve regression by nonlinearly mapping the input space into a higher dimensional feature space where a linear approximant hyperplane can be found. This is implicitly made by the use of a kernel function.

A version of a SVM for regression was proposed by Vapnik el al [16]. This method is called support vector regression (SVR). The model produced by SVR only depends on a subset of the training data, because the cost function for building the model ignores any training data that are close (within a threshold ε) to the model prediction. The relevant data points form a set of support vectors and they immediately lead to a sparse representation. On the other hand, computing the model is a Quadratic Programming (QP) problem. To simplify this QP problem, Least Squares Support Vector Machines were introduced [15]. In both methods the model is:

$$y(\mathbf{x}) = \mathbf{w}^T \varphi(\mathbf{x}) + b \tag{1}$$

The $\varphi(\mathbf{x})$ mapping is usually a non-linear function that transforms the data into a higher dimensional feature space, and is weighted by $\mathbf{w}$. Constant b is the bias term.

LS-SVM corresponds to solving the following constrained optimization problem:

$$\min_{\mathbf{w}} J = \frac{1}{2}\mathbf{w}^T\mathbf{w} + C\frac{1}{2}\sum_{k=1}^{N} e_k^2 \quad \text{s.t.} \quad z_k = \mathbf{w}^T\varphi(\mathbf{x}_k) + b + e_k \tag{2}$$

The $\mathbf{w}^T\mathbf{w}$ term stands for minimizing the length of the weight vector, while the C constant is the trade-off parameter between the complexity of the representation and the minimization of training data errors. The number of training samples, known as support vectors, is given by N.

Using Lagrange multipliers, in order to transform the problem into an unconstrained optimization problem, gives:

$$L = \frac{1}{2}\mathbf{w}^T\mathbf{w} + C\frac{1}{2}\sum_{k=1}^{N} e_k^2 - \sum_{k=1}^{N} \alpha_k[\mathbf{w}^T\varphi(\mathbf{x}_k) + b + e_k - z_k] \tag{3}$$

which is guaranteed to have a global minimum when:

$$\frac{\partial L}{\partial \mathbf{w}} = 0; \frac{\partial L}{\partial b} = 0; \frac{\partial L}{\partial e_k} = 0; \frac{\partial L}{\partial \alpha_k} = 0,$$

resulting in the following linear system of equations:

$$\begin{bmatrix} 0 & \mathbf{1}^T \\ \mathbf{1} & \Omega + C^{-1}\mathbf{I} \end{bmatrix} \begin{bmatrix} b \\ \alpha \end{bmatrix} = \begin{bmatrix} 0 \\ \mathbf{z} \end{bmatrix} \tag{4}$$

where Ω is the kernel matrix, $\Omega_{kl} = \Psi(x_k, x_l) = \varphi(x_k).\varphi(x_l)$, $k, l = 1, \ldots, N$, and Ψ is the kernel function.

The resulting LS-SVM is given by:

$$y(\mathbf{x}) = \sum_{k=1}^{N} \alpha_k \Psi(\mathbf{x}, \mathbf{x}_k) + b \tag{5}$$

Table 1. Common kernels

Linear:	$\Psi(\mathbf{x}_i, \mathbf{x}_j) = \mathbf{x}_i^T \mathbf{x}_j$
Polynomial:	$\Psi(\mathbf{x}_i, \mathbf{x}_j) = (\mathbf{x}_i^T \mathbf{x}_j + \theta)^n$
Exponential (RBF):	$\Psi(\mathbf{x}_i, \mathbf{x}_j) = \exp(\frac{-\|\mathbf{x}_i - \mathbf{x}_j\|^2}{\sigma^2})$
Hyperbolic Tangent:	$\Psi(\mathbf{x}_i, \mathbf{x}_j) = \tanh(\phi \mathbf{x}_i^T \mathbf{x}_j + \theta)$

The simplicity of (5) is not without a cost. While SVMs have a built in way of selecting the most significant data points from their training set, LS-SVMs do not. Sparseness is lost due to the usage of all the data points as support vectors (a large N). This adds a new complexity to the problem. It becomes necessary to judiciously select the training datapoints used to effectively cover the input space.

There are many kernels from which to choose from, some of which are shown in Table 1. In this work, we will focus exclusively on the RBF kernel since it has good empirical results and has a nice smooth behavior.

3   Kernel Tuning

The regression process is not totally automated, since there are a number of parameters that need to be selected, namely C (see (4)), σ (see Table 1) and the number of support vectors, N. We also have an option as to which kernel to use, however the exponential RBF kernel (Table 1) has been reported to perform particularly well under LS-SVM [12]. The analysis and results presented in the remainder of this paper were all obtained with this kernel.

3.1   Parameter C

As referred in Section 2.2, C is a constant that permits a tradeoff between the training error and the smoothness of the model. The training error in sample k is given by $e_k = \frac{\alpha_k}{C}$, indicating that larger values of C force the estimator to reduce the training errors. We have computed the errors obtained using different values of C, maintaining all remaining parameters constant ($\sigma = 2$ and with 2,000 SVs). These errors are obtained on a set of datapoints disjoint from the training set, and which is called the test set.

We use the following error functions to provide some insight into LS-SVM model's performance:

Relative error: $E_R = \{\frac{|z_k - y(\mathbf{x}_k)|}{z_k}\}_{k=1}^{N}$

Average relative error: $E_1 = \frac{1}{N} \sum\limits_{k=1}^{N} E_{R_k}$

Maximum relative error: $E_2 = \max_k E_{R_k}$

Fraction below 10% : $E_3 = \frac{|\{a \in E_R : a < 10\%\}|}{N}$

Ultimately we aim to achieve an E_3 of 100% and an E_1 smaller than 1%. Although the error values are not bounded, E_2 is a good representation of the worst-case scenario.

The graphs in Figure 1 show the test error variation with C averaged over all the benchmark circuits (given in Table 3). For all the circuits the behavior was similar so it is safe to derive conclusions from the average results. We can observe that the error decreases as C increases, but for values above $C = 10^4$ the error remains almost constant. Hence, both training and test errors benefit from larger C.

A new experiment was devised to show that the optimum C depends on the noise present in the data points. Consider the earlier data set $\{\mathbf{x}_k, z_k\}$ with added noise: $z'_k = (1 + \epsilon)z_k$ where ϵ follows a uniform distribution between $[-e; e]$.

Figure 2 shows the test errors for noisy data with maximum noise $e = 10\%$. It becomes clear that the value of C depends on the quality of the data set. We have set $C = 10^4$ since it is approximately optimal for the noiseless case and it is still good when there are small errors present.

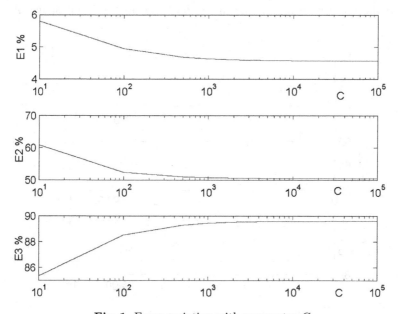

Fig. 1. Error variation with parameter C

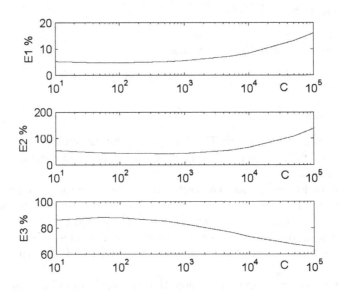

Fig. 2. Error variation with parameter C for noisy data (10%)

3.2 Parameter σ

In the exponential RBF kernel (Table 1), σ represents a width factor. If it is large, then the influence of each support vector (SV) spreads, smoothing the solution. If σ is small, each SV has a small influence over the space around it, which reduces the information the model has over all the input space. At the

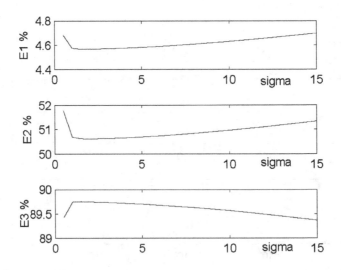

Fig. 3. Errors for different values of σ

extremes, if $\sigma \to \infty$ we obtain a constant function, and if $\sigma \to 0$ our model is only able to estimate input $\mathbf{x}$ equal to its SVs, having null generalization ability. Training error is then inversely proportional to σ values.Figure 3 presents the error obtained for different values of σ on test data ($C = 10^4$, obtained above, and the same 2,000 number of SVs were used). Test results indicate that a value of $\sigma = 1.1$ produces the best overall results (the training error is negligibly small for this σ). If we are to assume the same value of sigma for all the circuits, then this would be the value to use for σ.

Figure 4 shows how each support vector contributes to the final solution in an artificial two-dimensional problem, for two different values of σ, $\sigma = 1$ and $\sigma = 0.02$, respectively the top (a, b) and bottom (c, d) graphs. The graphs on the right (a, c) present a separate curve for each support vector and the graphs on the left (a, d) present the resulting model (summation of all components).

Three important conclusions are drawn:

1. for large values of σ the resulting surfaces are very smooth, and that might make it impossible to follow a steep function.
2. small values of σ allow more complex and steep surfaces, but unless all input space is well covered, bad generalization will occur.
3. as there is a single σ for all SVs, the only degree of freedom LS-SVMs have is the selection of the $\boldsymbol{\alpha}$ weights of each SV, which serves as a scaling factor to the respective component curve (the bias term, b, is one more degree of freedom, but it is only an added constant).

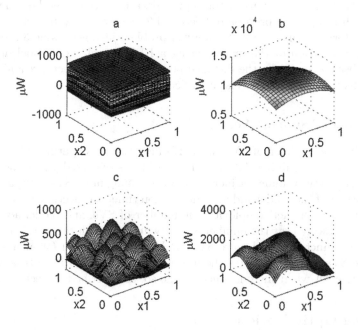

Fig. 4. Power surfaces for: a) $\sigma = 1$, components; b) $\sigma = 1$, sum; c) $\sigma = 0.02$, components; d) $\sigma = 0.02$, sum

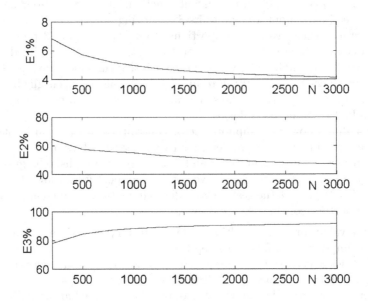

Fig. 5. Error dependence on the number of support vectors

Issues 1 and 2 could be solved by choosing an 'optimal' σ value, but it would still imply that all dimensions of the input space have the same behavior (all smooth or all steep). We propose in Section 4.2 an iterative approach to automatically determine the σ value for a given problem instance. Issue 3 seems to be a major restriction of the models using a RBF kernel. The model output, $y(\mathbf{x})$, is computed based on the distance between the input vector $\mathbf{x}$ and all of the model SVs. We address this issue in Section 4.1.

3.3   Number of Support Vectors

To determine the number of SVs, we performed similar experiments with increasing size of the training data set (Figure 5). As expected, errors decrease when the size of the training set increases. Since having more SVs translates linearly to the size of the model and its computation time, it is necessary to achieve a tradeoff between model complexity, the number of SVs, and model accuracy. One should be aware that the number of SVs will depend on the shape of power surface (steep functions need more SVs) and the σ value used (smaller sigmas imply more SVs). This motivates the use of an iterative algorithm to add SVs to the training set when there is a need to do so, as described in Section 4.2.

4   Model Optimization

In this section, we present the improvements we propose to the LS-SVM method.

4.1   Weighted Norm

Consider as an example a particular situation where:

1. $\mathbf{x} \in R^p$ are samples of the p inputs of a functional unit in a logic circuit.
2. one of them, x_r, has a huge effect on the power dissipated (for instance, a RESET signal).
3. we have a trained LS-SVM model with N support vectors, $N > p$.
4. two test vectors are given, $\mathbf{x}_1$ and $\mathbf{x}_2$, which are exactly the same except in their x_r component.

Since the only information the model uses to differentiate the output values $y(\mathbf{x}_1)$ and $y(\mathbf{x}_2)$ is their distance to all of the N support vectors, it is natural to assume that for $p \gg 1$ their distances to the N SVs would be almost the same which results in $y(\mathbf{x}_1) \approx y(\mathbf{x}_2)$. We know that their real outputs are very different and so the LS-SVM model can never give a good prediction of these values. A possible solution to this problem would be to get a very large number of SVs that would cover that critical input space where x_r varies. This is very costly and would prove to be extremely difficult since that means that there would be many SV close to each other, implying small σs and, thus, poor generalization ability.

To solve this problem, we introduce our proposed modification to the RBF kernel which spawns from a simple adaptation of the distance measure used. By adding weights, $\boldsymbol{\beta}$, to each dimension of the input space, we add significantly more flexibility to the LS-SVM training procedure. The norm becomes

$$||\mathbf{x}_i - \mathbf{x}_j|| = \sqrt{\frac{\sum\limits_{l=1}^{p} \beta_l (x_{i_l} - x_{j_l})^2}{\sum\limits_{l=1}^{p} \beta_l}} \tag{6}$$

Parameters $\boldsymbol{\beta}$ must be computed before training the model. In the case of power macromodeling, a formal method to obtain $\boldsymbol{\beta}$ would be to resort to the Shannon expansion for each circuit input [13]. In Section 5.2, we present a more expedite method.

Note that a similar weighing of the different dimensions can be applied to other kernels (Table 1), where the internal product needs to be modified to use a different coefficient for each dimension.

4.2   Iterative Process

As stated before, the best number of support vectors to use and the value of the σ parameter are interdependent. We propose an iterative method to automatically determine these parameters so that we maximize the generalization of the LS-SVM-based power macromodel.

The standard method of computing the kernel parameters is simply to solve the linear system given in Equation 4, using a set of data points $\{\mathbf{x}_k, z_k\}_{k=1}^{N}$, the training set. The model obtained can then be evaluated against a different and disjoint set of datapoints, the test set. From the obtained errors in each of these sets, we can conclude:

1. large errors on the test set might be due to two reasons: the 'area' of the input space where samples have large test errors is badly covered by the training set; or the kernel function is excessively local, which means that the influence of each SV is limited to a very small 'area' around it.
2. large errors on the training set indicate that the kernel function is smoother than it should be, not having enough flexibility to approximate steep surfaces.

To address these issues an extension to the training procedure was devised consisting of an iterative addition of SVs.

The iterative method developed starts from a given LS-SVM model and uses the following three sets:

- the final test set, with data points which will only be used to evaluate the final model (hence, after the iterative process has finished)
- an initial training set of size M_T of the given model.
- a validation set of size M_V, which can be much larger than M_T

The following steps are repeated while user specifications have not been met, namely that the average relative error, E_1, and the maximum relative error, E_2, on the validation set are smaller than given thresholds T_{E_1} and T_{E_2}:

1. to increase the generalization, we move k data points with the largest errors from the validation set into the training set.
2. if the error on the training set exceeded specifications, we reduce parameter σ by s. As discussed in the previous section, the σ parameter defines how local or global the impact of each support vector is. Hence, by reducing this value by multiplying it by a factor s, $s < 1$, the error is reduced on the training set. This may potentially lead to worse generalization, which is compensated by the extra data points that are moved to the training set. Nevertheless, σ should not be greatly reduced between iterations.

The initial σ value should be relatively large to start with a very smooth solution and steepening it only as much as necessary by reducing σ. Parameters k and s define the granularity of the process. Larger values will reduce the number of iterations, but may lead to a larger model. The size of the initial model and respective training set should be relatively small to give room for the addition of the more problematic data points in the validation set, but, at the same time, large enough to give reasonably good predictions. In our experiments, we start from a model of size 500 obtained from applying (7) to a training set of size 2,000.

5   Implementation

In this section, we describe the methodology for computing the power macromodel. We start by presenting how we obtain the data points used as the training set, then we describe the experiments we performed to tune the kernel parameters, and finally we discuss the size of the model and methods to reduce it.

5.1 Input Space Analysis

To generate the desired black-box macromodel it is necessary to obtain a set of data points to be plugged into the LS-SVM, $\{\mathbf{x}_k, z_k\}$. To analyze the performance of the LS-SVM method for power estimation, we need data points where z_k represents the power dissipation of a circuit under inputs $\mathbf{x}_k$. For this purpose, we can either use experimental values obtained from actual circuit measurements, or values computed by a simulator. Naturally, the accuracy of the model will be directly related to the quality of the data points.

Note that there is some flexibility in terms of what $\mathbf{x}_k$ represents. In this work, we are using the switching probability of each of the p inputs to the functional unit, hence a vector of size p with values between 0 and 1. Alternatively, we could aggregate all inputs and have their distribution probability (for example, in the case a set of bits represent some numerical value). Additionally, if specific information is available regarding joint probability distributions, it can be used to bias the choice of data points.

We should also observe that z_k can represent both static or dynamic power, or total power. The results we present in the next section were obtained from a logic simulator which only accounts for dynamic power. Yet, the results should easily extrapolate for static, and hence, total power.

As data points used during training represent the total knowledge LS-SVMs have for model construction, their selection method is of crucial importance. For each circuit, the objective is to generate N vectors $\mathbf{x}$ of size p with values within $[0, 1]$. To effectively cover the input space three distributions were tested:

1. UNIFORM, 100% follow an uniform distribution between 0 and 1.
2. NORM, 100% follow a normal distribution with 0.5 mean and a chosen variance γ (every value not contained in the [0,1] interval is resampled).
3. UNMIX, a mix of 1 and 2, 50% follow an uniform distribution and 50% follow a normal distribution.

Table 2. Comparison of input distributions

Distribution	E_1	E_2	E_3
UNIFORM	1.68	23.1	99.7
UNMIX ($\gamma = 0.1$)	1.53	24.8	99.5
UNMIX ($\gamma = 0.3$)	1.5	24.2	99.6
NORM ($\gamma = 0.1$)	2.24	34.2	97.7
NORM ($\gamma = 0.3$)	1.57	26.5	99.4

For the purpose of testing the generalization ability of our model, test sets of 8,000 points were constructed using equal quantities of each of the 3 methods presented, for each of the benchmark circuits. In Table 2 the errors defined earlier (Section 3.1) are shown, averaged over all the circuits.

We conclude that the difference in error performance between the tested methods is small, yet the UNMIX distribution seems to lead to slightly smaller error values. Adding to that, in practice, circuit input probabilities should be around 0.5 so we opted to use UNMIX with a variance $\gamma = 0.3$ to get a better representation in that area.

5.2   Computing the Input Weights

In order to gauge the relative importance of each input to the functional unit in terms of the impact in power consumption, we performed a set of experiments where we set all other inputs to a fixed value and measure the power as we change the value of the input under evaluation. Naturally, the results obtained depend on the values assigned to the other inputs. Ideally one would want to check the impact on power consumption of a single input for all possible combinations of the other inputs. Since this is impractical, we randomly sample 20 different combinations of values for the remaining inputs.

From these experiments, we compute the power range for each input, as the difference between the maximum and minimum power values. We use this value directly as the weight for this input in the computation of the modified norm.

5.3   Model Size

From Equation 5, we know that evaluating the LS-SVM model to compute the power requires the sum of N elements, and each element contains a norm (Equation 6) which is a sum of p elements. Hence, the model requires $O(Np)$ operations to compute $y(\mathbf{x})$. Computing the model's output is much faster than simulating the circuit. On a 3GHz AMD64 it took no more than 10 seconds to estimate 10,000 outputs for any of the tested circuits.

It terms of memory, we need to store: N SVs, each of size p; N α values; and the constant b. Hence, the non modified kernel has $O(N(p+1)+1) = O(Np)$ memory complexity. Our modified kernel adds p input weight coefficients (β), which has a negligible impact on memory usage.

If we use the float data type to store these values (usually 4 bytes long), a model of a circuit with 200 inputs ($p = 200$) and 2,000 SVs ($N = 2000$) will need $(2000 \times (200+1)+200+1) \times 4 = 1.53MB$ of storage space. It is affordable, but still expensive. Next, we discuss methods to reduce this size.

5.4   Model Pruning

There are two parameters that define the model size, N and p. There are methods that reduce N by searching for "redundant" SVs, i.e., SVs whose removal has minimal impact on the error [5].

In our work, we apply one of the methods prescribed in [5]. In each step the algorithm solves the linear system (eq. 4) and removes the least important SV which is the $\mathbf{x}_k$ with the smallest $d(\mathbf{x}_k)$:

$$d(\mathbf{x}_k) = [A.\Delta\mathbf{x}]_{k+1} = \frac{\alpha_k}{[A^{-1}]_{k+1}} \tag{7}$$

where A is the square matrix from Equation 4. This is an expensive method but has a good model-reduction to model-error ratio. For a more detailed description we refer the reader to the original paper.

Additionally, we investigate the reduction of p, which amounts to a form of feature selection. The process is to simply remove input dimensions with the lowest β values, as these are the ones which have less impact in defining the power characteristics of the circuit. Starting from lower β, we remove dimensions until the sum of removed betas (normalized) is below a user specified threshold $T \in [0, 1]$. Figure 6 shows the increase in error with the increase of T.

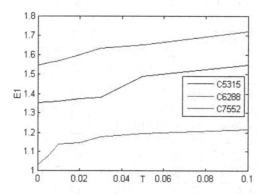

Fig. 6. Error increase with the increase of T

6   Results

In Table 3 we present results for circuits of the ISCAS benchmark set, obtained under different methods. Here we compare several modifications of the basic LS-SVM method with state of the art table lookup methods. In the table, E_1 represents average error, E_2 maximum error and E_3 estimates with error below 10%. Under "Usual Norm" we give the performance of the base LS-SVM models, computed using $C = 10^4$, $\sigma = 1.1$ (Section 3) and from training sets of $N = 2,000$ samples, generated as described in Section 5.1. Weighted norm tests are shown in columns "Weighted Norm", under the same conditions. Under "Iter. Weighted Norm" are the results after the iterative process, where N indicates how many support vectors were used. The results reported by [3] are given under "4D Tables". Finally, under "Pruned" are the results after applying the pruning technique described in Section 5.4, using a threshold value of $T = 0.08$.

Table 3. LS-SVM test results

Circuit	Info		Usual Norm			Weighted Norm			Iter. Weighted Norm				4D Table	
	Ins	Nodes	E_1	E_2	E_3	E_1	E_2	E_3	N	E_1	E_2	E_3	E_1	E_2
C499	41	202	3.5	21.3	98.0	0.4	4.0	100	500	0.5	3.7	100	3.9	16.3
C880	60	383	6.9	69.2	75.8	1.6	16.0	99.8	1000	1.4	17.6	100	3.6	14.0
C1355	41	546	3.1	17.2	98.9	0.5	5.3	100	500	0.5	3.7	100	4.0	15.0
C1908	33	880	4.9	41.7	91.6	1.0	10.8	99.9	695	1.1	9.8	100	3.7	15.7
C2670	233	1193	5.3	36.2	87.4	1.3	9.2	100	1000	1.2	7.2	100	2.2	10.2
C3540	50	1669	5.9	50.4	85.4	1.1	14.0	99.9	740	1.2	11.6	99.9	3.2	15.6
C5315	178	2307	4.0	21.5	96.5	1.0	5.9	100	600	1.1	5.9	100	2.1	12.2
C6288	32	2406	3.9	44.7	95.7	0.5	9.1	100	500	0.6	5.4	100	2.2	17.4
C7552	207	3512	4.4	27.1	96.2	1.3	13.4	99.9	1000	1.3	11.2	99.9	2.7	14.3
average:			4.7	36.6	91.7	1.0	9.73	99.9	726	1.0	8.46	99.98	3.1	14.5

Table 4. LS-SVM test results with pruning

Circuit	Ins	Nodes	Ins	E_1	E_2	E_3
C499	41	202	33	1.0	6.0	100
C880	60	383	39	1.7	16.6	99.8
C1355	41	546	33	0.9	5.9	100
C1908	33	880	28	1.3	11.1	100
C2670	233	1193	107	1.3	8.7	100
C3540	50	1669	29	1.2	15.1	99.9
C5315	178	2307	94	1.1	7.0	100
C6288	32	2406	29	1.0	10.7	100
C7552	207	3512	124	1.3	13.1	100
average:				1.2	10.5	99.97

Several interesting observations can be made from the results presented in Table 3. First, we note that the results obtained with the original kernel were already very good, with average error E_1 below 5%. However, maximum error E_2 can be large, with circuit C880 presenting an error close to 70%. The use of the proposed weighted norm is by itself very effective in reducing error. Its impact is especially visible on the maximum error, which on average reduces to just under 10%, with circuit C880 still presenting the largest maximum error, but reducing from 70% to 16%. On average, the E_1 comes to under 1% and only 0.06% of the samples have error above 10% (E_3)!

The next set of results demonstrates that the iterative process allows for significantly smaller models sizes, while practically maintaining the error levels. Whereas for the previous results a constant number of 2,000 support vectors is used in the model, the iterative process finds equally good solutions with only 726 support vectors on average, providing models almost 3× more compact.

Table 4 presents the results obtained after pruning. Note that the model size can still be effectively reduced using the proposed pruning method, without significant effect on the error level. For larger examples, the number of inputs effectively used in the model are close to half of the original circuit, leading a model half the size and half the evaluation time.

Moreover, we can observe that the results obtained clearly surpass existing state-of-the-art methods based on table lookup, both in terms of average (E_1) and maximum (E_2) errors.

7   Conclusions

Our experiments show that LS-SVM are a viable method for the generation of power macromodels. Modifying the basic RBF kernel so that it takes into account the impact of different circuit inputs on dissipated power proved to result in a huge improvement in model accuracy. It also opened doors to a new approach to model size reduction based on input dimension weights and the use of the weighted norm on other kernels. Further work involves applying kernels composed of more than one element [14].

Acknowledgments. This research was supported in part by the Portuguese FCT under program POCTI.

References

1. Bogliolo, A., Benini, L., De Micheli, G.: Regression-Based RTL Power Modeling. ACM Transactions on Design Automation of Electronic Systems 5(3), 337–372 (2000)
2. Chen, Z., Roy, K.: A power macromodeling technique based on power sensitivity. In: Proceedings of Design Automation Conference, pp. 678–683 (June 1998)
3. Gupta, S., Najm, F.: Power Modeling for High-level Power Estimation. IEEE Transactions on Very Large Scale Integration (VLSI) Systems 8, 18–29 (2000)
4. Gusmao, A., Silveira, L.M., Monteiro, J.: Parameter tuning in svm-based power macro-modeling. In: Quality of Electronic Design (ISQED 2009), pp. 135–140 (March 2009)
5. Hoegaerts, L., Suykens, J.A.K., Vandewalle, J., De Moor, B.: Primal space sparse kernel partial least squares regression for large scale problems. In: Proceedings of 2004 IEEE International Joint Conference on Neural Networks, vol. 1, p. 563 (July 2004)
6. Jochens, G., Kruse, L., Schmidt, E., Nebel, W.: A new parameterizable power macro-model for datapath components. In: Proceedings of Design, Automation and Test in Europe Conference and Exhibition 1999, pp. 29–36 (1999)
7. Landman, P.E., Rabaey, J.M.: Architectural power analysis: The dual bit type method. IEEE Transactions on Very Large Scale Integration (VLSI) Systems 3(2), 173–187 (1995)
8. Macii, E., Pedram, M., Somenzi, F.: High-level Power Modeling, Estimation, and Optimization. IEEE Transaction on Computer-Aided Design of Integrated Circuits and Systems, 1061–1079 (1998)

9. Marculescu, D., Marculescu, R., Pedram, M.: Information Theoretic Measures of Energy Consumption at Register Transfer Level. In: Proceedings of the International Symposium on Low Power Electronics and Design, pp. 81–86 (April 1995)
10. Najm, F.: Towards a High-Level Power Estimation Capability. In: Proceedings of the International Symposium on Low Power Electronics and Design, pp. 87–92 (April 1995)
11. Raghunathan, A., Dey, S., Jha, N.K.: High-level Macro-modeling and Estimation Techniques for Switching Activity and Power Consumption. IEEE Transactions on Very Large Scale Integration (VLSI) Systems 11(4), 538–557 (2003)
12. Shang, W., Zhao, S., Shen, Y.: Application of LSSVM with AGA Optimizing Parameters to Nonlinear Modeling of SRM. In: 3rd IEEE Conference on Industrial Electronics and Applications, pp. 775–780 (June 2008)
13. Shannon, C.: The Synthesis of Two-Terminal Switching Circuits. Bell System Technical Journal 28, 59–98 (1949)
14. Smits, G., Jordaan, E.: Improved SVM Regression using Mixtures of Kernels. In: Proceedings of the 2002 International Joint Conference on Neural Networks, IJCNN 2002, vol. 3, pp. 2785–2790 (2002)
15. Suykens, J., Van Gestel, T., De Brabanter, J., De Moor, B., Vandewalle, J.: Least Squares Support Vector Machines. World Scientific Pub., Singapore (2002)
16. Vapnik, V.: Statistical Learning Theory. John Wiley & Sons, Chichester (1998)
17. Wu, Q., Qiu, Q., Pedram, M., Ding, C.-S.: Cycle-accurate macro-models for rt-level power analysis. IEEE Transactions on Very Large Scale Integration (VLSI) Systems 6(4), 520–528 (1998)

Enhancing Electromagnetic Attacks Using Spectral Coherence Based Cartography

Amine Dehbaoui, Victor Lomne, Philippe Maurine,
Lionel Torres, and Michel Robert

LIRMM, CNRS - University of Montpellier 2
161, rue Ada, 34392 Montpellier, France
{amine.dehbaoui,victor.lomne,pmaurine,
lionel.torres,michel.robert}@lirmm.fr

Abstract. Electromagnetic Aattacks hve been recently identified as an efficient technique to retrieve the secret key of cryptographic algorithms. Although similar mathematically speaking, Power or Electromagnetic Attacks have different advantages in practice. Among the advantages of EM attacks, the feasibility of attacking limited and bounded area of integrated systems is the key one. However, efficient techniques are required to localize hot spots, characterized by partially *data dependent* electromagnetic emissions, at which DEMA may be applied with success. This paper aims at introducing a pragmatic technique to localize quickly and efficiently these points of interest.

Keywords: Side-Channel Attacks, EM emissions, Coherence analysis.

1 Introduction

In the last century, modern cryptology has mainly focused on defining cryptosystems resistant against theoretical attacks. However, with the increasing use of secure embedded systems like smartcards, researchers focused on exploiting the physical syndromes leaking from secure devices during cryptographic operations to disclose the key. As a result, a new kind of attack called Side-Channel Attacks (SCA) has appeared. Among the known attacks, some exploit the timing behavior of Integrated Circuits (IC) [1], while others exploit the global power consumed by IC such as the well known Differential Power Analysis (DPA) [2]. Recently, the Electro-Magnetic (EM) emanations of embedded systems have been identified as a major threat [3][4].

The efficiency of the EM channel is mainly due to the inner properties of EM emissions. Their ability to propagate through different materials is the most interesting one since it allows an attacker targeting the bounded hardware area integrating the cryptographic algorithm under attack or part of it. This is all the more interesting since it also allows getting round global hardware countermeasures against power attacks such as the use of detached power supplies [5] by focusing the attack on reduced die areas.

J. Becker, M. Johann, and R. Reis (Eds.): VLSI-SoC 2009, IFIP AICT 360, pp. 135–155, 2011.

However, this requires the use of small magnetic sensors to localize the leaking spots and thus implies a quadratic increase (with the square of the ratio between the length of the measured chip and the size of the sensor) of the number of points to be attacked using Differential Electro-Magnetic Analyses (DEMA) [3][4]. Thus, according to the magnetic sensor size, it could be very long and tedious for an attacker to apply DEMA on each possible position above the package or circuit.

Within this context, our contribution is a practical technique allowing the localization of hardware modules involved in the cryptographic operation, by localizing die areas with partially *data dependent* electromagnetic emanations. The proposed technique has several interesting properties.

Firstly, it requires only few EM measurements to be efficiently applied. Secondly, it remains efficient (a) even in presence of *data independent* EM emanations such as the ones generated by the clock tree or any *always on* analogue blocks but also (b) in presence fully *data independent* parasitic emissions such as noise. Thirdly, it allows finding positions where DEMA might be successful with a reduced set of EM traces. Finally, as last advantage, this non invasive and contactless technique can be applied with success, as demonstrated in section 4, even if the circuit under attack is encapsulated.

The remainder of this paper is organized as follows. Section 2 gives an overview of Differential ElectroMagnetic Analysis and its variants, but also some experimental results related to successful attacks performed on a standard Data Encryption Standard (DES) [13] mapped onto an Field Programmable Gate Array (FPGA). Section 3 introduces theoretical explanations about the proposed localization technique called Weighted Global Magnitude Squared Incoherence technique ($WGMSI$)and how to couple $WGMSI$ technique with EM near field scanning systems. Section 4 presents some concrete results related to the application of $WGMSI$ localization technique to different mappings on a FPGA of a same design. This section also demonstrates the efficiency of $WGMSI$ cartography to guide DEMA. Finally, conclusions are drawn in section 5.

2   DEMA Overview and Improvements

In this section, we first recall the principles of DEMA and the main known improvements, through a concrete example of a DEMA performed on a naive DES (mapped into a FPGA).

2.1   DEMA Overview

Differential Electromagnetic Analysis introduced in [3][4] is based on the fact that EM emissions radiated by a circuit during a cryptographic operation depend strongly on the manipulated data. This attack, like Power Analysis based attack, is usually performed in three steps: data collection, data sorting and data analysis.

- *Data collection* : it consists in sampling and recording, with a sensor, the direct EM emanations radiated by the circuit or part of it depending on the spatial resolution of the sensor. This is typically done for a large number of cryptographic operations leading to an important collection of EM traces.
- *Data sorting* : it consists in extracting from the whole set of EM traces several sub-sets of EM traces accordingly to one selection function. Different selection functions allow predicting, for each possible guess made on a small part of the secret key (denoted by sub-key afterwards), few bits of intermediate words necessarily computed during the algorithm execution. Thus, for each possible guess of the sub-key, a differential curve is computed.
- *Data analysis* : it consists in identifying which guess among all possible guesses of the sub-key is the correct one, by searching the differential curve with the greatest peak.

2.2   A Standard DEMA Example

DEMA is a known plaintext or known ciphertext attack. The adversary ciphers (resp. deciphers) N PlainText Inputs (PTI) (resp. N CipherText Outputs, CTO) with an unknown key stored in the device, and monitors the ElectroMagnetic (EM) radiations of the device during each ciphering (resp. deciphering). At the end of the first stage, he gets N $PTIs$ (resp. N $CTOs$) and N EM traces. Each EM trace is the evolution versus time of the EM radiations of the chip.

Note that these EM traces have to be well aligned, that means that the time index of the beginning of the ciphering has to be the same for all measurements. If measurements are not well aligned (due for instance to countermeasures like random clock frequency or dummy instructions), different preprocessing techniques allow to re-synchronize EM traces [6][7][8][9][10].

Fig.1 shows several EM traces corresponding to the DES encryption of different $PTIs$ with the same key, called Simple Electro-Magnetic Analysis (SEMA), monitored on an FPGA with the acquisition plateform described in section 4.

The second stage is a statistical processing of the N $PTIs$ (resp. N $CTOs$) with the N EM traces.

In the rest of the article, the DES will be used as example, because of it is the well-known block cipher and principles of SCA stay the same on others cryptographic algorithms as, for example, Advanced Encryption Standard AES) [14]. Moreover, we consider, for convenience, that the adversary is in the case of a known plain-text attack and tries to guess the round-key 1 of the DES (the remaining 8 bits could be found with a brute-force attack). A similar algorithm allows to disclose the round-key 16 in a known cipher-text attack [20].

Because of the set of all possible values for the round-key 1 is too big to test all of them, the adversary divides usually the round-key 1 in 8 parts of 6 bits (called here sub-key) and attacks each sub-key independently and sequentially. Thus, for each sub-key, there is 64 possible values.

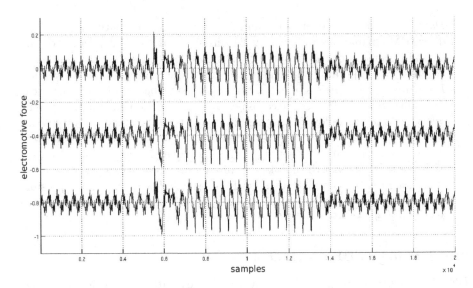

Fig. 1. Several SEMA of a DES encryption on FPGA

The adversary makes an hypothesis on the 6 bits of the attacked sub-key, and for each PTI, he computes the output (4 bits) of the corresponding sbox. This value is called the Intermediate Value (IV). In the state-of-the-art mono-bit DPA [2], the adversary targets one bit among the four, for instance the Less Significant Bit (LSB).

If the LSB of IV_1 (corresponding to the first plaintext, PTI_1) is equal to 0, the associated trace (T_1) is ranked in set A.

At the contrary, if the LSB of IV_1 is equal to 1, T_1 is ranked in set B. The adversary ranks all the traces, as explained above, in sets A or B, and then computes the difference of the means of sets A and B. The resulting curve is called a differential curve, and corresponds to an hypothesis of a sub-key.

The adversary computes the 64 differential curves corresponding to the 64 possible values for a given sub-key.

As explained in [2], the differential curve, noted Δ, for a sub-key hypothesis K_s, is calculated following equation 1:

$$\Delta_{K_s}[j] = \frac{\sum_{i=1}^{N} D(PTI_i, K_s)T_i[j]}{\sum_{i=1}^{N} D(PTI_i, K_s)} - \frac{\sum_{i=1}^{N}(1 - D(PTI_i, K_s))T_i[j]}{\sum_{i=1}^{N}(1 - D(PTI_i, K_s))} \quad (1)$$

where $\Delta_{K_s}[j]$ is the j-th sample of the differential curve, N is the number of EM traces used, PTI_i is the i-th plaintext, $T_i[j]$ is the j-th sample of the EM trace and D the decision function ranking EM traces in sets A or B, also called *selection function*.

If the hypothesis on the sub-key is wrong, all the computed intermediate values will be wrong in comparison with the data really processed in the chip. Then EM traces will be randomly classified in sets A and B. The mean curves of sets A and B will be similar, and the differential curve will look-like to a thick horizontal line (mainly composed of noise).

At the contrary, if the hypothesis on the sub-key is good, all the computed intermediate values will match with the real processed data in the chip, and EM traces in set A will have the same characteristic : at the time index where the intermediate value is computed, the LSB of IV equal to 0 will not lead to an excess of power consumption. Inversely, when the LSB of IV is equal to 1, a bit more energy will be consumed at the same time index and spikes corresponding to the clock cycle where IV is computed will be greater on traces in set B than on traces in set A. When computing the difference of the means of the 2 sets, a spike will appear at the considered time index of the differential curve, which indicates that the sub-key hypothesis is good.

Fig.2 represents the 64 differential curves computed following guesses of the sub-key 1 of the round-key 1 of the DES, using 500 EM traces. Differential curves corresponding to bad guess of the sub-key are drawn in cyan, whereas the curve corresponding to the good guess of the sub-key is drawn in black, and has the greatest peak.

This processing is applied on each sub-key to guess the eight parts of the round-key 1.

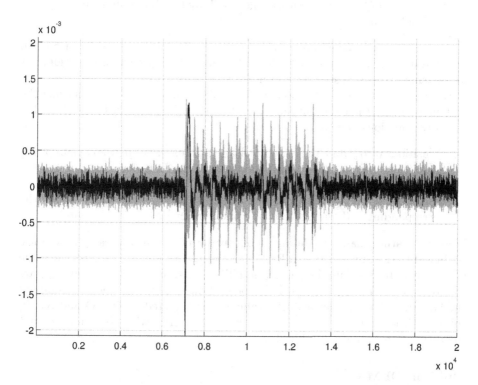

Fig. 2. Example of a successful DEMA: 64 differential curves computed following guesses of the sub-key 1 of the round-key 1 of the DES, using 500 EM traces

2.3   Improvements of DEMA

From this first idea, different improvements have been proposed.

Hamming Weight vs. Hamming Distance Power model

In the original DPA algorithm and as explained above, the selection function follows the Hamming Weight (HW) power consumption model. Actually this model does not match exactly with the reality. Indeed, the power consumption of devices built in CMOS technology is generally considered in terms of two components [11]:

- *Switching power component* : related to the charging and discharging of the load capacitance at the gate output.
- *Short circuit power component* : during the transition of the input line from one voltage level to the other, there is a period of time when both the PMOS and the NMOS transistors are on, thus creating a path from VDD to VSS.
- *Static power component* : due to leakage, that is present even when the circuit is not switching. This, in turn, is mainly composed of two components - gate to source leakage, which is directly though the gate insulator, mostly by tunneling, and source-drain leakage attributed to both tunneling and sub-threshold conduction.

The two first components are related to the processed data, and in case of an inverter, it is not its output state that leaks through its power consumption, but its switching from one state to another.

So the Hamming Weight power model could be improved by considering the switching rather than the output state [12] (the Hamming Distance (HD) between the previous and the new state) :

- transitions 0 to 0 and 1 to 1 do not lead to an excess of power consumption. So, in the example of part 1, if the value of the LSB does not change, EM trace associated to the considered IV has to be ranked in set A.
- transitions 0 to 1 and 1 to 0 involve an excess of power consumption and the corresponding EM trace has to be ranked in set B.

Moreover, rather than considering an output bit of a sbox, one can consider the bit linked to the previous one in R1 [13]. Thus, as the adversary knows the value of this bit in R0 (because he knows the PTI), and assuming that R0 and R1 are stored in the same register which is updated at each round, one can compute the hamming distance between the value of the targeted bit in R0 and R1. In this case, it is not the power consumption of an inverter which is estimated, but the power consumption of a flip-flop.

Multi-bit DEMA

Another way to improve DEMA attacks consists in considering the four bits linked to the output of the sbox rather than one. One can, as proposed in [15], compute the differential curve for each bit among the four of the output of the sbox, and sum the four differential curves.

One can also rank traces following another criterion [16]: we add the number of switching bits among the four considered, and if this sum is smaller than 2, we rank the associated trace in set A, and if the sum is greater than 2, the trace is ranked in set B.

Correlation ElectroMagnetic Analysis (CEMA)

The first class of *selection function* (also called *distinguisher*) described before, is called *Difference of Means*. But the main idea of the DEMA is to find which hypothesis of the sub-key is the most correlated to the EM radiations of the chip. From this idea, Brier and al. have proposed in [12] to use a well-known statistical tool, the Pearson correlation.

Considering that the adversary has ciphered N $PTIs$, and has obtained N EM traces, he can compute, for each sub-key hypothesis, the N IVs. Thus, for each time index j of the EM traces, he computes the Pearson correlation between the row-vector composed of the N IVs and the row-vector of the EM radiations of the N EM traces at time index j. Doing this computation for each j will give a differential curve as in the case of a DEMA.

3   Global Magnitude Squared Incoherence

As demonstrated in section 2, performing even a simple EM attack, requires collecting a significant number of EM traces, and thus could be time consuming even if the latter analysis is done at only one position above the attacked cryptographic modules.

The situation becomes much more critical or even unpractical, as discussed in section 1, if an adversary uses tiny sensors to attack a circuit or equivalently if a circuit provider aims at demonstrating the robustness of its designs against EM attacks performed with such tiny probes.

Considering our previous example, one may to plan collecting, at 71x71 positions above the Spartan3 core (displacement step of 100μm), 10000 EM traces, using a magnetic loop with a 100μm diameter, in order to determine if EM emissions may be exploited or not by an adversary. However, this would result, in our example, in collecting EM traces during approximately 70 days.

This situation leads to the following question: how efficiently and quickly position tiny probes ? One may naturally think, to solve this problem, in performing a standard EM near field scan of the surface in order to localize the cryptographic modules. However, as explain below, this is often insufficient.

3.1   Problem Definition

Let us consider, for simplicity, that there are only two local sources of EM emissions within the chip: the source CB (corresponding to the cryptographic

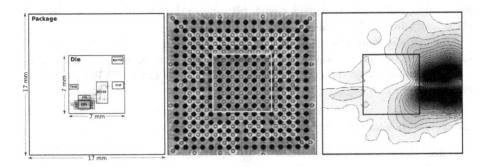

Fig. 3. (a) Design floor plan (b) X-Ray photography (c) Peak to Peak EM amplitude map

block) which is *data dependent*, and a source S (such as clock, or an *always on* analogue block), which is *data independent*.

In that case, if a probe placed close to the IC surface but far from CB and close to S collects: only a small fraction of the *data dependent* emissions radiated by CB (since the magnetic field amplitude decreases rapidly as the square or the cube of the distance [18]) and large portion of the emissions of S.

On the contrary, if the probe is placed really close to CB, the probe collects a large fraction of the *data dependent* emissions radiated by CB during its operation and a small portion of the emissions of S. From the considerations above, one may conclude that positioning the probe closed to the co-processor CB, results in collecting time domain traces differing significantly one from another, and therefore that it is easy to localize the cryptographic module. However, these last claims do not hold !

Indeed, if the EM emissions radiated by the source S are significantly greater than the emissions of the CB or, if S and CB sources are really close one from the other, it is still extremely difficult to localize CB, even if the probe is placed just above, since most of the signal collected by the probe is generated by S.

As a result, any localization technique based on time domain amplitude analyses may not work in presence of large EM *data independent* emanations sources such as clock generators, PLL or I/O interfaces, or even in presence of large environmental electromagnetic noise sources.

As an illustration, Fig.3c shows a map revealing the maximum amplitude of the EM emissions measured at several coordinates of the FPGA package surface during a DES ciphering (this EM emission maps has been obtained with the experimental setup introduced section 4). Fig.3b is an X-Ray photography of the package containing the circuit under attack. Finally, Fig.3a discloses the routing (obtained with Xilinx ISE tool suite) of the considered circuit, running at 50MHz and integrating a DES module, a finite state machine and a RS232 interface for communication purpose.

As shown, it appears impossible to correlate Fig.3a with Fig.3c even if the die area is roughly known thanks to the X-Ray photography Fig.3b. It thus appears all the more difficult to identify the DES module on this kind of EM cartography and thus to decide where to position the magnetic sensors above the package to perform a successful DEMA only on the DES module, in order to avoid potential global hardware countermeasures such as [5].

3.2   Fundamentals of Global Magnitude Squared Incoherence

About the behavior of EM emissions of IC

DPA exploits by statistical means the *data dependent* behavior of the switching current consumed by circuits during a computation of a cryptographic module. This behavior is due to inner properties of the CMOS logic which consumes energy (much more than in the idle state) only to switch from one logical state to another [17].

EM emissions of a circuit are mainly generated by flows of electrical charges through the different metal wires connecting logic gates but also trough wires supplying the circuit [18][19]. Since the switching of gates generates a current flow through the circuit interconnect, we may conclude that these switching generate some *data dependent* EM emissions at different points in the circuit according to the power distribution network [18][19]. These *data dependent* behaviors may be exploited by statistical means, using for example DEMA [3][4], to retrieve the secret key.

Even if the magnitudes of both power consumption and computation time of logic cells are roughly known, it is extremely difficult to deduce any characteristic about the EM emissions generated by gates due to the complexity of the power distribution grid of actual IC. As a result, the only conclusion we may draw and consider in the remainder of the paper is that gates generates some EM perturbations and more precisely generates some *data dependent* harmonics located somewhere in the whole EM emission spectrum.

Within this context, the proposed technique allows disclosing the *data dependent* behavior of EM emissions in the frequency domain without making any assumption on the EM emission characteristics. It is based on spectral incoherence analysis of two time domain signals as detailed below. The only observation on which is based the method is the following: considering two successive hardware operations, we are sure that some gates switch during one computation and does not switch during the other, while some gates switch during both operations. This leads to the following intuitive conclusion that guides the development of our proposal: between two cryptographic operations some characteristics of the EM emissions remain constant (coherent) from one operation to another, while some characterristics completely change (are incoherent). Such a behavior is said partially *data dependent* in the rest of the paper and the proposed $WGMSI$ technique aims at disclosing circuit areas characterized by this behavior.

Weighted Global Magnitude Squared Incoherence

The Magnitude Squared Coherence (MSC) between two signals $w_1(t)$ and $w_2(t)$ is a real-valued function of frequency with values between 0 and 1. It is defined by the following expression:

$$MSC_{w_1,w_2}(f) = \frac{P_{w_1,w_2}(f)^2}{P_{w_1,w_1}(f).P_{w_2,w_2}(f)} \tag{2}$$

where $P_{w_1,w_1}(f)$, $P_{w_2,w_2}(f)$ are respectively the power spectral density of $w_1(t)$, $w_2(t)$, and $P_{w_1,w_2}(f)$ is the cross power spectral density of $w_1(t)$ and $w_2(t)$. At a given frequency f, a $MSC(f)$ value of 1 indicates that the two signal spectra have exactly the same amplitude i.e. are coherent while a value of 0 means that the signal spectra are different i.e. incoherent. Alternatively, one may compute the Mean Squared Incoherence $MSI(f)$ defined by (2). This criterion has also its values between 0 and 1 but indicates rigorously the contrary of (1).

$$MSI_{w_1,w_2}(f) = 1 - MSC_{w_1,w_2}(f) \tag{3}$$

Considering the whole spectra of two sampled time domain signals, one may compute respectively the Weighted Global Magnitude Squared Coherence or Incoherence coefficients $(WGMSC$ and $WGMSI$ factors) between two time domain signals according to the definitions (3,4) that consider the signal $w_2(t)$ as a reference. In these definitions, nf is the number of frequency values at which the $MSC(f)$ and $MSI(f)$ coefficients are computed, BW is the considered frequency bandwidth and $A_{w_2(t)}$ is the power spectrum amplitude at the f frequency.

$$WGMSC = \sum_{f \in BW} \frac{MSC_{w_1,w_2}(f)}{nf} \cdot \frac{A_{w_2}(f)}{\max_{f \in BW}(A_{w_2}(f))} \tag{4}$$

$$WGMSI = \sum_{f \in BW} \frac{MSI_{w_1,w_2}(f)}{nf} \cdot \frac{A_{w_2}(f)}{\max_{f \in BW}(A_{w_2}(f))} \tag{5}$$

$WGMSI$ and $WGMSC$ have values ranging between 0 and 1. Considering the $WGMSI$, a high value indicates that $w_1(t)$ and $w_2(t)$ have perfectly incoherent spectra, while a low value indicates the contrary. It is to be noted that the right hand term of (4) is a key term. Indeed, it weights $MSI(f)$ value such that fully incoherent and high amplitude harmonics have more impact on the final $WGMSI$ value than fully incoherent but low amplitude harmonics.

Illustrations

To illustrate the proposed definitions, 5 time domain EM traces were acquired during 5 different ciphering of a DES module $(50MHz)$. These traces, shown

Table 1. *WGMSI* values

WGMSI values calculated between :	traces collected above clock nets	traces collected above the DES module	Ratio
data1 & data1	0	0	NaN
data1 & data2	$2.8 \ 10^{-5}$	$2.6 \ 10^{-3}$	90.9
data1 & data3	$2.1 \ 10^{-5}$	$2.5 \ 10^{-3}$	116.8
data1 & data4	$2.4 \ 10^{-5}$	$2.4 \ 10^{-3}$	100.4
data1 & data5	$2.4 \ 10^{-5}$	$1.7 \ 10^{-3}$	70.5

in Fig.4, have been collected with $500\mu m$ diameter probe placed respectively above a DES module (Fig.4a) and above some nets distributing the clock signal (Fig.4b). As a result, one may expect that curves Fig.4a are partially *data dependent* traces while, waveforms Fig.4b are completely *data independent*. To validate this assumption, $MSC(f)$ were computed.

Fig.4c gives the $MSC(f)$ evolution with respect to frequency for both partially *data dependent* and fully *data independent* traces. As shown, the $MSC(f)$ values obtained considering traces collected above some clock nets have, as expected, values closer to 1 over a wider frequency range than the $MSC(f)$ values computed with traces collected above the DES module, validating the above discussion.

The obtained $MSC(f)$ values were gathered to compute the $WGMSI$ coefficients. As expected again, $WGMSI$ values (Table 1) corresponding to acquisitions above the clock nets are two magnitude order lower than that corresponding to acquisitions above the DES. However, the latter values remain low meaning that only few harmonics are incoherent or that the amplitudes of those harmonics is significantly lower than those of coherent harmonics. Hence, the used term of partially *data dependent* EM emission.

Considering these results, one may consider that the $WGMSI$ criterion appears efficient enough to differentiate a partially *data dependent* behavior from a *data independent* one and may be used during a magnetic near field scan of a circuit to localize area with partially *data dependent* EM emissions.

3.3   Coupling *WGMSI* Criterion with EM near Field Scanning

Coupling $WGMSI$ analysis with near field scanning system to localize the points characterized by partially *data dependent* EM emissions and thus leaking spots is straightforward. The basic idea is to collect for each (X,Y) coordinates above

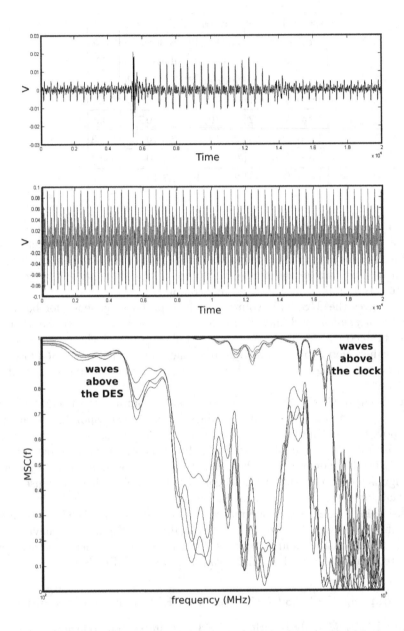

Fig. 4. (a) EM traces collected above the DES (b) EM traces collected above clock nets (c) Evolution with frequency of the corresponding MSC coefficients

the integrated circuit at least two different time domain traces of the magnetic field corresponding to two different data processing. Finally, $WGMSI$ values are computed for all (X,Y) positions. This provides $WGMSI$ cartographies revealing positions characterized by partially *data dependent* EM emissions.

Note however, that computing $WGMSI$ values for more than two data and averaging the results is not theoretically required but may lead to better results in practice.

4   Experimental Results

To validate the effectiveness of the $WGMSI$ analysis in localizing spots with partially *data dependent* EM emissions, 2 kinds of validation were performed. The one aimed at correlating the obtained $WGMSI$ cartographies with the design floorplans while the second aimed at demonstrating that spots characterized by the highest $WGMSI$ values are good candidates for DEMA.

4.1   Experimental Setup

These two experimental validation campaigns were achieved with the measurement platform showed Fig.5. It is composed of:

- an oscilloscope, with a 2.5GHz bandwidth, to sample at 40GS/s the time domain evolutions of the measured signals,
- a low noise 63dB amplifier with a 1GHz bandwidth,
- an handmade magnetic loop with a $500\mu m$ diameter, and a bandwidth greater than 1GHz,
- a motorized stage allowing positioning along X, Y and Z axes the probe with a resolution of $10\mu m$,
- a PC to controls the whole measurement setup, i.e. provides data to the DES module through an on chip RS232 module and store the measured EM traces from the scope, and controls the motorized stage.

4.2   Analyzed Design

The two aforementioned validation steps were performed considering a design mapped onto a FPGA circuit and more precisely a Spartan3-1000 Digilent board. Note the Spartan die is encapsulated in a cavity-up Ball Grid Array (BGA) package. The mapped design integrates a RS232 block to communicate with the PC, a finite state machine that manages the communications and the behavior of the chip. Three different floorplans of this design were elaborated with ISE tool suite as shown Fig. 6. This was done to definitively validate the efficiency of $WGMSI$ map in disclosing area with partially *data dependent* radiations.

Fig. 5. Near field scan and DEMA attack platform

4.3   *WGMSI* Maps vs. Design Floorplans

WGMSI maps aim at disclosing (X,Y) coordinates at which the EM emissions captured by the probes are partially *data dependent*. As a first validation, we therefore scanned the whole package surface during DES ciphering operations and computed the *WGMSI* maps for the 3 considered mappings. The expected result was, at least, to localize the DES module and more precisely to define an area (characterized by higher *WGMSI* values) containing the DES module or part of it since (a) the probe was placed at roughly 500μm from the die and (b) since EM waves are dispersive. Note that the distance from the probe to the die was estimated by removing the package of an identical FPGA and measuring the package thickness. This procedure also allowed measuring the die dimensions (incorporating the IO pads): roughly 7mm by 7mm.

The whole package was scanned with a displacement step of 500μm. This resulted in acquiring EM emissions at 1225 coordinates for each mapping. It tooks 2 hours, for one mapping, to collect the EM emissions corresponding to 5 different encryptions. Note that to increase the Signal to Noise Ratio, each ciphering was performed 20 times and the average computed.

Fig.6 shows the 3 obtained *WGMSI* maps. The lower left map of Fig.6 is to be compared to Fig.3c. This comparison demonstrates that *WGMSI* map provides more valuable information than a maximum time domain amplitude analysis.

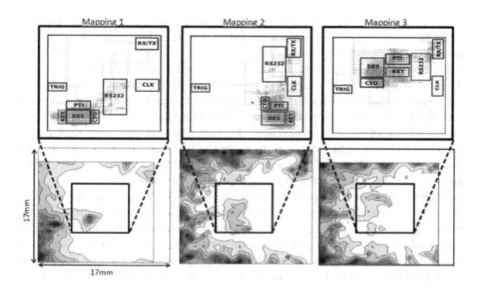

Fig. 6. Circuit oorplans and related full package *WGMSI* maps obtained for the three considered mappings of the design

Moreover and as expected the comparison of these maps with the corresponding floorplans demonstrates, considering the accuracy of the die size measure (0.5mm), that $WGMSI$ criterion allows disclosing the hardware area corresponding to the DES module. One surprising point is that areas with partially *data dependent* EM emissions have different size even if the DES module occupied roughly the same number of slices.

This is especially true for $WGMSI$ maps corresponding to mappings 1 and 2 that disclose significantly larger and smaller areas than that effectively occupied by the DES module. This is probably due to the power/ground network specificities effectively involved in the supply of the DES module in each mapping; supply rails being recognized as important sources of EM emanations [18][19].

Nevertheless, as illustrated by Fig.7, $WGMSI$ cartographies allow selecting rationally a small number of points (typically 20 to 30 in our testcases) above the die among 225 as interesting candidates for DEMA. Next paragraph aims at evaluating if these points are effectively good candidates for EM attacks.

4.4 $WGMSI$ and DEMA Attacks

In order to further evaluate the efficiency of the $WGMSI$ criterion, a last validation step has consisted in elaborating a DEMA map of the mapping 3. Several EM attacks were thus performed at different positions of a package area above the die.

The architecture of the DES co-processor being iterative with a fully parallel computation of a round in a clock period, it was therefore possible to use the Hamming distance model, considered as the most efficient when applicable.

For each attacked position, 5000 EM traces were acquired; each trace was obtained by averaging 20 times the signal to increase the Signal to Noise Ratio. Then, we launched on each selected position CEMA attacks on first and sixteenth rounds, following the original CPA attack from Brier and al. [12]. More precisely, a correlation coefficient was computed, for each time sample, every time a new trace was collected. This was done to check the key guess stability by fixing an arbitrary threshold at 100 iterations with the good key to decide that CEMA has definitely found the key accordingly to the DPA contest rules [20].

Following this protocol, several maps were obtained; Fig.7 groups some of them. Fig.7a gives the percentages of correct guesses (among 4900 guesses done during the CEMA), of the sub-key provided to Sbox1 during round 1. On this map, darkest areas correspond to highest percentages of correct guesses while (a) the black curve represents the boundary of the design 3 and (b) black rings correspond to the 25 highest $WGMSI$ points (among 225 values computed). It is to be noted that most of these points coincide with coordinates at which the percentage of right sub-key guesses is greater than 45%, which is a sufficiently high threshold to consider CEMA as successful.

Fig.7b reveals areas at which the full key is obtained with the lowest number of traces. This map must be interpreted according to the following criterion: the darkest the area is, the lower is the number of traces required to disclose the full key. Note that white areas correspond to coordinates at which the CEMA failed. Once again, the right hand darkest areas coincide with some high $WGMSI$ points.

The above results partially demonstrate the efficiency of the $WGMSI$ criterion in selecting rationally few points to be attacked. Indeed, some coordinates at which an attacker may obtain a high percentage of correct guesses or the full key are not detected by $WGMSI$ cartographies. To our opinion, these points correspond to a Gnd or Vdd rail close to the clock pad. This close vicinity with the clock pad reduces the weights involved in (4) due to high amplitude harmonics generated by the clock. As a result, the rank of these coordinates is lowered. There is thus room to improve the weighting policy of the MSI coefficients.

To definitively demonstrate the interest of the $WGMSI$ criterion as defined in this paper, we computed the percentage of points falling into $WGMSI$ bins. This binning of the whole population done, we computed the percentage of successful CEMA attack in each bin. Fig.8 gives the results. As shown, the percentage of successful CEMA by bin increases with the $WGMSI$ value validating the interest our proposal, while the percentage of points falling into the corresponding bins decreases with the $WGMSI$ value.

4.5 WGMSI vs. EM Analysis Maps

If the above results demonstrate the efficiency of the $WGMSI$ technique in disclosing some of the main hot spots from an attack point of view, they do not allow quantifying what could be the benefits in term of data collecting time reduction. This paragraph aims at providing a first order evaluation of this time reduction considering our DES implementation (design 3). In order to quantify the time cost of elaborating a $WGMSI$ map, Tables 2 and 3 report respectively the time required to collect:

- 10000 different EM traces (corresponding at 10000 data ciphering) to elaborate an attack cartography, i.e. map disclosing the leaking points of the package surface,
- 3 averaged EM traces corresponding to 3 different data ciphering (repeated 20 times) to obtain a WGMSI map.

As shown, the time required, to obtain a $WGMSI$ map, represents less than 3% of the time spent to collect EM traces for attacks at all positions. This definitively demonstrated the interest of the $WGMSI$ technique to guide the EM analysis by ranking the positions to be attacked. Note that the values reported in tables 2 and 3 were extrapolated from the measurement of the time spent to collected 10000 data at a given position.

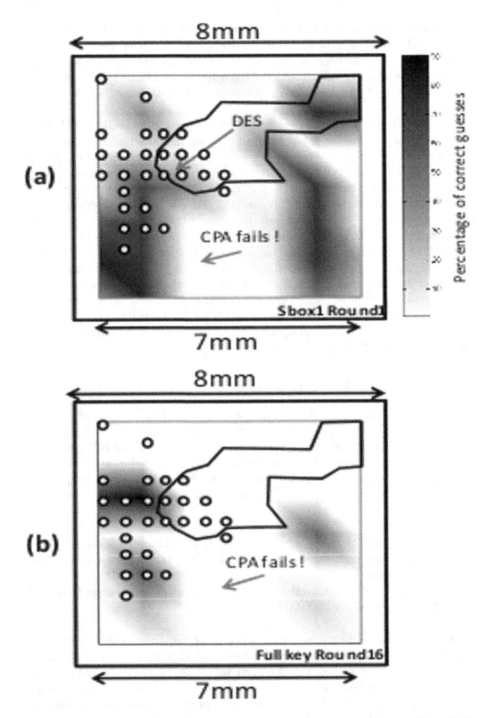

Fig. 7. Percentage of the successful CEMA by WGMSI bin and Percentage of the whole population by bin

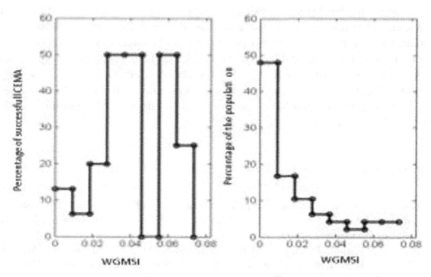

Fig. 8. Percentage of the successful CEMA by *WGMSI* bin and Percentage of the whole population by bin

Table 2. Data collecting time to obtain attack cartographies

probe size attacked area	1mm	500μm	100μm
1x1mm	20 min	3 hours	1.5 day
7x7mm	21 hours	3 days	70 days
17x17mm	4.5 days	17 days	406 days

Table 3. Data collecting time to obtain *WGMSI* cartographies

probe size attacked area	1mm	500μm	100μm
1x1mm	1 min	9 min	121 min
7x7mm	64 min	4 hours	3.5 days
17x17mm	5.5 hours	20 hours	20 days

5   Conclusion

In this paper, a new technique has been introduced. It is based on the assumption according to which: from a data processing to another one, EM emissions radiated by an integrated circuit have some coherent characteristics and some incoherent characteristics. This claimed property, called partially data-dependence of EM emissions, has been first validated experimentally by verifying its correctness with some measured traces. Then, we deduced from this observation, a localization technique. This technique allows (a) localizing cryptographic modules and more precisely leaking points thanks to EM near field mapping and (b) selecting rationally a reduced set of points of interests for electromagnetic analyses. Finally, concrete results have been given on an iterative DES mapped on a FPGA. These results have demonstrated the interest of using incoherence analysis of EM emissions.

References

1. Kocher, P.: Timing Attacks on Implementations of Diffie-Hellman, RSA, DSS, and Other Systems. In: Koblitz, N. (ed.) CRYPTO 1996. LNCS, vol. 1109, pp. 104–113. Springer, Heidelberg (1996)
2. Kocher, P., Jaffe, J., Jun, B.: Differential Power Analysis. In: Wiener, M. (ed.) CRYPTO 1999. LNCS, vol. 1666, pp. 388–397. Springer, Heidelberg (1999)
3. Gandolfi, K., Mourtel, C., Olivier, F.: Electromagnetic Analysis: Concrete Results. In: Koç, Ç.K., Naccache, D., Paar, C. (eds.) CHES 2001. LNCS, vol. 2162, pp. 251–261. Springer, Heidelberg (2001)
4. Peeters, E., Standaert, F.X., Quisquater, J.J.: Power and electromagnetic analysis: Improved model consequences and comparisons. Integration, the VLSI Journal, Special Issue: Embedded Cryptographic Hardware 40(1), 52–60 (2007)
5. Shamir, A.: Protecting Smart Cards from Passive Power Analysis with Detached Power Supplies. In: Paar, C., Koç, Ç.K. (eds.) CHES 2000. LNCS, vol. 1965, pp. 121–132. Springer, Heidelberg (2000)
6. Clavier, C., Coron, J.S., Dabbous, N.: Differential Power Analysis in the Presence of Hardware Countermeasures. In: Paar, C., Koç, Ç.K. (eds.) CHES 2000. LNCS, vol. 1965, pp. 252–263. Springer, Heidelberg (2000)
7. Moyart, H.D., Bevan, R.: A Method for Resynchronizing a random clock on smartcards. Eurosmart (2001), http://www.nmda.or.jp/nmda/ic-card/proceedings/30-1440-DMoyart.pdf
8. Pelletier, H., Charvet, X.: Improving the DPA attack using wavelet transform. In: NISTs Physical Security Testing Workshop (2005), http://csrc.nist.gov/groups/STM/cmvp/documents/fips140-3/physec/papers/physecpaper14.pdf
9. Homma, N., Nagashima, S., Imai, Y., Aoki, T., Satoh, A.: High-Resolution Side-Channel Attack Using Phase-Based Waveform Matching. In: Goubin, L., Matsui, M. (eds.) CHES 2006. LNCS, vol. 4249, pp. 187–200. Springer, Heidelberg (2006)
10. Kafi, M., Guilley, S., Marcello, S., Naccache, D.: Deconvolving Protected Signals. In: Proc. of the International Conference on Availability, Reliability and Security (ARES), pp. 687–694 (2009)
11. Coron, J.S., Naccache, D., Kocher, P.: Statistics and secret leakage. ACM Transactions on Embedded Computer Systems 3, 492–508 (2004)
12. Brier, E., Clavier, C., Olivier, F.: Correlation Power Analysis with a Leakage Model. In: Joye, M., Quisquater, J.-J. (eds.) CHES 2004. LNCS, vol. 3156, pp. 16–29. Springer, Heidelberg (2004)
13. Data Encryption Standard, FIPS PUB 46-3
14. Advanced Encryption Standard, FIPS 197

15. Bevan, R., Knudsen, E.: Ways to Enhance Differential Power Analysis. In: Lee, P.J., Lim, C.H. (eds.) ICISC 2002. LNCS, vol. 2587, pp. 327–342. Springer, Heidelberg (2003)
16. Messerges, T., Dabbish, E., Sloan, R.: Investigations of power analysis attacks on smartcards. In: Proc. of the USENIX Workshop on Smartcard Technology on WOST, p. 17 (1999)
17. Yeap, G.: Practical Low Power Digital VLSI Design. Springer, Heidelberg (1997)
18. Dhia, S., Ramdani, M., Sicard, E.: Electromagnetic Compatibility of Integrated Circuits: Techniques for low emission and susceptibility. Springer, Heidelberg (2005)
19. Ordas, T., Lisart, M., Sicard, E., Maurine, P., Torres, L.: Near-Field Mapping System to Scan in Time Domain the Magnetic Emissions of Integrated Circuits. In: Svensson, L., Monteiro, J. (eds.) PATMOS 2008. LNCS, vol. 5349, pp. 229–236. Springer, Heidelberg (2009)
20. DPA contest (2008/2009), http://www.dpacontest.org

A Multistep Extrapolated S-Parameter Model for Arbitrary On-Chip Interconnect Structures

Petru B. Bacinschi and Manfred Glesner

Department of Electrical Engineering and Information Technology,
Institute of Microelectronic Systems,
Technische Universität Darmstadt,
Karlstr. 15, 64283 Darmstadt, Germany
{pbb,glesner}@mes.tu-darmstadt.de
http://www.mes.tu-darmstadt.de

Abstract. Accurate high-frequency interconnect models are needed for the precise estimation of signal delays, crosstalk, and energy losses in complex on-chip communication structures, such as hierarchical bus architectures and networks-on-chip. In this chapter we introduce a computationally-efficient wide-bandwidth characterization method based on an incremental extrapolation of S-parameters for arbitrary interconnect structures. Our method defines a systematic set of *a priori* parameter extractions and performs on-demand multistep extrapolations for interconnect segments with specified wire length, widths, spacings, metal layer, and neighboring routing information. Experimental evaluations show a maximum absolute error of less than $2 \cdot 10^{-2}$ (magnitude) and 7 degrees (angle) between our model and an industry-standard full-wave field simulator for a 90-nm CMOS process. We consistently enforce the passivity of the admittance matrices for each set of measured or generated parameters to eliminate the possible errors introduced during parameter measurements and extrapolation. Circuit-level simulations with the extrapolated model show a maximum signal delay error of less than 12.5% across multiple metal layers and wire configurations.

1 Introduction

At gigahertz frequencies, bus data and clock signals in integrated circuits are entering the microwave-specific range and the global on-chip interconnects become a more and more critical bottleneck in the global system performance [3, 14]. Moreover, numerous vias, crossing lines, and dielectric discontinuities, as well as a high wire packing density, are common attributes of state-of-the-art CMOS processes, but constitute nevertheless a frequent cause of crosstalk and reflections [5]. In addition, important signal quality drops generated through skin effects and dielectric losses augment with the frequency and cannot be ignored anymore in the present interconnect wires. In this respect, an increasingly high percentage of the final circuit performance becomes dictated by the interconnects [3], although devices and, recently, device parameter variability continue

J. Becker, M. Johann, and R. Reis (Eds.): VLSI-SoC 2009, IFIP AICT 360, pp. 156–180, 2011.

to influence a significant performance amount. Thus, with increasingly high integration scales, the electrical performance of interconnects must be accurately characterized, modeled, and seamlessly integrated into IC design flows.

There are two common approaches in the analysis, measurement, and description of interconnect structures, namely in the time domain (using e.g. time-domain reflectometry or eye diagrams) and in the frequency domain (employing e.g. S-parameters) [14]. Although the two approaches may embed the same information in different forms, for practical circuit modeling purposes there are other factors, such as simulator support or the amount of computation overhead vs. accuracy, which decide which method becomes more appropriate. Furthermore, the analysis of on-chip interconnects is significantly burdened by challenging factors like high losses, scaled aspect ratios, increased number of wires, and strong non-uniformities in the dielectric stack [11], which contribute to the difficulty of employing standard measurement and simulation techniques.

In order to enable the accurate characterization of such parasitic effects within a practical workflow, designers need efficient performance estimation models at lower abstraction levels, which are capable to describe arbitrary interconnect structures [5] and are developed to support an integration with industry standard simulation frameworks. For instance, signal integrity analyses in digital communication structures operating at gigahertz frequencies [9] require the interconnect models to be valid over very wide frequency ranges.

1.1   Interconnect Modeling Challenges

The parasitic effects which affect the densely-packed interconnect wires, such as dielectric and substrate-induced dispersion, skin effects, and proximity effects, are strongly dependent on frequency [21] and need to be carefully considered by the interconnect models. Further, the evaluation of self and mutual impedances requires finding the current return paths for each individual wire, which are also frequency-dependent [15]. In addition, the actual return paths are difficult to estimate in interconnects, since there is no ground plane between the metal layers. Finally, the rapidly-switching signals exhibit very narrow rise and fall times and therefore contain significant spectral components within wide frequency ranges.

Interconnect models have traditionally evolved from simple, lumped capacitance, through lumped and distributed RC, until the state-of-the-art transmission-line distributed RLCG chains. Lumped and distributed RC models neglect inductive effects and fail to model lossy interconnect lines with propagation delays comparable or larger than the signal rise time [16]. Inductively and capacitively coupled, distributed RLCG models are today generally preferred [4,13,21], as they provide a good tradeoff between accuracy and model complexity. Within a distributed RLCG representation, the wires are divided into cascaded segments of circuit elements, extracted to reflect the interconnect response up to the desired significant frequency. These models are designed to enclose high-frequency effects, they achieve a perfect circuit-level compatibility with simulators, and are fast to simulate. On the other hand, they rely on coupled mutual inductances between all the segments from all chains, as illustrated in Fig. 1 for only one

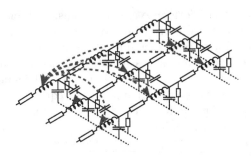

Fig. 1. Complexity of mutually-coupled inductances in distributed RLCG models

inductance of a single chain segment. As a consequence, the modeling complexity increases exponentially with the number of cascaded segments and it becomes extremely hard to compute the value of each mutually coupled inductance pair.

Field solvers are commonly employed for computing accurate capacitance values [17], and for resistance and inductance [12] extractions. Nevertheless, for fast estimations of arbitrary interconnect structures needed in the early design stages, analytic expressions have been developed for capacitance [25] and self inductance [23] computation. On the other hand, mutual inductance values can only be estimated for two parallel running lines of equal wire length [19], hence they are restricted to a small number of cases. Field solver extractions of wire parameters, while being very accurate, are not applicable for real-time estimations, due to the time overhead and complex structural setup they imply. Moreover, the extracted models exhibit a decreasing accuracy with frequency increase and their maximum frequency of validity is specified in terms of the acceptable error [16]. In addition, distributed RLCG models rely on the quasi-TEM (transverse electric and magnetic) propagation of electromagnetic waves in transmission lines [4], which does not account for radiation losses and steep discontinuities (vertical vias, wire segment bends) [21] and assumes that the cross-sectional wire dimensions are much smaller than the wavelength at the maximum frequency of interest. In such cases, more precise electromagnetic analyses might be required.

Full-wave characterization methods [21] are ideal for accurate wide frequency-range modeling purposes, as they rely on a direct discretization of Maxwell's equations and find a numerical solutions at every frequency. Such methods include differential-based approaches, such as either frequency-domain finite element solvers [8] or time-domain finite difference solvers [7], and integral-based techniques, such as the method of moments [18] and the partial element equivalent circuits (PEEC) [22, 21]. The complexity implied by the discretization and numerical solving of Maxwell's equations in differential or integral form is requiring however a substantial computational overhead [21]. Hence, while holding the highest accuracy, these methods are not directly applicable for interconnect synthesis applications, unless a method exists to extract fast characterizations of arbitrary interconnect segments.

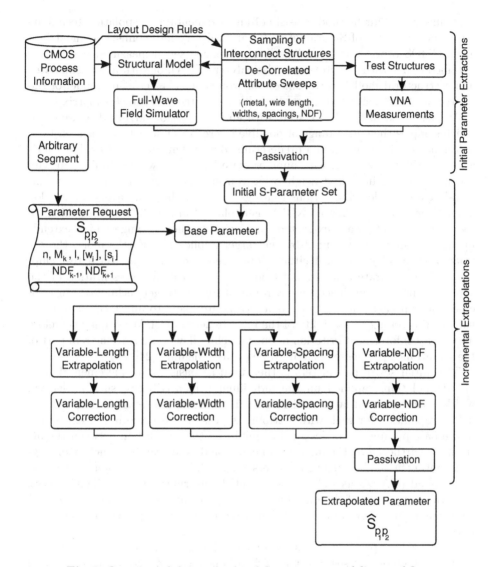

Fig. 2. Overview of the extrapolated S-parameter modeling workflow

1.2   Multistep Extrapolated S-Parameter Model

As discussed in Sec. 1.1, there are two main directions in the high-frequency interconnect modeling: first, the full-wave numerical methods, with high accuracy but restricted by their large computation time, and second, the transmission-line distributed RLCG circuit models, with a good accuracy over the frequency range, but with a very complex tracking of the mutual inductive couplings between the distributed segments. We propose here a third approach with limited complexity and exhibiting a modeling performance close to the precision of a field simulator. Our method consists of an incremental extrapolation technique for generating a set of S-parameters for an arbitrary interconnect segment in a given CMOS process, which relies on a predefined set of measured parameters obtained either with a vector network analyzer (VNA), or with a field simulator and a structural model of the silicon environment. The resulting model of the interconnect segment is an n-port with its associated S-parameter matrix.

As illustrated in Fig. 2, we start with an initial set of extracted parameters, which samples the entire range of possible interconnect structures, as seen from a designer's point of view, in a predetermined way. This initial set explores variations in the metal layer, wire number, wire length, as well as individual wire widths, wire spacings, and neighboring routing configurations in the adjacent metal layers. To describe various routings in the neighboring layers, we employ a neighboring density factor (NDF), as explained in Sec. 3.1. Within this process, the parameters are extracted for a wide frequency range which extends up to the bandwidth required by the target application. Furthermore, the extracted set can be obtained either from direct measurements on a test chip, or using an accurate field simulator and a multi-layered representation of the substrate, metal, and dielectric environment for the target technology. In both cases, measurement or computational errors are likely to affect the parameter values, threatening the stability of the interconnect model. We employ therefore a passivity enforcement criterion in our modeling flow, requiring the real part of the admittance-parameter matrix to be positive definite [24].

The initial set of parameters is then used as basis for an incremental suite of extrapolations, applied on the individual wire attributes, such as length, width, spacing, metal layer, and neighboring routing information. The individual extrapolation for each wire attribute is possible since the initial extraction of the base parameters is designed to minimize the correlation between the attributes. Furthermore, the inclusion of common design practices, such as orthogonal routing in neighboring metal layers and shielding of bus segments with V_{DD} and ground (GND), as well as the layout design rules for a specified process, limit the complexity of the initial extraction procedure to a polynomial $O\left(N^{2}\right)$ for a maximum of N minimum-width wires between the power grid shielding lines.

Several n-port parameter sets are available for representing the frequency behavior of interconnect segments, including impedance (Z), admittance (Y), and scattering (S) parameters. In Fig. 3 we have plotted the magnitude of a Z, Y, and S parameter for a 100-μm wire in a 90 nm technology (metal 5). The plot shows that the Z and Y parameters vary across several orders of magnitude within the considered frequency range, whereas the S parameter value remains between 0.8 and 1. If we consider the extrapolation of parameters across the entire frequency range, then the amount of variation of each parameter within this range will directly affect the extrapolation performance. As a result of this observation, we have chosen the S-parameter representation for our modeling methodology, since it exhibits the least amount of variations across the frequencies of interest.

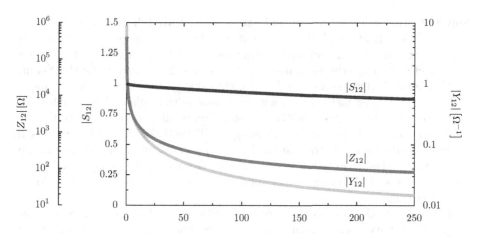

Fig. 3. Magnitude plot of the Z_{12}, Y_{12}, and S_{12} parameters for a single-wire segment

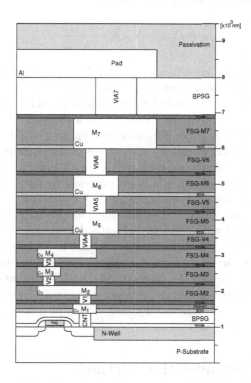

Fig. 4. Cross-section through the structural model of the CMOS process

2   Parameter Extraction Framework

Our incremental extrapolation method relies on an initial set of S-parameters, which can be obtained either from direct VNA measurements, or with a field solver. In this work we use an industry-standard 3D full-wave finite element method-based field simulator [1] to extract the base parameters from an interconnect structural model representing the target technology. Fig. 4 depicts a cross-section through the simulated 7-metal-layer (4-2-1) structure for the 90-nm, 1.0-V digital CMOS process employed within this work. The structure includes a total of 7 copper metal layers within a fluorosilicate glass (FSG) dielectric, separated by spin-on-glass (SOG) etch stop layers, silicon nitride dielectric diffusion barriers, and borophosphosilicate glass (BPSG), and finally bounded by a p-type doped silicon substrate at the bottom and an aluminum-pad grid on the top. This stacked material structure models effectively the complex dielectric environment and the inter-wire couplings present in tightly-integrated CMOS digital circuits.

For each metal layer, all the wire structures required for the subsequent extrapolations have been simulated across a frequency range from DC up to the maximum significant frequency. We have selected the maximum frequency for employing the model in SPICE simulations as:

$$F_{max} = F_{knee} \cdot N_{steps} \approx \frac{0.5}{t_{rise_{min}}} \cdot 5 \tag{1}$$

where F_{knee} denotes the knee frequency and N_{steps} is the number of required time steps per rise time (t_{rise}) during a SPICE transient simulation. A number of 5 steps together with a rounded upper bound for the knee frequency have been chosen for increased frequency validity. As a consequence, for an arbitrary minimum rise time of e.g. 10 ps, a maximum frequency of 250 GHz is obtained.

The extracted S-matrices usually contain generalized parameters, which are normalized to the impedances of each port. Since the port impedance depends on the attached load or driver, it's more practical to have all the parameters normalized to a single known impedance value. For convenience, the results have been normalized to the standard specific impedance of 50 Ω. In many cases, the solution of the solver would consider only the dominant mode. If higher-order modes are present in the structure, they should also be included. In such a case, a multi-mode analysis can be performed and the propagation constant $\gamma = \alpha + j\beta$ can be inspected for each mode. Nevertheless, each additional mode at a port adds an additional set of S-parameters. In our case however, the results show that a multi-mode analysis is not necessary, and the coupled lines can be accurately modeled with one mode per terminal.

3   Multistep Extrapolation Method

3.1   Extraction of the Initial Parameter Set

The target of our extrapolation procedure is to compute a requested parameter $S_{p_1 p_2}$ from the available set of extracted results, given the following specifications: the requested frequency f_k, the requested ports p_1 and p_2, and the structural details of the interconnect segment, such as the metal layer M_k, the wire

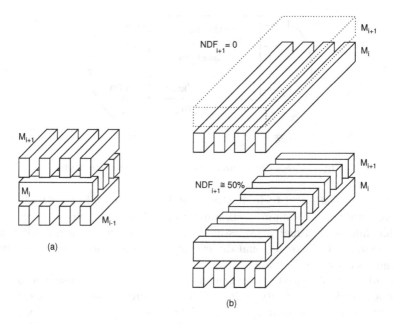

Fig. 5. (a) Orthogonal routing directions in adjacent metal layers. (b) NDF values of 0, respectively 50%.

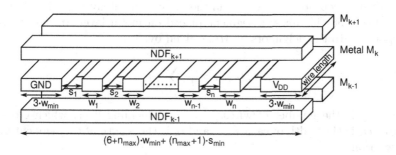

Fig. 6. Structural model of an n-wire interconnect segment

length l, the set of wire widths $[w_i]$, the set of wire spacings $[s_i]$, and the neighboring routing configurations. In order to extrapolate the requested parameter values, we must have an initial set of extracted S-parameters for every metal layer $M_1, \ldots, M_N$, a variable number of wires, variable wire lengths, variable wire widths, variable wire spacings, and variable routings in the neighboring metal layers.

To keep the problem tractable, we need to make a series of simplifying assumptions, which actually reflect common best practices in the design of state-of-the-art high-density digital signal processors. First, the number of parallel running wires is limited to n_{max} by introducing a power grid consisting of V_{DD} and GND shielding lines, in order to ensure a controlled low-impedance

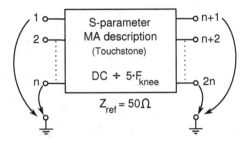

Fig. 7. Associated n-port model for an n-wire segment

current return path and to limit the inductive-coupling effects [20, 13]. In our case, we assume a maximum of six minimum-width signal wires between every two shielding lines. Finally, we assume that the routing in neighboring metal layers occurs only in orthogonal directions, to further minimize the inductive coupling, as shown in Fig. 5(a).

The influence of routed wires in the neighboring layers is considered by introducing a *neighboring density factor* (NDF). We further model the existence of routed wires in the adjacent metal layers by considering a density factor between 100% (i.e. a metal plane or a very thick wire which covers 100% of the considered segment) and 0% (i.e. no routing in the neighboring layer, as illustrated in Fig. 5(b) for e.g. 0 and 50%. Accordingly, we define an NDF value for each side of the metal, except for the lowest and the highest metal layers, which have only one neighbor. For instance, a segment placed on metal layer M_k has an NDF corresponding to the neighbors in M_{k+1} given by:

$$NDF_{k+1} = \frac{1}{l_k} \sum_{j=1}^{n_{k+1}} w_j \qquad (2)$$

where n_{k+1} is the number of wires, including shielding lines, which cross the segment, w_j is the width of each wire, and l_k is the length of the segment under consideration.

The structural model of an n-wire interconnect segment routed on a given metal layer M_k is depicted in Fig. 6. All wires within the segment have the same length l, but individual widths w_i and spacings s_i. Additionally, interconnects with distinct wire lengths can be modeled by concatenating several n-port segments [4]. The associated n-port model of the segment is shown in Fig. 7.

A complete base of initial parameters for the subsequent extrapolation must cover all metal layers and all numbers of wires in a segment, from 1 to n_{max}. As stated before, the number of parallel-running wires is restricted by the presence of a shielding grid, thus the distance between two subsequent GND and V_{DD} lines allows for the routing of maximum n_{max} minimum-width, minimum-spacing wires. Furthermore, the minimum wire width w_{min} and wire spacing s_{min} are dictated by the layout design rules for each metal layer.

Since the model applies an incremental sequence of extrapolations for each individual wire characteristic, the initial extracted set must be chosen in such a

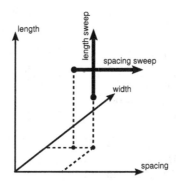

Fig. 8. Orthogonal sweeps of the wire attributes, illustrated here for length and spacing (NDF axis not shown)

way, as to minimize the correlation between wire attributes. More specifically, we can describe the sequence of extrapolations for a requested $S_{p_1 p_2}$ as:

$$\hat{S}_{p_1 p_2} = \sum_{a_i \in \{a_1, a_2, \dots\}} extrap\left(\hat{S}_i^{p_1 p_2}, F_{s_i}\right) \tag{3}$$

where $\hat{S}_{p_1 p_2}$ is the extrapolated parameter value, $a_1, a_2, \dots$ are the individual wire attributes, $\hat{S}_i^{p_1 p_2}$ is the extrapolated contribution of wire attribute a_i to the final parameter value, and F_{s_i} is the sweep function for wire attribute a_i. In order to apply the extrapolations individually on each attribute and sum the contributions, the sweep functions F_{s_i} must be orthogonal, i.e. they must not introduce correlations between the attributes during the sweeps.

We can achieve orthogonality between the attribute sweeps if we vary only one attribute at a time, while keeping the other attributes constant. In the attribute space, such sweeps would correspond to orthogonal lines, parallel to each of the attribute axes, as exemplified in Fig. 8 for wire length and spacing sweeps. An additional orthogonal NDF axis can not be displayed in Fig. 8, however it only adds a fourth dimension to the attribute space.

It is to be noted, that the individual wire attributes are not completely independent one from each other. For instance, the assumption of having a fixed power grid introduces a relatively strong dependence between wire width and spacing. Specifically, we cannot vary the width of a wire without affecting also the spacing to its neighbors. This generates a residual correlation between the attribute sweeps which must be taken into account and corrected afterwards. A controlled weighting of the incremental attribute correction steps is performed during the subsequent extrapolations, which are described in Sec. 3.2.

Given these observations, we exploit the orthogonality of the parameter sweeps to the maximum, by sweeping each individual wire attribute while keeping the other attributes at a neutral value (i.e. the minimum, or the average value, depending on the attribute). The algorithm applied for the extraction of the base parameter set is given in Listing 1. First, the length of the segment is varied

EXTRACTINITIALSET()
```
 1  for  each metal layer $M_k$
 2  do for $n \leftarrow 1$ to $n_{max}$
 3      do /* Length Sweep */
 4          $NDF_{k-1} \leftarrow NDF_{k+1} \leftarrow 0$;
 5          for $i \leftarrow 1$ to $n$
 6          do $w_i \leftarrow w_{min}$;
 7              $s_i \leftarrow \frac{n_{max}-n}{n+1} w_{min} + \frac{n_{max}+1}{n+1} s_{min}$;
 8          for $l \leftarrow l_{min}(M_k)$ to $l_{max}(M_k)$
 9          do EXTRACT-S-PARAMETERS();
10
11          /* Width Sweep */
12          $l \leftarrow l_{mean}(M_k)$;
13          for $i \leftarrow 1$ to $n$
14          do for $w_{sweep} \leftarrow w_{min}$ to $(n_{max}-n)(w_{min}+s_{min})+w_{min}$
15              do $w_i \leftarrow w_{sweep}$;
16                  $s_i \leftarrow \frac{(n_{max}-n+1)(w_{min}+s_{min})+s_{min}-w_{sweep}}{2}$;
17                  for $j \leftarrow 1$ to $n$, $j \neq i$
18                  do $w_j \leftarrow w_{min}$;
19                      $s_j \leftarrow s_{min}$;
20                      if $i < n$ then $s_{i+1} \leftarrow \frac{(n_{max}-n+1)(w_{min}+s_{min})+s_{min}-w_{sweep}}{2}$;
21                  EXTRACT-S-PARAMETERS();
22
23          /* Spacing Sweep */
24          for $i \leftarrow 1$ to $n$
25          do $w_i = w_{min}$;
26          for $i \leftarrow n$ downto 1
27          do for $s_{sweep} \leftarrow s_{min}$ to $(n_{max}-n)(w_{min}+s_{min})+s_{min}$
28              do $s_i \leftarrow s_{sweep}$;
29                  for $j \leftarrow 1$ to $n$, $j \neq i$
30                  do $s_j \leftarrow s_{min}$;
31                      if $i < n$ then $s_{i+1} \leftarrow (n_{max}-n)(w_{min}+s_{min})+2s_{min}-s_{sweep}$;
32                  EXTRACT-S-PARAMETERS();
33
34          /* NDF Sweep */
35          for $i \leftarrow 1$ to $n$
36          do $w_i \leftarrow w_{min}$;
37              $s_i \leftarrow \frac{n_{max}-n}{n+1} w_{min} + \frac{n_{max}+1}{n+1} s_{min}$;
38          for $NDF_{k-1} \leftarrow NDF_{min}$ to $NDF_{max}$
39          do for $NDF_{k+1} \leftarrow NDF_{min}$ to $NDF_{max}$
40              do EXTRACT-S-PARAMETERS();
```

Listing 1: Extraction of the base parameter set

across the relevant domain for metal layer M_k, i.e. from $l_{min}(M_k)$ to $l_{max}(M_k)$, with all the wires set to the minimum width and equally-spaced between the bounding power grid. From this first set of simulations we collect parameter sets

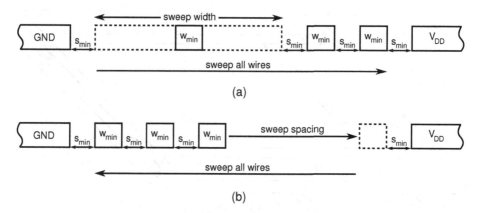

Fig. 9. Variable-width (a) and variable-spacing (b) sweeps during the initial parameter extraction

which reflect only changes in wire length, while the influence of wire width and spacing is minimized. Next, the length is kept constant at an average value for the given metal layer ($l_{mean}(M_k)$) and the width of each wire is varied from w_{min} up to the maximum allowed by the minimum spacing to its neighbors, with all the other wires kept to the minimum width and spacing. While doing this, the varying wire is placed exactly in the middle of the distance between its two direct neighbors. This approach minimizes the influence of wire length and spacing on the results obtained from the variable-width sweeps. An illustration of the variable-width sweep procedure is shown in Fig. 9(a). After that, a variable-spacing sweep is performed sequentially for every wire, as illustrated in Fig. 9(b), with all the wires kept at minimum width. Again, the influence of wire length and width on the results is minimized. During all the previous sweeps, the NDF of both upper and lower metal layers was set to zero, to avoid any influence of neighboring routed wires on these first results. Finally, the NDF sweeps add the information related to the presence of wires routed in the neighboring layers. During the sweeps, the density factors are varied from a minimum value NDF_{min}, which corresponds to either 0 (i.e. no routed wire), or to the value computed from the presence of only the GND and V_{DD} lines, depending on the position of the metal layer. The maximum value NDF_{max} corresponds to the maximum routing density present in the adjacent layer, including the power lines and maximum-width thick wires covering all the length of the segment. An illustration of such a maximum NDF case is shown in Fig. 10, where a single wire extends to the maximum width allowed by the fixed power grid. The EXTRACT-S-PARAMETERS() call designates the extraction of the S-parameter matrices for the given segment in a frequency sweep from 0 (DC) up to F_{max} with a step dictated by the application requirements.

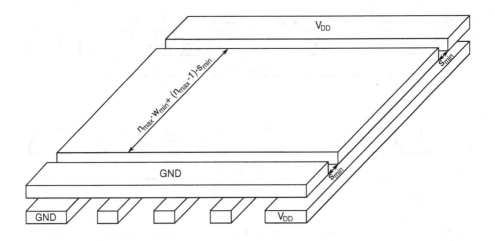

Fig. 10. Maximum NDF in the upper metal layer, with power grid and maximum-width signal line

3.2   Incremental Extrapolation

The input for the extrapolation procedure consists of the following:

- The request for computing a parameter $S_{p_1 p_2}$ for a multi-wire interconnect segment, described by its length, metal layer, individual wire widths and spacings, as well as the NDF information for the adjacent metal layers.
- An initial set of extracted base parameters for the target CMOS process, built as described in Sec. 3.1.

The result of the extrapolation method is the computed value $S_{p_1 p_2}$ for the specified segment, at all frequencies from DC to F_{max} (with the same step as the input data), written in the standard Touchstone magnitude-angle (MA) format.

First, the initial set of extracted parameters is parsed in a search for a base parameter for the extrapolation. This base parameter must be the closest-matching value for the requested parameter, i.e. a parameter describing an interconnect segment with the closest attributes to the requested one. To do this, a *matching rank* is first evaluated and the parameter with the highest matching rank will be afterwards selected. Considering a requested parameter $S_{p_1 p_2}$, the factors which contribute to the matching rank and their respective weight are as follows:

- The wire length, which contributes to the wire resistance, coupling capacitance, and coupling inductance, thus having a high weight.
- The widths of the primary wires (connected to the ports p_1 or p_2), which contribute mainly to the wire resistance and coupling capacitance, having a high weight.
- The spacings of the primary wires, which mainly affect the coupling capacitance, with a medium weight.

- The widths of the secondary wires (not attached to the requested ports p_1 and p_2), which mainly influence the coupling inductance, with a relatively low weight.
- The spacings of the secondary wires, with a relatively low weight.
- The NDF, which affects only the coupling capacitance, hence with a relatively low weight.

The matching rank of an extracted parameter is computed as the sum of the individual weights for the structural details that match with the requested segment. If a closest-matching parameter is found, then it is used further as the base parameter for the extrapolation. If no structural attributes can be matched with any of the already-extracted results, then the base parameter must be extrapolated from e.g. the variable-length set. Concretely, if the wire length for the requested parameter $S_{p_1 p_2}$ is l_r, then the extrapolated base parameter is computed as:

$$
\begin{aligned}
M_b^{p_1 p_2} &= \text{extrap}\left([l_i], \left[M_{l_i}^{p_1 p_2}\right], l_r, \text{'method'}\right) \\
A_b^{p_1 p_2} &= \text{extrap}\left([l_i], \left[A_{l_i}^{p_1 p_2}\right], l_r, \text{'method'}\right)
\end{aligned}
\tag{4}
$$

where $M_b^{p_1 p_2}$ and $A_b^{p_1 p_2}$ are the magnitude, respectively angle, of the base parameter for the extrapolation of $S_{p_1 p_2}$, $[l_i]$ represents the set of wire lengths available in the initial extracted set, while $M_{l_i}^{p_1 p_2}$ and $A_{l_i}^{p_1 p_2}$ are the magnitude, respectively angle, of $S_{p_1 p_2}$ for the segment with wire length l_i from the initial extracted set. The keyword 'method' designates the desired extrapolation function, which can be based either on linear interpolation, piece-wise cubic hermite polynomials, cubic interpolation, or cubic spline interpolation with smooth derivatives, to name only a few. The results shown in this work have been obtained with a cubic spline interpolation method, which proved to offer the best precision.

The base parameter represents the very first approximation of the requested $S_{p_1 p_2}$ value. Because in the most cases the structural attributes of the requested segment do not coincide with the attributes related to the base parameter, a set of incremental corrections for each structural element must be further applied as explained in the following. Let's first assume that the wire length related to the base parameter is l_b. We extrapolate two parameter values from the length-sweep results, one for l_b and one for the requested wire length l_r:

$$
\begin{aligned}
M_{l_b}^{p_1 p_2} &= \text{extrap}\left([l_i], \left[M_{l_i}^{p_1 p_2}\right], l_b, \text{'method'}\right) \\
M_{l_r}^{p_1 p_2} &= \text{extrap}\left([l_i], \left[M_{l_i}^{p_1 p_2}\right], l_r, \text{'method'}\right)
\end{aligned}
\tag{5}
$$

The corresponding angle values $A_{l_b}^{p_1 p_2}$ and $A_{l_r}^{p_1 p_2}$ are computed in a similar way:

$$
\begin{aligned}
A_{l_b}^{p_1 p_2} &= \text{extrap}\left([l_i], \left[A_{l_i}^{p_1 p_2}\right], l_b, \text{'method'}\right) \\
A_{l_r}^{p_1 p_2} &= \text{extrap}\left([l_i], \left[A_{l_i}^{p_1 p_2}\right], l_r, \text{'method'}\right)
\end{aligned}
\tag{6}
$$

Next, two variable-length *correction terms* $\Delta_l M^{p_1 p_2}$, respectively $\Delta_l A^{p_1 p_2}$ are computed as the following differences:

$$\Delta_l M^{p_1 p_2} = M^{p_1 p_2}_{l_r} - M^{p_1 p_2}_{l_b}$$
$$\Delta_l A^{p_1 p_2} = A^{p_1 p_2}_{l_r} - A^{p_1 p_2}_{l_b} \tag{7}$$

and the *variable-length correction* is applied to the base parameter as follows:

$$M^{p_1 p_2}_b = M^{p_1 p_2}_b + w_c \cdot \Delta_l M^{p_1 p_2}$$
$$A^{p_1 p_2}_b = A^{p_1 p_2}_b + w_c \cdot \Delta_l A^{p_1 p_2} \tag{8}$$

where w_c is a correction weighting factor for the parameter inter-correlations and is therefore data-dependent.

Further, to take into account the influence of wire width and spacing, for each wire in the segment the following parameter values are extrapolated:

$$M^{p_1 p_2}_{w_{b,i}} = \text{extrap}\left([w_{j,i}], \left[M^{p_1 p_2}_{w_{j,i}}\right], w_{b,i}, \text{'method'}\right)$$
$$M^{p_1 p_2}_{w_{r,i}} = \text{extrap}\left([w_{j,i}], \left[M^{p_1 p_2}_{w_{j,i}}\right], w_{r,i}, \text{'method'}\right) \tag{9}$$

$$M^{p_1 p_2}_{s_{b,i}} = \text{extrap}\left([s_{j,i}], \left[M^{p_1 p_2}_{s_{j,i}}\right], s_{b,i}, \text{'method'}\right)$$
$$M^{p_1 p_2}_{s_{r,i}} = \text{extrap}\left([s_{j,i}], \left[M^{p_1 p_2}_{s_{j,i}}\right], s_{r,i}, \text{'method'}\right) \tag{10}$$

where $w_{b,i}$ and $w_{r,i}$ represent the width of wire i (with i varying from 1 to n) for the base and the requested parameter, respectively, while $s_{b,i}$ and $s_{r,i}$ are the corresponding spacing values. The sets $[w_{j,i}]$ and $[s_{j,i}]$ contain the width and spacing arrays employed in the sweeps from Sec. 3.1 (see Listing 1 lines 14, respectively 28). In addition, the angle components $A^{p_1 p_2}_{w_{b,i}}$, $A^{p_1 p_2}_{w_{r,i}}$, $A^{p_1 p_2}_{s_{b,i}}$, and $A^{p_1 p_2}_{s_{r,i}}$ are obtained in a similar way.

After computing the correction terms $\Delta_{w_i} M^{p_1 p_2}$, $\Delta_{w_i} A^{p_1 p_2}$, $\Delta_{s_i} M^{p_1 p_2}$, and $\Delta_{s_i} A^{p_1 p_2}$ as the corresponding differences from the previously-extrapolated values, we apply the *variable-width* and *variable-spacing corrections*:

$$M^{p_1 p_2}_b = M^{p_1 p_2}_b + w_c \sum_{i=1}^{n} \left(\Delta_{w_i} M^{p_1 p_2} + \Delta_{s_i} M^{p_1 p_2}\right)$$
$$A^{p_1 p_2}_b = A^{p_1 p_2}_b + w_c \sum_{i=1}^{n} \left(\Delta_{w_i} A^{p_1 p_2} + \Delta_{s_i} A^{p_1 p_2}\right) \tag{11}$$

Finally, the *variable-NDF correction* is computed and applied:

$$M^{p_1 p_2}_b = M^{p_1 p_2}_b + w_c \cdot \Delta_{NDF} M^{p_1 p_2}$$
$$A^{p_1 p_2}_b = A^{p_1 p_2}_b + w_c \cdot \Delta_{NDF} A^{p_1 p_2} \tag{12}$$

where the correction terms $\Delta_{NDF} M^{p_1 p_2}$ and $\Delta_{NDF} A^{p_1 p_2}$ represent the differences between the extrapolated parameters for the base NDF and for the requested NDF values.

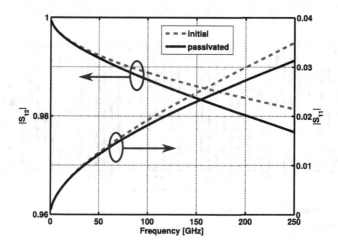

Fig. 11. Passivation example for a single-wire interconnect segment (metal 1, $l = 10\,\mu\text{m}$, $w = 400\,\text{nm}$, $s = 810\,\text{nm}$)

The correction steps applied to the base parameter are incremental and the influences of various wire attributes on the S-parameters are treated as independent. Although minimized, a non-zero residual correlation still exists between the individual influences, especially in the case of wire width variation, which has a significant influence on the spacing, see e.g. Fig. 9(a). Thus, a correction weighting factor $w_c < 1$ is employed, which accounts for the residual correlation and prevents therefore an overscaling of the final corrected value. A further correction of the extrapolated parameters is provided in Sec. 3.3.

3.3 Passivity Enforcement

Both measured and extrapolated S-parameters must exhibit a passive behavior, i.e. the interconnect model must dissipate active power, as opposed to generate it, at any value of the input voltage and at any frequency. We employ here a passivation enforcement criterion based on the correction of the eigenvalues of the admittance matrix [6]. First, the Y-parameter matrix can be computed from the S-parameter matrix as follows [10]:

$$\mathbf{Y} = \mathbf{G}_{ref}^{-1} \cdot \mathbf{Z}_{ref}^{-1} \cdot (\mathbf{S} + \mathbf{E})^{-1} \cdot (\mathbf{E} - \mathbf{S}) \cdot \mathbf{G}_{ref} \qquad (13)$$

where, in our case, $\mathbf{Z}_{ref} = Z_{ref} \cdot \mathbf{E}$ is the reference impedance matrix, $\mathbf{G}_{ref} = \frac{1}{\sqrt{|Z_{ref}|}} \cdot \mathbf{E}$ is the reference conductance matrix, and $\mathbf{E}$ is the identity matrix. The passivity criterion requires the real part of the $\mathbf{Y}$ matrix to be positive definite [6], i.e. the eigenvalues of $Re\,\{\mathbf{Y}\}$ to be all positive. This relatively simple technique ensures both the passivity and the stability of the model. A more detailed discussion on passivity and stability conditions can be found in [24].

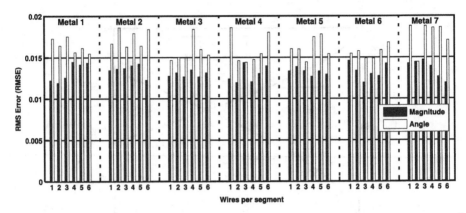

Fig. 12. RMS error between extrapolated and extracted results for the entire range of tested interconnect segments

We set the negative eigenvalues of $Re\{\mathbf{Y}\}$ to zero as in [9], then we recompute the real part as:

$$Re\{\mathbf{Y}\} = \mathbf{V} \cdot \mathbf{D}_{corr} \cdot \mathbf{V}^{-1} \qquad (14)$$

where $\mathbf{V}$ contains the eigenvectors of $Re\{\mathbf{Y}\}$ and $\mathbf{D}_{corr}$ is a diagonal matrix with the corrected eigenvalues. The S-parameter matrix is recomposed from the corrected admittance matrix as:

$$\mathbf{S} = \mathbf{G}_{ref} \cdot (\mathbf{E} - \mathbf{Z}_{ref} \cdot \mathbf{Y}) \cdot (\mathbf{E} + \mathbf{Z}_{ref} \cdot \mathbf{Y})^{-1} \cdot \mathbf{G}_{ref}^{-1} \qquad (15)$$

Fig. 11 shows two extracted S-parameters before and after the passivation, for a 10-μm single-wire interconnect segment placed on the M_1 layer. We observe that the passivity correction becomes more substantial as the frequency increases, which shows that measurement and numerical computation errors increase with frequency.

4   Experimental Validation

In order to assess the overall precision of the extrapolation method we have tested a wide range of interconnect segments in the 90-nm technology, with up to six wires per segment and varying from metal 1 up to metal 7. In every case, the evaluation has been performed on a "difficult", non-standard segment configuration, with each wire having an individual width and spacing, randomly assigned with a uniform distribution between the minimum and maximum values allowed by the design rules.

We computed the RMS error (RMSE) between the extrapolated parameters and the parameters obtained with the field simulator, from all the $(2n)^2$ S-parameters of each segment as:

$$RMSE = \sqrt{\frac{1}{N_f \cdot 4n^2} \sum_{i,j=1}^{2n} \sum_{f_k}^{N_f} \left(\hat{S}_{ij}^{f_k} - S_{ij}^{f_k}\right)^2} \qquad (16)$$

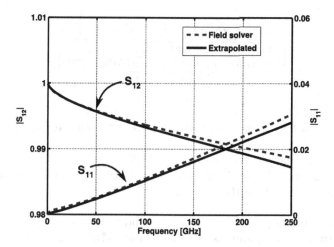

Fig. 13. Magnitude of extrapolated and extracted parameters for a single-wire interconnect segment

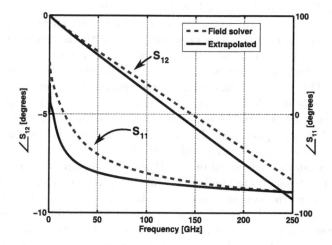

Fig. 14. Angle values for the extrapolated and extracted parameters of a single-wire segment

where $\hat{S}_{ij}$ and S_{ij} represent the extrapolated, respectively the extracted parameter values, and f_k is the frequency index, indicating the steps from DC up to the maximum frequency of interest. The results for all the investigated configurations are summarized in Fig. 12, where the angle values have been normalized to $360°$. The maximum absolute errors were $1.8 \cdot 10^{-2}$ in magnitude and 6.8 degrees in angle. The main causes for the exhibited deviations are given by:

Table 1. Wire attributes for a three-wire M_4-segment

Wire	Length	Width	Spacing	NDF$_3$	NDF$_5$
1		140 nm	200 nm		
2	2.5 mm	300 nm	290 nm	70%	25%
3		300 nm	295 nm		

- The residual correlations between the wire attributes, especially width and spacing.
- The non-optimal passivity correction [24,6].
- The precision of the extrapolation method, which is limited by the number of samples available in the initial set.

A more detailed example is shown in Fig. 13 and 14 for a single-wire M_1-segment with $l = 10\,\mu m$, $w = 580\,nm$, $s = 420\,nm$, and NDF = 35%. The plots show the values for S_{11} and S_{12}, while the other two parameters, S_{22} and S_{21}, are virtually identical with S_{11}, respectively S_{12} due to the inherent symmetry of the wire. From Fig. 13, one can see that $|S_{12}|$, which reflects the power wave transmission from port 2 to port 1, reaches a maximum of 1 at DC and starts to drop relatively fast as the frequency increases into the multi-GHz range. This behavior shows the rate of losses in signal power with the frequency increase, for a direct transmission across the line from port 2 to port 1, and points out the expected signal integrity issues which influence the interconnect at high frequencies. The level of signal reflections at port 1 is shown by the plot of $|S_{11}|$, which indicates that reflections are essentially zero at DC, but increase with the frequency. Again, the expected signal reflections within the wire are here illustrated and quantified. The extrapolated model is overall in a good agreement with the directly-extracted parameter data.

A further example is depicted in Fig. 15 for a three-wire segment in metal 4, with the attributes presented in Tab. 1. Only six parameters have been selected for the plot from the complete set of 36, in order to maintain a reasonable amount of visible detail. S_{14}, S_{25}, and S_{36} represent the direct signal transfer along the three wires, and show substantial losses at the maximum frequency of interest. S_{13}, S_{24}, and S_{35} reflect the crosstalk between wires 3 and 1, 1 and 2, respectively 2 and 3. Here we see that the crosstalk also increases significantly with the frequency. Thus, we can clearly observe that a wide-frequency interconnect model is extremely important to quantify the amount of performance losses at very high switching speeds. Beyond these observations, we can also notice a very good agreement between the extrapolated model and the directly-extracted parameters. In order to obtain a more detailed quantitative evaluation of the modeling performance we have computed the RMS error for every parameter across the investigated frequency range. The results are displayed in Fig. 16 where we omitted the parameters which are identical due to the wire symmetry, i.e. S_{44} with S_{11}, S_{41} with S_{14}, S_{55} with S_{22}, S_{52} with S_{25} etc. The measured errors are in line with our previous evaluations from Fig. 12.

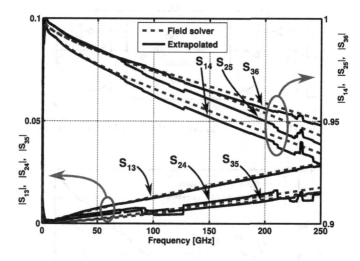

Fig. 15. Magnitude plot of six S-parameters for a three-wire M_4-segment

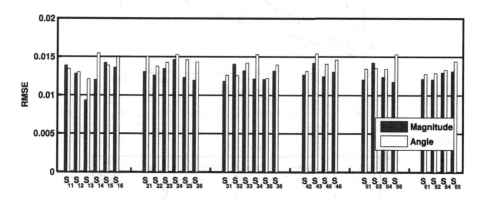

Fig. 16. RMS errors between extrapolated and directly-extracted parameters (three-wire M_4-segment)

Next, we have tested the extrapolated S-parameter models within transient circuit-level simulations. For this purpose we used a SPICE-level simulator which supports the direct modeling of n-port elements using S, Y, or Z-parameter descriptions [2]. Within our modeling framework, the extrapolated S-parameters are saved as standard Touchstone files which are directly supported by the simulator. The circuit configuration employed for the tests is shown in Fig. 17, where each wire of the interconnect model is driven and terminated independently.

We have measured the signal delay across each wire with both quiet and switching neighboring lines and we compared the results obtained using our extrapolated S-parameters and the parameters extracted with the field solver. A detailed view of the results is shown in Fig. 18 for three-wire interconnect

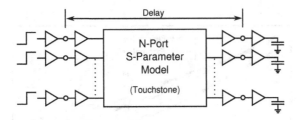

Fig. 17. Circuit employed for the transient simulations

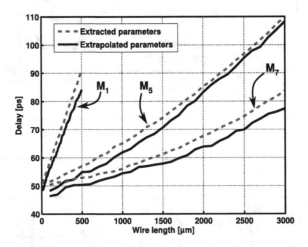

Fig. 18. Signal propagation delays from three-wire interconnect segments placed on three metal layers

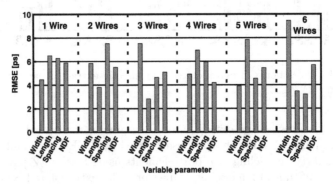

Fig. 19. Delay RMSE for the transient simulations of interconnect segments on metal 5

segments of various lengths placed on M_1, M_5, and M_7, in each case with one neighbor switching at the same time in opposite direction. To better quantify the differences we have measured the RMS and relative errors for every series of simulations. First, we have measured the RMS errors on each metal layer, for

Table 2. Maximum relative delay error across all considered metal layers and wires per segment

		Number of wires per segment				
		1	2	3	4	5	6
Metal layer	1	4.28%	7.37%	7.77%	10.01%	10.47%	11.88%
	2	5.04%	6.69%	8.19%	10.39%	10.24%	11.46%
	3	5.46%	5.56%	6.94%	8.28%	9.51%	11.50%
	4	6.93%	5.34%	7.78%	8.83%	9.94%	11.74%
	5	6.79%	7.32%	6.21%	9.32%	10.39%	10.51%
	6	6.37%	5.78%	7.41%	8.60%	11.27%	**12.21%**
	7	5.56%	7.18%	8.38%	8.97%	9.29%	11.14%

each number of wires per segment, and for each sweep of the wire attributes. A detailed plot of the RMS errors in the case of metal 5 is depicted in Fig. 19. Each RMSE value is computed across the parameter sweep range, across the investigated frequency range, and across all S-parameters.

After computing the RMSE values we have evaluated the maximum relative delay error obtained across all metal layers and numbers of wires per segment. For each metal layer and for each wire number we have varied individually the segment length, wire widths, wire spacings, and the NDF, and we evaluated the maximum error as:

$$
\varepsilon_r^{max} = \max \left\{ \max_{l_i} \left\{ \left| \frac{\hat{\delta}_{l_i} - \delta_{l_i}}{\delta_{l_i}} \right| \right\}, \max_{w_{j,i}} \left\{ \left| \frac{\hat{\delta}_{w_{j,i}} - \delta_{w_{j,i}}}{\delta_{w_{j,i}}} \right| \right\}, \right.
$$
$$
\left. \max_{s_{j,i}} \left\{ \left| \frac{\hat{\delta}_{s_{j,i}} - \delta_{s_{j,i}}}{\delta_{s_{j,i}}} \right| \right\}, \max_{NDF_i} \left\{ \left| \frac{\hat{\delta}_{NDF_i} - \delta_{NDF_i}}{\delta_{NDF_i}} \right| \right\} \right\} \quad (17)
$$

where $\hat{\delta}$ is the delay measured with the extrapolated model and δ is the delay obtained using the directly-extracted parameters. It is to be noted that the attribute variations during these tests have been selected in such a way that they do not include the same values found in the initial set, for a better evaluation of the extrapolation performance. Wire length has been varied between 1 and 500 μm for the local layers (M_1 to M_4), between 100 μm and 5 mm for intermediate layers (M_5 and M_6) and from 3 mm to 5 cm for the global layer (M_7). Wire width and spacing have been varied from the minimum design rule for each metal layer up to the maximum allowed by the shielding grid and the number of wires between two successive power lines (see Listing 1 lines 14 and 28). Additionally, the minimum NDF was always zero, while the maximum NDF varied between 85% and 100% depending on the wire length (see Fig. 10).

The evaluated maximum relative errors are shown in Tab. 2. The maximum error generally increases with the number of wires per segment, since the total number of S-parameters increases quadratically with the number of wires. As it can be seen, our method achieved during the tests a maximum delay error of 12.21% for six-wire segments placed on the 6th metal layer.

5   Conclusions

Technology-accurate wide-bandwidth interconnect models are needed for the precise estimation of signal delays, crosstalk, and energy losses across the complex on-chip communication structures. Traditional transmission-line distributed models offer a good accuracy at the expense of limited frequency validity and complex mutual inductance extractions, therefore they always imply a tradeoff between precision and computational efficiency. On the other hand, full-wave interconnect analyses provide a high accuracy at all frequencies, but require extensive numerical computations which can not be performed in real time. In addition, the amount of possible wire configurations across various lengths, widths, spacings, and metal layers increases exponentially the complexity of the modeling problem.

This chapter has introduced a computationally-efficient wide-bandwidth characterization method for arbitrary interconnect structures, which is based on the incremental extrapolation of S-parameters. The method defines a set of *a priori* parameter extractions, designed to reflect the particularities of a given manufacturing process. This initial set of parameters can be extracted with high precision within an independent time frame prior to the application, and represents a data base for the subsequent computations. Further, it has been shown how the initial set can be extracted by means of a full-wave field simulator and a structural model reflecting the technological process. It has also been shown that the complexity of covering the large set of possible wire attributes can be substantially reduced by minimizing the correlations between the segments employed in the initial set. A further measure to limit the complexity is to consider a fixed power grid and orthogonal routing directions. Moreover, the presence of wire segments in the neighboring metal layers has been modeled by introducing a density factor which indicates the amount of coupling capacity between the metal layers. Next, an incremental extrapolation procedure is performed in real time for every parameter request, which includes a search for a best-matching base parameter and a suite of extrapolated corrections applied for every wire attribute. A passivation enforcement criterion has been also described, which ensures that the obtained model is stable and exhibits a passive behavior.

The model has been tested across all metal layers and up to six wires per segment and the results have been compared with an industry-standard field simulator. The results show a good agreement with the directly-extracted parameters and lie within $2 \cdot 10^{-2}$ and 7 degrees for magnitude and angle values, respectively. Another suite of extensive tests has been performed in the time domain, within circuit-level simulations. The results summarized in Tab. 2 show a maximum error of less than 12.5%.

References

1. Ansoft Corp.: HFSS: 3D Full-wave Electromagnetic Field Simulation (September 2008), http://www.ansoft.com/products/hf/hfss
2. Cadence Design Systems: Virtuoso Spectre Circuit Simulator User Guide, product Version 5.1.41 (July 2004)

3. Cong, J.: An Interconnect-Centric Design Flow for Nanometer Technologies. Proceedings of the IEEE 89, 505–528 (2001)
4. Deutsch, A., Coteus, P.W., Kopcsay, G.V., Smith, H.H., Surovic, C.W., Krauter, B.L., Edelstein, D.C., Restle, P.J.: On-Chip Wiring Design Challenges for Gigahertz Operation. Proceedings of the IEEE 89(4), 529–555 (2001)
5. Devarayanadurg, G.V., Soma, M.: An interconnect model for arbitrary terminations based on scattering parameters. Analog Integrated Circuits and Signal Processing 5, 31–45 (1994)
6. Gustavsen, B., Semlyen, A.: Enforcing Passivity for Admittance Matrices Approximated by Rational Functions. IEEE Trans. on Power Systems 16(1), 97–104 (2001)
7. Heinrich, W., Beilenhoff, K., Mezzanotte, P., Roselli, L.: Optimum Mesh Grading for Finite-Difference Method. IEEE Trans. on Microwave Theory and Techniques 44(9), 1569–1574 (1996)
8. Hill, V., Farle, O., Dyczij-Edlinger, R.: A Stabilized Multilevel Vector Finite-Element Solver for Time-Harmonic Electromagnetic Waves. IEEE Trans. on Microwave Theory and Techniques 39(3), 1203–1206 (2003)
9. Huang, C.C.: Using S parameters for signal integrity analysis. eeDesign (EE Times EDA News) (February 2004)
10. Jahn, S., Margraf, M., Habchi, V., Jacob, R.: The Qucs Project: Technical Papers (November 2008), http://qucs.sourceforge.net/tech/technical.html
11. Jiao, D., Mazumder, M., Chakravarty, S., Dai, C., Kobrinsky, M., Harmes, M., List, S.: A novel technique for full-wave modeling of large-scale three-dimensional high-speed on/off-chip interconnect structures. In: International Conference on Simulation of Semiconductor Processes and Devices (SISPAD), pp. 39–42 (September 2003)
12. Kamon, M., Tsuk, M., White, J.: FastHenry: A Multipole-Accelerated 3D Inductance Extraction Program. IEEE Trans. on Microwave Theory and Techniques 42(9), 1750–1758 (1994)
13. Kaul, H., Sylvester, D., Blaauw, D.: Performance Optimization of Critical Nets Through Active Shielding. IEEE Trans. on Circuits and Systems I: Regular Papers 51(12), 2417–2435 (2004)
14. Loyer, J.: S-parameters and digital-circuit design. EDN Magazine (February 2003)
15. Mezhiba, A.V., Friedman, E.G.: Properties of On-Chip Inductive Current Loops. In: Great Lakes Symp. on VLSI (GLSVLSI), pp. 12–17 (April 2002)
16. Moll, F., Roca, M.: Interconnection Noise in VLSI Circuits. Kluwer, Dordrecht (2004)
17. Nabors, K., White, J.: FastCap: A Multipole-Accelerated 3D Capacitance Extraction Program. IEEE Trans. on Computer-Aided Design (CAD) of Integrated Circuits and Systems 21(11), 50–62 (1991)
18. Naishadham, K., Misra, P.: Order Recursive Method of Moments (ORMoM) for Iterative Design Applications. IEEE Trans. on Microwave Theory and Techniques 44(12), 2595–2604 (1996)
19. Pamunuwa, D.: Modelling and Analysis of Interconnects for Deep Submicron Systems-on-Chip. Ph.D. thesis, Royal Inst. of Technology, Stockholm, Sweden (2003)
20. Rabaey, J.M., Chandrakasan, A., Nikolić, B.: Digital Integrated Circuits. In: A Design Perspective, 2nd edn. Prentice Hall, Upper Saddle River (2003)
21. Ruehli, A.E., Cangellaris, A.C.: Progress in the Methodologies for the Electrical Modeling of Interconnects and Electronic Packages. Proceedings of the IEEE 89(5), 740–771 (2001)

22. Ruehli, A.E., Heeb, H.: Challenges and Advances in Electrical Interconnect Analysis. In: Design Automation Conf. (DAC), Anaheim, California, pp. 460–465 (June 1992)
23. Shepard, K.L., Zian, T.: Return-Limited Inductances: A Practical Approach to On-Chip Inductance Extraction. IEEE Trans. on Computer-Aided Design (CAD) of Integrated Circuits and Systems 19(4), 425–436 (2000)
24. Triverio, P., Grivet-Talocia, S., Nakhala, M.S., Canavero, F.G., Achar, R.: Stability, Causality, and Passivity in Electrical Interconnect Models. IEEE Trans. on Advanced Packaging 30(4), 795–808 (2007)
25. Wong, S.C., Lee, T.G.Y., Ma, D.J., Chao, C.J.: An Empirical Three-Dimensional Crossover Capacitance Model for Multilevel Interconnect VLSI Circuits. IEEE Trans. on Semiconductor Manufacturing 13(2), 219–227 (2000)

Techniques for Architecture Design for Binary Arithmetic Decoder Engines Based on Bitstream Flow Analysis

Dieison Antonello Deprá and Sergio Bampi

PPGC, GME, Informatics Institute (II)
UFRGS, Federal University of Rio Grande do Sul
Porto Alegre, RS, Brazil
{dadepra,bampi}@inf.ufrgs.br

Abstract. The design and implementation of a hardware accelerator dedicated to Binary Arithmetic Decoding Engine (BADE) is presented. This is the main module of the Context-Adaptive Binary Arithmetic Decoder (CABAD), as used in the H.264/AVC on-chip video decoders. We propose and implement a new approach for accelerating the decoding hardware of the significance map by providing the correct context for the regular hardware engine of the (CABAD). The design development was based on a large set of software experiments, which aimed at exploiting the characteristic behavior of the bitstream during decoding. The analysis gave new insights to propose a new hardware architecture to improve throughput of regular engines for significance map with low silicon area overhead. The proposed solution was described in VHDL and synthesized to standard cells in IBM 0.18 μm CMOS process. The results show that the developed architecture reaches 187 MHz with a non optimized physical synthesis.

Keywords: Hardware Dedicated Architectures for Decoding H.264/AVC Video Standard, Arithmetic Entropy Coding, CABAC, CABAD.

1 Introduction

The growing importance of high definition digital videos, mainly for real-time application, is calling for higher video compression efficiency to save storage space and transmission bandwidth [1]. The most advanced standard is the H.264/AVC, currently at the commercial state-of-the-art, defined by the ITUT/ISO/IEC [2]. This standard defines a great set of tools, which act in different domains of image representation to get higher compression ratios, roughly doubling the ratio obtained, by the MPEG-2 compressors [2]. The H.264/AVC introduces many innovations in the techniques used to explore the elimination of the redundancies found in digital video sequences.

The H.264/AVC standard specifies two alternative entropy methods: CAVLC (Context-Adaptive Variable Length Coding) and CABAC (Context-Adaptive Binary Arithmetic Coding) [1]. Both are based on the fact that the digital video sequences present non-stationary but predictable statistical behavior [3]. Moreover, this

J. Becker, M. Johann, and R. Reis (Eds.): VLSI-SoC 2009, IFIP AICT 360, pp. 181–197, 2011.

statistical behavior is highly dependent on the type of content that is being processed and on the video capture technique [1, 2]. To address this issue, the H.264/AVC adopts an innovative approach that provides dynamic adaptive probabilities estimation, which is introduced in the CAVLC and CABAC [3] coding schemes.

The CABAC is the most important entropy encoding method defined by the H.264/AVC standard, allowing the H.264/AVC to reach 15% coding gain over CAVLC [2]. However, to obtain these coding gains a significant computational complexity is added in the coding hardware. Moreover, the coding algorithm is essentially sequential, as each step iteration produces only one bit and the next step depends on the values produced in the previous iterations [1]. The sequential nature of the CABAD leads to significant performance bottlenecks in the decoder. Many works found in the literature address these constraints trying to break data dependencies inherent to the nature of CABAC.

The goal of this work is to present a new hardware architecture to improve the throughput of the CABAD arithmetic engines. The architectural design aims to achieve a very efficient implementation, based on our experiments for a detailed bitstream flow analysis.

Next section presents an overview on context-adaptive binary arithmetic codec and the arithmetic engines are also detailed. Section 3 presents related works found in the literature. The bitstream flow analysis by simulation is discussed in Section 4. The architecture proposal is detailed in Section 5. The results of our architecture after synthesis are presented in Section 6. Section 7 the validation process applied in this case study are discussed. Finally, Section 8 addresses some conclusions and future work.

2   Context Adaptive Binary Arithmetic Codec Overview

The context-adaptive binary arithmetic codec as defined by H.264/AVC standard is a framework for entropy encoding that transforms the value of a symbol in a word of code, with variable length near the theoretical limit of entropy [3]. It works with recursive interval divisions combined with context models that allow better coding efficiency [3]. Each subinterval represents a unique source symbol, and the size of the interval is proportional to that symbol probability of occurrence [3]. However, modeling occurrence probabilities of each symbol brings increasing computational complexity. One way to decrease this computational complexity is to use a binary alphabet [3].

The H.264/AVC standard, in its main and high profiles, supports the binary arithmetic coding/decoding, from the macroblock layer, to deal with information generated by the tools that act on the transform redundancies of the following kinds: spatial, temporal, and psycho-visual [2]. In the entropy methods of H.264/AVC standard the information that is arriving at the inputs of the encoding process or at the outgoing outputs in the decoding process are named Syntax Elements (SE) [3]. The SE is composed by the following information: i) type, used for codec control to determine the encoding process to be used; ii) and the value to be encoded based on the control information provided [2].

The decoding process is named CABAD and the encoding is referred to as CABAC. The encoding process receives at the input SEs with its type and value. Considering the SE type, a binarization method is applied to convert the SE value into a binary alphabet [2]. Then, the context model selects the appropriate context and sends it to the stage of arithmetic coding, responsible for generating the output bitstream and updates the context models. In Fig. 1 the integrated encoding and decoding dataflow is presented. Both encoding and decoding processes are composed by three steps that can be organized into four modules, which are described in the following subsections.

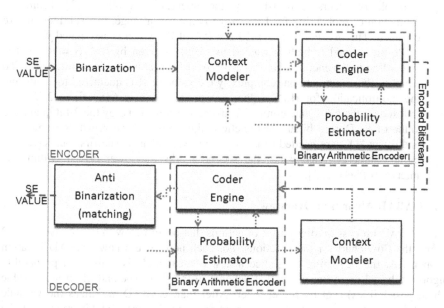

Fig. 1. CABAC and CABAD dataflow diagram with the three stages and four modules that compose the encoder and decoder

As shown in Fig. 1 both encoding and decoding processes are composed by four modules can be organized into three stages that are described below:

Binarization/Anti-Binarization: The binarization process consists of mapping SE values for a unique sequence of bits that represents the original value. This mapping is done to reduce the symbols in the encoding alphabet, thus simplifying the amount of elements to be modeled and minimizing the costs of the context modeling and facilitating the task of arithmetical coding. Each bit, generated through this process, is denoted as "bin" and the set of all "bins" (bits) is named "binstring". From a total of seven binarization methods, four are fundamental: unary; truncated unary; fixed length; and exponential Golomb [2, 3].

Probability modeling: A context is a probabilistic model that represents a statistical distribution of a particular symbol on the basis of the review of the symbols previously processed and the probability of occurrence of the current symbol. To adequately model all probabilities of occurrence of each symbol, CABAC defines 460 different contexts. Each bin of an SE can be associated with one or more contexts. During the encoding the probabilistic estimates must be kept updated to ensure the accuracy of the process. Each context model is composed by a pair of values, a 6-bit state value for the probability index (63 possible probability states), and a binary value for the most probable symbol "MPS". The state value is used as an index to the estimated probability value of the least probable symbol "LPS"[2, 3].

Binary Arithmetic Coder (BAC), or Decoder (BADE): It works based on the principle of recursive division of the interval of width R [3]. From the estimation of probability for LPS (pLPS) on a given range, two subintervals are obtained. The first is given by: rLPS = R * pLPS which is associated with LPS while the second (which is related to MPS) is given by: rMPS = R - rLPS. According to the encoded bin the rMPS or rLPS is chosen as new interval R. To simplify the computational complexity the value of R is quantized to 2 bits and the multiplication for rLPS values are pre-stored in a 64x4 fixed 2-D table indexed by the 6-bit state coming from context model and by the 2-bit quantized value of R. During binary arithmetic coding process two registers (range "R" and offset "O") are needed to keep the interval updates. The first one saves the current interval range while the second marks the lower bound within this interval (offset) [2, 3].

2.1 CABAD Algorithm Overview

The CABAD process involves a set of actions that occur below the slice layer. Fig. 2 shows the flow chart for these actions. For each new slice a new CABAD iteration happens. At the beginning of a slice a new context table is built from probability algorithm based on initial tables that depend on the slice type and of an index value (three possibilities) sent by the encoder. After that, CABAD initializes the variable CodlOffset getting the first nine bits reading from the encoded bitstream and the variable CodlRange si set to default value [2].

The CABAD decoding of macroblock layer of SE values are performed until an "End One Slice" (EOS) SE type is found. The first step in the SE decoding is the decision of its type and, based on this information it chooses an anti-binarization method [2]. After that, if the SE type is an EOS, then terminal decoding process is selected. Otherwise, for each bin of SE one of two other decoder processes, regular or bypass, must be chosen. For bins being decoded by regular process a context table address calculation must be done. The information retrieved from context table includes the MPS and its probability estimate index denoted by pState variable. The CABAD uses an offset fixed for each SE type combined with an increment defined by different possible forms, according to the SE type in conformance with [2] to generate context table addresses. For some SEs, obtaining increment index involves referring to SE from the left, top and current macroblock and, for others, the bin index is used for this purpose.

For bins that use the regular decoding process the CABAD obtains new rLPS from a look-up in a fixed pre-stored table indexed by pState and then one of four possible values is selected by value of quantized CodlRange (CodlRange>>6) [2]. Then, new value of CodlRange is calculated and the comparison between CodlRange and CodlOffset define if MPS or LPS happens. After that, the context table must be updated with new values for MPS and pState which are obtained from a fixed table with state transition with different values for MPS or LPS occurrence. Next, the CodlRange and CodlOffset registers are available for the normalization process. In this case one or more bits of bitstream can be consumed [2]. Finally, one step of regular decoding process is finished; the contexts model and decoding environment register are updated. For other bins the bypass decoding process is applied. The bypass mode is simpler than the regular mode. Then, anti-binarization module is performed and the results of this operation determine if the binstring produced by the decoding environment matches with the method expected or not.

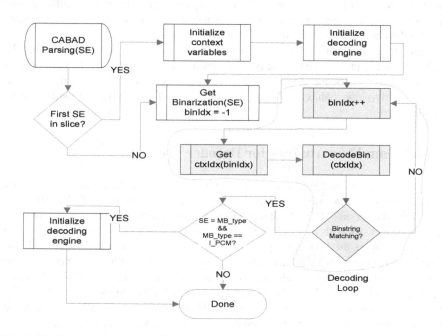

Fig. 2. CABAD algorithm flow diagram shows the action sequence released by CABAC Decoder to process each one SE inside of the slice layer

3 Related Work

Techniques to reduce the latency and data dependency of CABAD have been widely discussed in the literature and they follow five basic approaches: pipeline; contexts pre-fetching and cache; elimination of renormalization loop; parallel decoding engines; and memory organization. The pipeline strategy is used in [4] to increase the bins/cycle rate. An alternative to solve the latency of renormalization process is presented in [5]. The speculative processing through the use of engines decoding parallel is explored first in [6], then in [7] and [8]. High efficiency in the decoding process using pre-fetching and cache contexts is discussed in [6] and [9], respectively. Memory optimization and reorganization are addressed in [4].

The work of [8] presents optimizations in the arithmetic engine through the parallel execution in speculative mode and the adoption of leading zero anticipation that allows counting of consecutives zeros in CodlRange. These two approaches bring reductions in the delay in the critical path.

The hardware architecture proposed in [6] is based on analysis of the relationship between bins count for each SE type and the occurrence of each SE type in one macroblock. The usage rate imposed by each SE in each of the three decoder engines is a relevant aspect that is used to optimize the overall decoding process.

An evaluation of the data dependencies in the regular mode of decoder arithmetic engine is presented in [7]. In this study, the frequency of changes to CodlRange and CodlOffset registers are considered for cases where renormalization process happens combined with the observation of MPS or LPS decision.

Considering the various architectures proposed by different authors for the CABAD, a static characteristics analysis of constraints for decoding bitstream process was considered and some experiments were conducted by software simulations to extract the dynamic behavior of the decoder flow. This analysis is addressed in Section 4.

4   Bitstream Flow Analysis for Decoder Process

All our analyses were based on results obtained from statistical data collected by software routines that we introduced into the decoder module of the reference software (JM), version 10.2 [10]. To reach more representative data set in our analysis we decided to work with four different digital video resolutions, in YUV video format 4:2:0, more often used in the reports found in the literature: QCIF, CIF, D1 and HD1080p. Moreover, we evaluated the impact of the quantization parameters on the bitstream behavior. For our statistics we selected all 18 QCIF, 17 CIF, 18 D1 video sequences available in [11], and also seven additional HD1080p video sequences. The last are designated as: rush-hour; riverbed; blue-sky; tractor; sunflower; station2; pedestrian area. In total, there were 60 digital video sequences in this analysis, each with 200 frames. Fig. 3 show one frame of the HD1080p video sequences used in this case study in additional to QCIF, CIF and D1 listed in Table 1.

Fig. 3. Samples of HD1080 video sequence, that named: rush-hour; riverbed; blue-sky; tractor; sunflower; station2; pedestrian area, respectively

Table 1. All video sequence used in this case study

Video Sequences			
QCIF (176×144)	CIF (352×288)	D1 (720×480)	HD1080 (1920×1080)
Akiyo	Bridge-close	Abstract	Bluesky
Bridge-close	Bridge-far	Artant	Pedestrian
Bridge-far	Bus	Chips	Riverbed
Carphone	Coastguard	Concert	Rush-hour
Claire	Container	F1	Station2
Coastguard	Flower	Football	Sunflower
Container	Foreman	Ice	Tractor
Foreman	Hall	Leaves	
Grand-mother	High Way	Letters	
Hall	Mobile	Mobile	
Highway	Mother-daughter	Parkrun	
Miss-america	News	Rafting	
Mobile	Paris	Rugby	
Mother-daughter	Silent	Seawall	
News	Stefan	Suzie	
Salesman	Tempete	Tempete	
Silent	Waterfall	Toweres	
Suzie		Waterfall	

The encoding parameters employed for coding all sequences were: Profile IDC = 77, Level IDC = 40, SymbolMode = CABAC, GOP=IPBB and RDO=ON. Our experimental procedure was to perform, for all the video sequences, six different encoding processes, varying the parameters of quantization QPISlice and QPPSlice in pairs; namely the pairs were: 0:0, 6:0, 12:6, 18:12, 24:18, and 36:26, resulting in a total of 420 digital video sequences encoded. The decoding process was done for all encoded sequences using the JM v.10.2 decoder, to collect the statistics data and to obtain feedback for the validation process. The relations and statistical behavior were studied and synthesized, and they will be presented next.

One of the problems of CABAD is to determine the actual throughput needed for the decoding process to occur in real-time. This happens because the length of codeword generated by CABAD is variable and may change significantly between iterations, since the coding method is context-adaptive. Furthermore, for some SE types it can be difficult to determine the binstring length and the SE sequence, as they vary according to the slice type and the macroblock type. However, H.264/AVC standard in its level 4.0 defines the upper-limit bit/rate at 20Mbps. We analyzed the bit count at the input and output of the CABAD, before quantization, and the ratio between them varies between 1.3 and 2.1 times. Then, we can consider that, in the worst case, the architecture has to process at nearly 42Mbps, to reach throughput enough for real-time decoding at 30 frames per second in the 1080 x 1920 format (1080p).

The Binary Arithmetic Decoder Engines (BADE) are the CABAD kernels. They are responsible for regenerating the binstring since of the bitstream and internal variables. Each bin is produced by one of three BADE kinds. Considering that the decoding process is done bin by bin, it requires high performance because inside this module resides the CABAD critical path. The BADE basic organization is shown in Fig. 4.

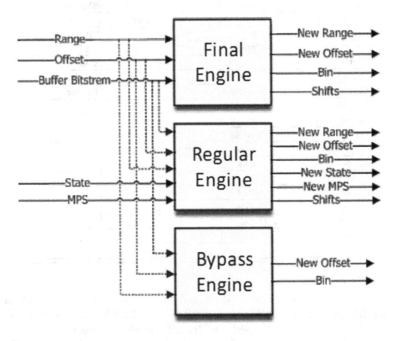

Fig. 4. The three kinds of Binary Arithmetic Engines present into CABAC core, its organization and they connection with the internal registers

The H.264/AVC standard defines which type of BADE engine each SE must use. Moreover, part of binstring of one SE type can be produced by one BADE type while another part can be produced by other one. The regular engine is the most complex BADE block and is used on most SEs. The bypass engine is only used by the suffix part of motion vector differential (MVD) and transforms coefficient (COEF). Additionally, the signal bits of COEF have to be treated in the bypass engines. During software profiling, the BADE engine utilization by each SE type was observed to determine the better strategy for the dedicated architecture design.

By analyzing the bins count occurrence in the bitstream we observed that just four SE types (coded_block_flag, coeff_level, sig_coeff_flag and last_sig_flag) account for more than 93% of all bins, in average, for all types of macroblocks. Thus, a deeper analysis of the behavior of these SE types was performed to improve the gain in the BADE. In the first study we investigated the bins distribution for different SE types in each one macroblock types. In the Table 2 the results obtained are summarized.

Table 2. Distribution of bins by different SE types for each macroblock type

	Information	Code Block Flag (%)	Sig & Last Flags (%)	Coefficient Levels (%)	Other SEs (%)
I MB	Total occurs	2.32	60.38	34.30	3.00
	Bins generated	0.67	17.62	80.00	2.31
	Regular Process	0.86	22.31	74.68	2.15
	Bypass Process	0	0	100	0
P MB	Total occurs	2.51	58.50	37.07	1.92
	Bins generated	1.47	34.21	62.05	2.27
	Regular Process	1.76	40.95	54.90	2.39
	Bypass Process	0	0	98.33	1.67
B MB	Total occurs	2.61	57.58	38.56	1.25
	Bins generated	1.80	39.75	46.29	12.16
	Regular Process	2.17	47.98	37.46	12.39
	Bypass Process	0	0	98.97	1.03
Average	Total occurs	2.55	58.07	37.65	1.73
	Bins generated	1.54	35.14	61.10	2.22
	Regular Process	1.86	42.41	53.30	2.43
	Bypass Process	0	0	98.78	1.22

The results show that there are, on the average, seven significant coefficient flag (SE_SIG) and five least significant coefficient flag (SE_LAS) for each 4x4 residual blocks. The utilization of arithmetic engines shows that regular engines produce 80.8% of bins count while the bypass produced 19.2% of them. Another interesting fact is that many bins produced by regular and bypass is generated in a consecutive way, 84.92% and 29.35%, respectively.

The occurrence of bins related to the SEs of the significance map (SE_SIG and SE_LAS) also deserve emphasis, since together they represent between 27% and 36% of all bins processed by the CABAD. Moreover, they have special interest for decoding engines since they usually occur in sequence, i.e. each SE_SIG is followed by a SE_LAS. However, this does not occur when the value of SE SE_SIG is zero, in this case the next SE decoded should be another SE SE_LAS. Fig. 5 illustrates the

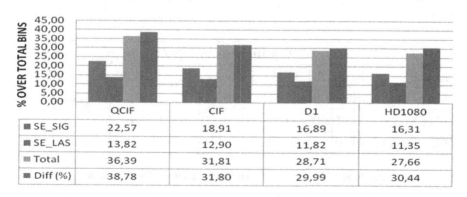

Fig. 5. Bin occurrences for Significance Map SE in each resolution used

relationship between bins occurrence of the significance map for each of the resolutions discussed, highlighting the percentage difference occurrences between SE_SIG and SE_LAS.

5 Design Architecture

The proposed architecture development was based on observations made on the behavior of the bitstream for many coding scenarios and on few previous works found in the literature. The bitstream flow analyses have shown that for some specific situations using an approach with specialized processing can provide throughput gains in the decoding process. As presented in section 2, 3 and 4, the exploration of the parallel speculative execution of BADE engines is a good alternative to reach greater throughput without excessive area increase.

Our design is based on the work presented in [12] which applies multiple parallel engines for speculative execution. In this work we include few extensions mainly in the regular branch. The new arrangements in the regular engine interconnections aim at exploring characteristics behavior of the SE_SIG and for the SE_LAS kinds of the syntax element to reach high throughput in the significance map decoding.

From the work presented by Yu and He in [6] a significant part of the new proposed architecture for CABAD makes use of two regular engines for decoding a variable number of bins per cycle. Depending on each implementation, the context modeling can provide one or two context models for regular engines branch, thus varying the efficiency of the decoding. But, for special situations this approach may not improve efficiency because according to the decision of the first regular engine the second bin for each one of these engines needs to use a different context.

The H.264/AVC standard defines that each 4x4 coefficient block should refer to one significance map [2]. This map set is composed by two types of SE (SE_SIG and SE_LAS) which should occur in a specific order. The significance map is generated according to the process order and the coefficients value. The process for generation of the significance map for a 4x4 coefficient block example is shown in Fig. 6. The Index line shows the index or the values in zig-zag scan order while the Value line shows each one coefficients value for a 4x4 example block. The lines with Flag SIG and Flag LAST show the composition of the significance map for the 4x4 example block.

	Coefficients in Zig-Zag Order															
Index	0	1	2	3	4	5	6	7	8	9	10	11	12	13	14	15
Value	24	2	0	-1	1	1	0	0	0	3	0	0	0	0	0	0
Flag SIG.	1	1	0	1	1	1	0	0	0	1						
Flag LAST	0	0		0	0	0				1						

Fig. 6. Significance Map generation for a 4x4 coefficients block

As shown in Fig. 6 for each SE_SIG with value equal to one there is one SE_LAS, but when the SE_SIG is equal to zero then the SE_LAS element does not occur. Based on the results analysis, summarized in the Fig. 5, it is possible to identify that this mismatching between SE_SIG and SE_LAS pair happens, in average, for roughly 30% of the cases in the HD1080 video sequences that we tested. This fact opens the opportunity to explore decoding optimizations, specifically as to when one specialized process to supply the correct context for BADE can be used.

The proposed architecture employs multiple engines instances for the case of variable number of bins per cycle, and also adopts specialized mechanism for context selection. Our design basic structure is shown in Fig. 7.

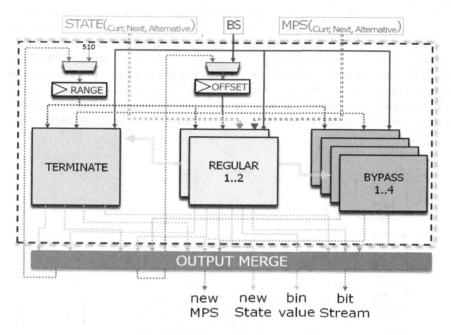

Fig. 7. BADE core with arrangement

As Fig. 7 shows, the three kinds of engines present in CABAD are organized in one hierarchical arrangement, namely: one terminate engine, two regular engines and four bypass engines. The BADE block (in Fig. 7) receives three context pairs (STATE and MPS) and the bitstream buffer (BS). According to the SE kind, one of its engines is used. The Regular and Bypass engine instances are organized into two distinct branches. Inside the Regular branch two bins can be produced in one cycle while in the Bypass branch at most four bins can be produced in a single cycle. The Regular engine is more complex than the other engines, and contains the critical path of this module. We used optimizations to reduce the delay of this block.

Initially an operations reordering is made by the regular engine, as the approach presented in [7]. This results in two parallel paths inside the regular engine, one to treat the occurrence of the MPS and another for the LPS. Another important aspect is the access to static memories to retrieve information about the next state (access the MPS_TABLE, and the LPS_TABLE) and the rLPS estimate probabilities (RLPS_TABLE). These memories are addressed by pState, which is provided from the context model stored in the context memory. The fact that these memories are inside the regular engine affects the critical path. Furthermore, when we concatenate two regular engines, two accesses to these memories in the same cycle is required. To solve this problem we apply an approach similar to that adopted in [13], in which the memories are concatenated and combine the information about current, the next MPS states, the next LPS states and rLPS estimate probabilities. Thus, we can obtain all information needed to decode two bins that reference the same context with just one access to the static memory.

Finally, we applied the first one detect (FOD) strategy to solve the renormalization problem in an approach similar to [5]. The special approach used to resolve the renormalization allows it to save between 2 to 8 cycles, because the loop is eliminated and the renormalization always happens in only one cycle. To reduce the FOD delay, the FOD is broken in two segments, one for the low interval part and another for the high interval part, as illustrated by Fig. 8. Then, adding just one multiplexer we can select the renormalization part between the low and high ranges. To finish, the Range first bit is used to choose between new and old register values for the renormalization process.

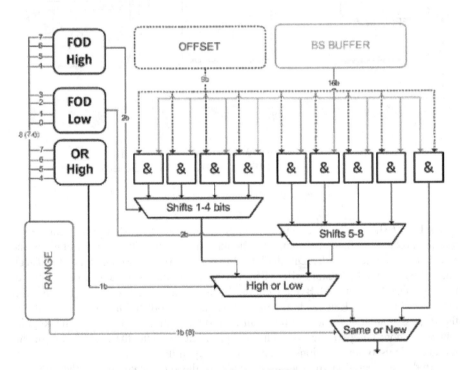

Fig. 8. Renormalization block with FOD accelarates

Considering that the regular engine is responsible for most of the bins produced by the CABAD, it seems a good alternative to increase the parallelism level in this engine, instantiating additional regular engines. Meanwhile, the regular engine is in the BADE critical path due to its long combinational logic depth (that includes adders, comparators, ROM and renormalization). Thus, it is not advantageous to use a larger number of regular engines concatenated because this would cause performance degradation for all other CABAD stages and the throughput may not be satisfactory. Moreover, our analysis has shown that the Regular engines are underutilized because the context modeling cannot be efficient for all situations, especially for significance map decoding.

A new interconnection approach, namely of SP_SIGMAP, for regular engines was developed to improve throughput in the regular branch. The BADE block can receive three context pairs from context modeling. These context pairs can be used in significance map decoding to explore the characteristic behavior of these SEs. The first regular engine receives one context to decode one SE_SIG, while the second regular engine receives two contexts, being one to decode one SE_LAS and other to decode the next SE_SIG. If the first regular engine result was MPS then the second regular engine receives the second context else the third context will be delivered to the second regular engine. The interconnections for regular branch engines are shown in Fig. 9.

The next section analyzes the results obtained by our architectures when processing digital video test sequences, the same utilized in the simulation analysis discussed in section 4.

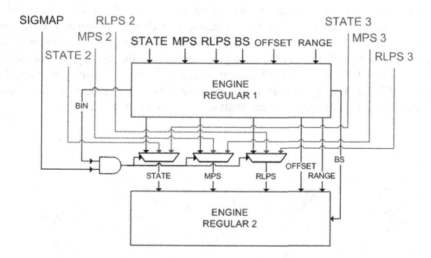

Fig. 9. Regular engines interconections inside the Regular Branch

6   Experimental Results

The developed architectures were described in VHDL and synthesized to 0.18 um CMOS standard cells based on the IBM cell library using the Cadence RTL compiler.

The Modelsim tool, version 6.01a, was used during the simulation and architectural validation process. The architecture development presents a new arrangement for binary arithmetic decoders of CABAD that is able to generate up to 4 bins per cycle, in the best case. The utilization of four decoding bypass engines inside the BADE increases the hardware resources required, while providing more efficiency compared to the BADE architecture with just two decoder bypass engines. Table 3 shows the hardware synthesis results for the architecture proposed. It compares the solutions with two and four decoder bypass engines in the architecture and our design.

Table 3. Distribution of bins by different SE types for each macroblock type

Information	Architectures for multi bin BADE engines			
	[6][1]	[12]	Our Proposal	Differences (percent)
Gates	3671	3928	4022	94 (**+2.4%**)
Max. Frequency	191.86	190.25	187	-3,25 (**-1.7%**)
Max. Bins/Cycle	3(2R1B)	4(4B)	4(4B)	0

[1] Our implementation of the author´s proposal.

The results in Table 3 indicate that the increase in the hardware costs is around 2.4% for our design and the maximum frequency decreases 1.7%, both when compared to the design proposed in [12]. A large number of test-benches were developed and run to evaluate the performance of our architecture with data extracted from the reference software during the decoding process of the 440 digital video sequences listed in Section 4. For these video test-benches we observed that the two main approaches adopted can improve the throughput when compared to previous works presented in [6] and [12]. So, the potential gain for the four Bypass engines (4 BYPASS) and for the specialized context selection for significance map in regular engines (SP SIGMAP) were analyzed for each different resolution of the video sequences tested. The results of these analyses are shown in Fig. 10.

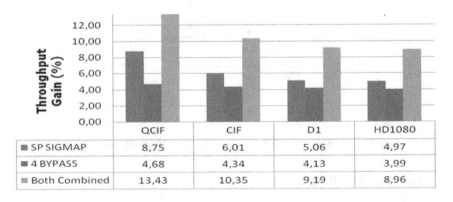

	QCIF	CIF	D1	HD1080
■ SP SIGMAP	8,75	6,01	5,06	4,97
■ 4 BYPASS	4,68	4,34	4,13	3,99
■ Both Combined	13,43	10,35	9,19	8,96

Fig. 10. Performance analysis to four classic resolutions

The data presented in Fig. 10 shows that the SP SIGMAP approach can improve the throughput from 4.97% for HD1080 up to 8.75% for QCIF video sequence resolutions. Furthermore, the 4 BYPASS approach offers additional gain from 3.99% up to 4.68% for HD1080 and QCIF, respectively. The proposed design adopts both approaches, and when compared to [6] which does not use neither of these techniques, it reaches 8.96% to 13.43% throughput gains. When compared to [12] the proposed design shows the throughput gains indicated in the SP SIGMAP line of Fig. 10.

The strategy to evaluate the performance of our hardware was also employed to validate our design: in these simulations we compared the outputs generated by our architecture to the results generated by the JM10.2 decoding module [10]. To this end, we introduced extra code (routines) in this software to save the inputs and the outputs of the BADE engines for later comparison with the hardware simulations. This strategy was used for extensive architecture validation.

7 Validation Process

In the development cycle of integrated circuits, the validation process can reach 70% of the design time. This information indicates the challenge of this process. The approach used in this work to minimize this time was to make a hierarchical and incremental validation. In this approach, several validation steps were made according to the complexity and the abstraction level of the developed blocks.

In the first step, the blocks of lower abstraction level were validated as standalone block. This was accomplished by generating the intermediate data from the specifications given in the H.264/AVC standard. These stimuli were used in each of the blocks and the verification was done by comparing the waveforms in the simulator to the functional definition of that block.

In the second step, the blocks were grouped according to their function and the validation was done for the entire group. In this step a software implementation of the norm was used to produce the input stimuli and the expected output. The software model used to generate the stimuli and the expected results was based on the

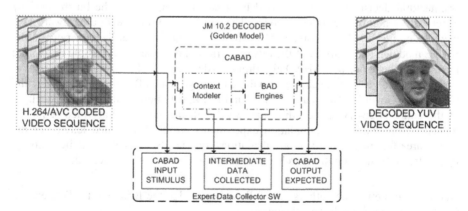

Fig. 11. Data extraction process for functional validation of the individual blocks and the complete architecture

reference software of the H.264/AVC (Surking, 2009). Modifications were done in this software to get the right data for the hardware validation. Fig. 11 illustrates the data extraction process for validation.

The data extraction process for the production of input stimuli and the results for comparison were done using the same standard video sequences of the section 4. Actually these stimuli were produced at the same time the data for static and dynamic analysis were produced. This approach allowed us to significantly reduce the time spent, once we had to process all the video sequences only once. It also made the data used for analysis and validation consistent with each other.

The second step followed the flow showed in Fig. 12. Inside a test-bench file, the input stimuli were injected into the validating block (Design Under Test - DUT). The outputs of the DUT were stored for later comparison to the expected outputs.

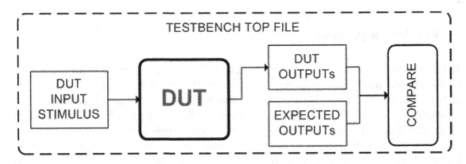

Fig. 12. Processo de extração de dados para a validação funcional dos blocos individuais e da arquitetura completa

8   Conclusions and Future Work

This work presented a novel dedicated hardware architecture for the BADE of the CABAD block that supports the decoding of up to four bins per cycle. The architectural decisions were supported by a detailed analysis of the bitstream flow generated by a software video decoder. The results show that, with a hardware cost increase of just 2.4%, we obtain 5% efficiency gain in the utilization rate of the BADE module. The analysis of the bitstream flow shows that it is possible to explore the dynamic behavior of CABAD algorithms to develop novel hardware solutions.

The next step in this development will be to integrate this BADE module inside the CABAD top-level hardware architecture and to evaluate performance and throughput of the entire H.264/AVC decoding hardware with the same digital video sequence inputs. Given that in our simulation experiments we used a limited length for the search area for the motion vector calculations, one needs to analyze the behavior of the bitstream flow when the search area for motion estimation is increased.

Acknowledgment. The authors gratefully acknowledge the Brazilian R&D agencies, CNPq and CAPES, for financial support.

References

1. Wiegand, T., Sullivan, G., Bjøntegaard, G., Luthra, A.: Overview of the H.264/AVC Video Coding Standard. IEEE Transactions on Circuits and Systems for Video Technology 13(7), 560–576 (2003)
2. Draft ITU-T Recommendation, H.264 and Draft ISO/IEC 14 496-10 AVC. In: Joint Video Team of ISO/IEC JTC1/SC29/WG11 & ITU-TSG16/Q.6 (March 2003)
3. Marpe, D., Schwarz, H., Wiegand, T.: Context-Based Adaptive Binary Arithmetic Coding in the H.264/AVC Video Compression Standard. IEEE Transactions on Circuits and Systems for Video Technology 13(7) (July 2003)
4. Yang, Y.-C., Lin, C.-C., Chang, H.-C., Su, C.-L., Guo, J.-I.: A High Throughput VLSI Architecture Design for H.264 Context-Based Adaptive Binary Arithmetic Decoding With Look Ahead Parsing. In: 2006 IEEE International Conference on (ICME) Multimedia and Expo, pp. 357–360 (July 2006)
5. Eeckhaut, H., Christiaens, M.: Stroobandt. D., Noolet, V.: Optimizing the critical loop in the H.264/AVC CABAC decoder. In: IEEE International Conference on Field Programmable Technology, FPT 2006 (December 2006)
6. Yu, W., He, Y.: A High Performance CABAC Decoding Architecture. IEEE Transactions on Consumer Electronics 51(4), 1352–1359 (2005)
7. Kim, C.-H., Park, I.-C.: High speed decoding of context-based adaptive binary arithmetic codes using most probable symbol prediction. In: Proceedings of 2006 IEEE International Symposium on Circuits and Systems, ISCAS 2006 (May 2006)
8. Bingbo, L., Ding, Z., Jian, F., Lianghao, W., Ming, Z.: A high-performance VLSI architecture for CABAC decoding in H.264/AVC. In: 7th International Conference on ASICON 2007, pp. 790–793 (October 2007)
9. Zhang, P., Gao, W., Xie, D., Wu, D.: High-Performance CABAC Engine for H.264/AVC High Definition Real-Time Decoding. In: Digest of Technical Papers. International Conference on Consumer Electronics, ICCE 2007, Las Vegas, NV, USA, pp. 1–2 (January 2007)
10. Suhring, K.: H.264/AVC Reference Software. In: Fraunhofer Heinrich-Hertz-Institute, http://iphome.hhi.de/suehring/tml/download/ (accessed: March 2008)
11. Reisslein, M.: YUV Video Sequences. Video Traces Research Group, http://trace.eas.asu.edu/yuv/index.html (accessed: March 2008)
12. Depra, D.A., Rosa, V.S., Bampi, S.: A novel hardware architecture design for binary arithmetic decoder engines based on bitstream flow analysis. In: Proceedings of the 21st Annual Symposium on Integrated Circuits and Systems Design. SBCCI 2008, pp. 239–244 (September 2008)
13. Mei-Hua, X., Yu-Lan, C., Feng, R., Zhang-Jin, C.: Optimizing Design and FPGA Implementation for CABAC Decoder. In: International Symposium on High Density packaging and Microsystem Integration. HDP 2007, pp. 1–5 (June 2007)

Author Index